Library Evaluation

A Casebook and Can-Do Guide

Danny P. Wallace

Director and Professor
School of Library and Information Studies
University of Oklahoma
Norman

Connie Van Fleet

Associate Professor
School of Library and Information Studies
University of Oklahoma
Norman

Editors

2001
LIBRARIES UNLIMITED, INC.
Englewood, Colorado

Libraries Unlimited, Inc.
P.O. Box 6633
Englewood, CO 80155-6633
1-800-237-6124
www.lu.com

Library of Congress Cataloging-in-Publication Data

Library evaluation : a casebook and can-do guide / Danny P. Wallace, Connie Van Fleet, editors.
    p. cm.
  Includes bibliographical references and index.
  ISBN 1-56308-862-2 (softbound)
    1. Libraries--Evaluation. 2. Libraries--United States--Evaluation. 3. Library administration. 4. Library administration--United States. I. Wallace, Danny P. II. Van Fleet, Connie Jean, 1950-

Z678.85 .L535 2000
025.1--dc21
                                                  00-050705

CONTENTS

1—The Culture of Evaluation 1
Danny P. Wallace and Connie Van Fleet

2—Measuring Organizational Effectiveness 11
Richard E. Rubin

2—Measuring Organizational Effectiveness (*continued*)

FIGURES/TABLES/APPENDIXES

Figures

Tables

Appendixes

PREFACE

THE ORIGIN OF LIBRARY EVALUATION: A CASEBOOK AND CAN-DO GUIDE

Library Evaluation: A Casebook and Can-Do Guide grew out of the S:OLE (Seminar: Ohio Library Evaluation) project, carried out at Kent State University during 1997-98. This effort, sponsored by the Kent State University School of Library and Information Science and supported by a $99,563 U.S. Department of Education Library Education and Human Resource Development Program grant (R036A70035), brought together nearly 100 public library staff members from the state of Ohio for a week-long exploration of the motivations for and approaches to library evaluation. S:OLE Co-Directors included School of Library and Information Science Director Dr. Danny P. Wallace, faculty members Dr. Connie Van Fleet and Dr. Richard E. Rubin, and Assistant to the Director Julie A. Gedeon, with the support of Graduate Assistant Sharon Nahra.

The goals of S:OLE were straightforward: to present participants with practical information regarding library evaluation and to provide them with direct experiences in applying evaluation tools and techniques. From early afternoon on a Sunday in May 1998 until noon on the following Friday, S:OLE participants listened to presentations by expert, experienced speakers and interacted with each other in hands-on working group sessions. Participants learned and worked together for five days, and many of them continued the experience into the evenings, gathering in the computer labs of the School of Library and Information Science to explore electronic resources or catching up on e-mail and communing in the common areas of the Kent State University dormitory where many of the participants were housed during S:OLE. It was an invigorating environment in which presenters learned from participants, and peers shared their personal evaluation experiences. The added bonding value of more than one tornado-alert trip to the basement area of the Kent Student Center was invaluable in building the team spirit that emerged early and characterized the week.

The presentations provided a mixture of conceptual overviews and pragmatic case studies. If the expertise of the 14 featured speakers was the heart of S:OLE, the 11 working group sessions were its soul. Each of the case studies was paired with a working group experience in which participants experimented with carrying out the technique described in the case study.

Topics and speakers for S:OLE included

1. *The Nature of Evaluation*, by Dr. Danny P. Wallace, Director, Kent State University School of Library and Information Science

2. *Measuring Organizational Effectiveness*, by Dr. Richard E. Rubin, Kent State University School of Library and Information Science

3. *Case Study: Total Quality Management*, by Paula J. Miller, Director, Westlake (Ohio) Porter Public Library

4. *Case Study: Cost-Benefit Analysis*, by Glen E. Holt, Director, St. Louis (Missouri) Public Library

5. *Case Study: Focus Groups*, by Roger G. Verny, Deputy State Librarian of Ohio

6. *Availability, Interpretation, and Use of Federal, State, and Local Data*, by Mark L. Smith, Director of Communications, Texas Library Association

7. *Gathering and Using State Level Data*, by Michael S. Lucas, State Librarian of Ohio

8. *Putting Statistics to Work: Interpreting and Presenting Library Data*, by Mark L. Smith

9. *Evaluation of Reference and Information Services: Issues, Trends, and Strategies*, by Dr. Mary Stansbury, Kent State University School of Library and Information Science

10. *Case Study: The Ohio–Wisconsin Project*, by Carolyn Radcliff, Coordinator of Reference Services, Kent State University, and Barbara Schloman, Director of Library Information Services, Kent State University

11. *Case Study: Reference Service Evaluation at the Columbus Metropolitan Library*, by Wendy Ramsey, Staff Development Coordinator, Columbus (Ohio) Metropolitan Library

12. *The Responsive Library Collection: Approaches to Evaluating Collections*, by Dr. Sharon L. Baker, University of Iowa School of Library and Information Science

13. *The Responsive Virtual Library Collection: Evaluating Access to Electronic Resources*, by Erica Lilly, Coordinator of Electronic Information Services, Kent State University

14. *Evaluating Network Services*, by Carol Lynn Roddy, Executive Director, Ohio Public Library Information Network (OPLIN)

15. *The Evaluation Action Plan*, by Dr. Connie Van Fleet, Kent State University School of Library and Information Science

16. *The Culture of Evaluation*, by Dr. Danny P. Wallace

Many of the S:OLE presentations found their way into *Library Evaluation: A Casebook and Can-Do Guide*. In some cases, S:OLE presenters were not available to serve as authors. In others, the editors wanted to expand the scope of the book to bring into play topics that were not covered at S:OLE. It is the editors' intent that the mixture of intellectual substance, directly applicable practicality, and the excitement of inquiry that were the spirit of S:OLE carry forward into the *Casebook*. As a means of encouraging continuation of that spirit, the editors and contributors have agreed that all royalties for *Library Evaluation: A Casebook and Can-Do Guide* will go directly to the Kent State University Center for the Study of Librarianship to support future experiences related to library evaluation.

ACKNOWLEDGMENTS

The editors wish to thank the U.S. Department of Education for the grant that supported S:OLE, the skilled and effective library managers and other professionals who made up the core group of presenters for S:OLE, the enthusiastic participants who made the experience an unqualified success, the staff of the School of Library and Information Science, and our devoted and determined Graduate Assistant, Ms. Sharon Nahra.

INTRODUCTION

THE PURPOSE OF LIBRARY EVALUATION: A CASEBOOK AND CAN-DO GUIDE

This book is about library evaluation, about the purposes and processes of evaluating library programs, services, and resources. It is not a review of all the possible types of evaluation or approaches to evaluation. It is not a textbook. Its focus is evaluation, not research, although evaluation and research are very closely related. The purpose of this book is to familiarize the reader with the motives for and purposes of evaluation and the major contexts and models for evaluation—and to provide explicit examples of how evaluation projects have been and can be carried out in a variety of library contexts.

The need for research in librarianship has been felt at least since Beals (1942) lamented that the literature of librarianship was dominated by "glad tidings" and "testimony," with "research" a distant third. "The research record of librarianship is uneven. Those who have assessed the previous research of librarians have been of a consensus that the quantity and quality leave something to be desired" (Powell 1997, 1). The perceived need for a sound base of true research on library issues and problems led to the founding of the first graduate program in the field, the late Graduate Library School at the University of Chicago, and can be credited with transforming the process of educating library professionals.

Research continues to play an important role in understanding the societal needs to which libraries should be responsive, assessing the effectiveness of approaches to delivering library services, and guiding the evolution of library processes, practices, and policies. Practitioners often view research and researchers as being removed from and uninterested in pragmatic problems. A study conducted by Van Fleet and Durrance (1993) suggests that there is a communication gap between researchers and public library leaders. "Researchers and practicing librarians view the field from different perspectives, attempt to meet different standards, and are driven by different motives. One of the participants in the study noted that 'We need to find a line between what is good and what is practical.' Another suggested that 'the language of research procedure is different than the language of practical management and provision of service' " (145).

Systematic evaluation is the nexus between the need to conduct true research into library operations and the need to provide direct evidence of the value of libraries. *Library Evaluation: A Casebook and Can-Do Guide* is an attempt to bridge the gap between researchers and practitioners by presenting examples of approaches to library evaluation that are methodologically sound but at the same time pragmatic. The tools and techniques described have been selected to represent practical approaches to assessing the value of the library that are on a scale that can be easily implemented in most library environments.

This book is intended for library managers, for individuals who include evaluation among their responsibilities and duties. The central feature of this book is the presentation of concrete, real-life cases that document the development and application of approaches to evaluating library operations. These cases reflect real uses of evaluation models, tools, and measures. Overviews of broader concepts and function areas that are frequent targets for evaluation accompany and introduce the individual cases. This is not strictly speaking a how-to-do-it book so much as a how-it-has-been-done book. Readers interested in a broader survey of measurement and evaluation in libraries may want to turn to Baker and Lancaster's *The Measurement and Evaluation of Library Services*, while those more interested in how-to-do-it may find Lancaster's *If You Want to Evaluate Your Library* or Smith's *Collecting and Using Public Library Statistics: A How-To-Do-It Manual* useful. Hernon and McClure's *Evaluation & Library Decision Making* provides an overview of the evaluation process. There are many useful research methods books, including Powell's *Basic Research Methods for Librarians*, that can guide individuals interested in the motives, methods, and mechanisms of true research.

WHY EVALUATE?

The answer to the question "Why evaluate?" is frequently "Because it is required." Evaluation is a prominent concern in a wide variety of environments. The public increasingly demands accountability from government agencies and elected officials. Elected officials, if they are wise, transfer that demand to government employees and call upon them to demonstrate that what they do is right and good. Shareholders in public companies expect to see profitability, efficiency, and—increasingly—social responsibility in the actions and decisions of management. Consumer activism creates a need to ascertain the quality of products and services.

The need for evaluation is felt very keenly in libraries, particularly in libraries that are supported by public funds. The sharpened focus on evaluation has led to a number of excellent publications over the last three decades, many of which carry the imprimatur of major organizations such as the American Library Association. The impressive number of publications and presentations on evaluation as a topic, however, do not necessarily ensure that the tools and techniques of evaluation are being delivered to and explicated for the front-line library employees who are responsible for carrying out evaluation activities.

> Librarians are feeling growing pressure, as are many others charged with the administration of public agencies. Shrinking federal resources and eroded local tax bases, combined with pressing social problems, result in intense competition among agencies for resources. Social scientists have recognized for some years that the allocation of funds is a political act; in such a case, evaluation measures become political tools. Public librarians recognize that their tools are inadequate. They appear frustrated that they cannot defend what they know to be a crucial and threatened public good: free public library service available to all citizens. They know that the case for public libraries cannot be supported in the current terms of business or politics, but researchers have not developed alternative measures that are compelling in a hostile political environment. They see a need for a new generation of evaluation tools that better explain what librarians do and what impact libraries have on the future. (Van Fleet and Durrance 1994, 5–6)

In times of rapid and profound societal and technological change, evaluation is essential to preserving the viability and the visibility of libraries. Although most librarians probably reject the notion that libraries will be summarily replaced by some mythical digital beast, there are clearly members of the general public—who have extensively bought into the notion of a truly paperless society and who equate libraries with the ancient traditions of print on paper. Some of those believers in the digital epoch serve as municipal administrators, members of governing boards, school principals, and university executives. Evaluation of the library and its benefits ultimately may be essential to the survival of the library itself.

Evaluation leads to enhanced efficiency and avoidance of errors. The history of libraries is rich with examples of inappropriate policies, processes, tools, and techniques that were promulgated for protracted periods of time because they were never properly evaluated or—much too frequently—were never evaluated at all. The history of research into the usability of library catalogs, for instance, is a depressing tale of the precedence of rule over role. Similarly, studies of library fines have found that their impact is generally much more negative than positive, but fines remain an entrenched aspect of library practice. Such mistakes as creating catalogs that please librarians more than they serve patrons and imposing fine systems that discourage library use can be avoided through the relatively simple means of evaluating local needs, policies, and processes.

The emphasis on planning for library services that has dominated library practice at least since the publication of *A Planning Process for Public Libraries* (Palmour, Bellassai, and DeWath 1980) carries with it an essential need for evaluation. Planning is fruitless if not accompanied by evaluation of the appropriateness of the planning process, the efficacy of the plan, and the outcomes of implementation of the plan.

Even when evaluation is not required for purposes of accountability, for demonstrating the need for libraries, for avoiding costly mistakes, or for planning, systematic evaluation is desirable as an expression of the library's concern for its public trust. Libraries are among the most service-oriented and consumer-friendly of all institutions. The focus on the public that pervades all types of libraries and library services in itself suggests a need for evaluation, for exploring ways to do things better, for demonstrating that the library's administration and staff want to provide the best possible library. The desire to improve, to grow, and to provide ever better services and products, is a deeply rooted part of the librarian's philosophy.

ORGANIZATION OF LIBRARY EVALUATION: A CASEBOOK AND CAN-DO GUIDE

This book comprises six major sections. Chapter 1, by Danny P. Wallace and Connie Van Fleet, provides an overview of the need for evaluation and the processes required to make evaluation an integral component in library management, administration, and operation. Evaluation is discussed in terms of the systems approach to understanding phenomena. Procedures are outlined for developing an evaluation action plan as an approach to nurturing the habits of evaluation.

Chapter 2 addresses evaluation in the context of organizational effectiveness, beginning with an overview of the nature of and models for understanding organizational effectiveness, and Case Studies 2.1 through 2.4 showcase efforts to evaluate and improve organizational effectiveness. The models for assessing organizational effectiveness presented by Richard E. Rubin in Chapter 2 form a basis for understanding the potential use and impact of the 11 cases that are the heart of *Library Evaluation: A Casebook and Can-Do Guide*. In addition to delineating the essential criteria for evaluation of organizational effectiveness, Rubin discusses seven models for understanding organizational effectiveness. Those models are revisited throughout the book.

In Case Study 2.1, Paula J. Miller examines the application of a simplified Total Quality Management model for effecting beneficial organization change in a public library. Total Quality, a philosophy as well as a set of techniques, arose with roots in the corporate manufacturing world, but has been successfully used in a variety of library settings. Miller's chapter provides an understanding for how Total Quality can revolutionize the management of a medium-sized suburban public library without requiring an overwhelming expenditure of resources.

Roger Verny and Connie Van Fleet discuss focus groups and their use in soliciting constituent group feedback in Case Study 2.2. The popularity of focus groups has increased rapidly due to their potential for yielding high-quality indications of group perceptions of important issues in a timely manner at a relatively low cost. Verny and Van Fleet describe the use of a focus group approach to solicit constituent group feedback and input on the programs and operations of a school of library and information science.

Case Study 2.3 presents an innovative approach to combining existing sources of data in building a case for library support. Traditional approaches to presenting quantitative analyses of library operations have tended to emphasize library-centric measures that are frequently appealing only to the library cognoscenti. Mark L. Smith presents a model for incorporating nonlibrary data to convincingly make the case for library support by comparing costs and expenditures for libraries to costs and expenditures for other popular activities. This innovative approach to cost-benefit analysis has substantial potential in the arena of marketing libraries and their services.

Case Study 2.4 outlines a process for completely redesigning the quantitative measures used in evaluating and comparing libraries at the state level. Jay Burton provides a detailed account of how the measures of public library performance used in the state of Ohio were completely overhauled to recognize the changes that have taken place in the library environment. The procedures employed in developing and implementing new measures are an exemplar of systematic evaluation and redesign.

Chapter 3 and associated case studies deal with evaluation of reference services and provide a general overview of the evaluation of reference services and resources. Kathryn Dana Watson summarizes the issues, trends, and strategies pertinent to the evaluation of reference activities. Her discussion introduces quantitative, qualitative, and obtrusive–unobtrusive methods in reference evaluation as well as exploring the use of surveys, sampling, interviews, observation, and case studies.

Case Study 3.1 focuses on the use of a standardized survey that can be used to evaluate local reference effectiveness and compare local performance to that of other libraries. Carolyn J. Radcliff and Barbara F. Schloman present the Wisconsin–Ohio Reference Evaluation Program (WOREP), a standardized survey for assessing the quality of reference services. Surveys are an important tool in the evaluation of all varieties of library services, programs, and functions. The use of surveys in the evaluation of reference services has a substantial history. A specific advantage of the WOREP is that it is based on input from librarians and patrons. A second advantage is the provision of data comparing the local library to other libraries.

Case Study 3.2 presents a method for unobtrusively examining reference behaviors. Unobtrusive evaluation has been used extensively to assess the accuracy of answers to reference questions. Jeffrey N. Gatten and Carolyn J. Radcliff document the successful use of unobtrusive observation of the behaviors of reference librarians. Specific attention is given to the role of unobtrusive observation in determining the effectiveness of a training program intended to improve the reference service behaviors of public library reference staff.

Chapter 4 presents an overview of evaluating collections, with Case Studies 4.1 through 4.3 providing specific cases of approaches to collection evaluation. Connie Van Fleet discusses the relative roles of quantitative and qualitative data in collection evaluation. Detailed attention is given to measures of extent, efficiency, quality, performance, and effectiveness.

Case Study 4.1 presents an overview of the use of systematic expert judgment and consistent criteria in evaluating specific reference resources and the reference collection as a whole. Miriam J. Kahn provides guidance on the role of expert judgment, list checking, and frequency of use in evaluating individual reference sources. She also provides guidelines for evaluating a reference collection as a whole.

In Case Study 4.2, Blane Halliday presents list checking as a technique for determining the adequacy of library holdings in a specific subject area. Comparison against standard lists is a frequently used traditional approach to judging the adequacy of entire collections and has been used to assess subject-specific subcollections. Halliday presents a unique technique based on tools not explicitly designed for collection evaluation and incorporating data on consumer demand. This method and its results introduce an innovative new way of assessing collection strength in a focused subject-format area.

Case Study 4.3 introduces the use of citation analysis to understand the origins and nature of a subject literature and to guide collection-building decisions. Citation analysis is a vastly underused tool with great potential for adding to librarians' understanding of specific-subject literatures and the patrons who use them and for guiding the decisions and actions necessary to supporting subject collections. Gina R. Barkett provides a straightforward summary of how a citation analysis can be planned, carried out, and interpreted. Her chapter concludes with an analysis of the implications of citation analysis for collection building in the area of art history. This can be extended to many circumstances in which efficiency in collection building is paramount, such as assessing a specific area of a library's professional collection to provide important tools for use in library management.

Chapter 5 and its case studies are devoted to evaluation in the digital environment and serve as a global view of evaluating electronic collections and services. Erica B. Lilly emphasizes the importance of access, which includes intellectual access (authority, sponsoring organization, accuracy, objectivity, currency, coverage, scope, access, design, ease of use-navigability, general content, and external validation-evaluation), library user instruction, physical access, and technological access.

Case Study 5.1 presents guidelines for the evaluation of World Wide Web search engines. The proliferation of the World Wide Web and of search engines for retrieving information via the Web leads to an intensive need to develop procedures for determining the relative effectiveness of Web search engines. Thomas J. Froehlich has developed a rating scale for search engine evaluation that can be used to examine the quality and utility of search engines and that can readily be adapted and updated as the state of the art of search engines advances.

Case Study 5.2 provides guidance for the process of ensuring that World Wide Web pages are accessible to individuals with disabilities. Erica B. Lilly and Pamela R. Mitchell explore the problems of providing equitable access to the Web, describe the need for accessible workstations, and provide guidance on how institutional guidelines for the design of accessible Web pages can be developed, introduced, and monitored.

Chapter 6 provides an overview of the nature of evaluation and ties evaluation to its conceptual origins and contexts. Danny P. Wallace discusses the contexts in which evaluation can be understood, including the societal, professional, institutional, administrative, functional, technological, and patron contexts. The chapter continues with an exploration of ways of assigning value, including values, benefits, goals, quality, and quantity. The chapter concludes with a discussion of decision making, including types of decisions to be made, and details the prominent approaches to evaluation.

Each of the 11 case studies is preceded by a pair of introductory "@ A Glance" summaries, one to introduce the general method or focus of the case study, the other to provide a brief sketch of the case itself. The "@ A Glance" summaries serve to provide the reader with a thumbnail sketch of the ways in which the methods, tools, and techniques described in the cases have the potential for contributing to the solution of specific library evaluation problems. Each "@ A Glance" includes the following information for the methodology and the case:

1. The *purpose* of the methodology and of the specific case.

2. A *description* of the methodology and of the specific case.

3. Guidance on when to *use* the methodology and how it was used in the specific case.

4. A general description of the *data needed* to implement the methodology.

5. The *sources of data* required for the evaluation.

6. The *organizational model* or models most closely aligned with the methodology.

7. The *procedure* required for implementing the methodology or actually used in the specific case.

The role of "@ A Glance" is not to substitute for the case study that follows, but to provide the reader with a quick view of what to expect from the case and to provide guidance on how the general method presented in the case can be understood in the broader context of evaluation. It is the editors' hope that the combination of overview chapters, "@ A Glance" summaries, and detailed case studies will serve to build a framework on which to understand evaluation and—most importantly—to put the methods presented into action while building toward the culture of evaluation described in Chapter 1.

Each chapter and case study ends with a "Resources" section that includes both items referenced in the text and additional materials related to topic of the chapter or case study. The purpose of the "Resources" sections is to provide readers with further opportunities to learn and to acquire those tools and skills necessary to effective evaluation. References to World Wide Web sources reflect accessibility at the time the authors of chapters and cases referred to those sources; some Web sources may no longer be available or may have been modified since examined by the authors.

RESOURCES

Baker, Sharon L., and F. W. Lancaster, 1991, *The Measurement and Evaluation of Library Services,* 2d ed. Arlington, VA: Information Resources Press.

Beals, Ralph, 1942, "Implications of Communications Research for the Public Library," pp. 159–81 in *Print, Radio, and Film in a Democracy,* ed. Douglas Waples. Chicago: University of Chicago.

Hernon, Peter, and Charles R. McClure, 1990, *Evaluation & Library Decision Making.* Norwood, NJ: Ablex.

Lancaster, F. W., 1993, *If You Want to Evaluate Your Library. . . .,* 2d ed. Urbana, IL: University of Illinois, Graduate School of Library and Information Science.

Palmour, Vernon, Marcia C. Bellassai, and Nancy V. DeWath, 1980, *A Planning Process for Public Libraries.* Chicago: American Library Association.

Powell, Ronald R., 1997, *Basic Research Methods for Librarians*, 3d ed. Greenwich, CT: Ablex.

Smith, Mark L., 1996a, *Collecting and Using Public Library Statistics: A How-To-Do-It Manual.* New York: Neal-Schuman.

Van Fleet, Connie, and Joan C. Durrance, 1993, "Public Library Leaders and Research: Mechanisms, Perceptions, and Strategies," *Journal of Education for Library and Information Science* 34 (Spring): 137–53.

———, 1994, "Public Library Research: Use and Utility," pp. 1–16 in *Research Issues in Public Librarianship: Trends for the Future,* ed. Joy M. Greiner. Westport, CT: Greenwood.

CONTRIBUTORS TO LIBRARY EVALUATION: A CASEBOOK AND CAN-DO GUIDE

Gina R. Barkett (M.L.S., Kent State University) works at the Cleveland Heights-University Heights Public Library and at the Wickliffe Public Library.

Jay Burton (M.L.I.S., Brigham Young University) is Head of Library Programs and Development at the State Library of Ohio.

Thomas J. Froehlich (M.A., Pennsylvania State University; M.S., University of Pittsburgh; Ph.D., Duquesne University) is a professor in the School of Library and Information Science at Kent State University.

Jeffrey N. Gatten (M.A., Kent State University; M.L.S., Kent State University) is an associate professor and Director of Library Collection Management for Libraries and Media Services at Kent State University.

Blane Halliday (M.L.S., Kent State University) is a reference librarian at the Michigan City (Indiana) Public Library.

Miriam J. Kahn (M.L.S., Queens; M.A., Hunter College) is a partner in MBK Consulting, Columbus, Ohio.

Erica B. Lilly (M.L.S., University of Maryland) is an assistant professor and Coordinator of Electronic Information Services for Libraries and Media Services at Kent State University.

Paula J. Miller (M.L.S., University of Maryland) is Director of the Westlake Porter Public Library in Westlake, Ohio.

Pamela R. Mitchell (M.A., The Ohio State University; Ph.D., The University of Wisconsin) is an associate professor in the School of Speech Pathology and Audiology at Kent State University.

Carolyn J. Radcliff (M.L.S., Kent State University) is an associate professor and a coordinator of Reference Services for Library and Media Services at Kent State University.

Richard E. Rubin (M.L.S., Kent State University; Ph.D., University of Illinois at Urbana-Champaign) is a professor in the School of Library and Information Science at Kent State University.

Barbara F. Schloman (M.S.L.S., University of Wisconsin-Madison; Ph.D., Kent State University) is a professor and Director of Library Information Services for Libraries and Media Services at Kent State University.

Mark L. Smith (M.L.I.S., University of Texas at Austin), formerly Director of Communications for the Texas Library Association, is a library consultant in Riverside, California.

Connie Van Fleet (M.L.I.S., Louisiana State University; Ph.D., Indiana University) is an associate professor in the School of Library and Information Studies at the University of Oklahoma.

Roger Verny (M.Ed.Media, University of Toledo) is Deputy State Librarian for Planning, Evaluation and Research at the State Library of Ohio.

Danny P. Wallace (M.A.L.S., University of Missouri-Columbia; Ph.D., University of Illinois at Urbana-Champaign) is Director and Professor in the School of Library and Information Studies at the University of Oklahoma.

The Culture of Evaluation

Danny P. Wallace and
Connie Van Fleet

ENVIRONMENTAL IMPACT: THE SYSTEMS APPROACH

Evaluation, at its best, is a mechanism for understanding a system. In the library context, evaluation has to do with understanding library systems. The *systems approach* to evaluation is based on a number of key concepts:

1. All phenomena take place in the context of systems. No action, event, process, or product can be divorced from the system to which it belongs.

2. Understanding the phenomenon requires understanding the system.

3. Every system is linked to other systems and to its environment. No system exists in isolation. There are no *closed* systems.

4. Any change to a system affects other systems. No system is an island.

Systems analysis is the process of understanding and evaluating systems and is a highly structured set of tools and processes that, when properly employed, yields reliable data to describe the system, its inputs, its outputs, its processes, and its products. *Operations research* is a highly quantitative adjunct to systems analysis in which systems and events are described in terms of predictable mathematical and statistical formulae.

Systems analysis and operations research are tools and processes; they are also ways of thinking. The most important aspect of a systems approach to evaluation is learning to think in a systematic manner. As evaluation is adopted and nurtured in an institutional setting, evaluation takes on an important systems role that places it on a level with basic and familiar library systems such as collection management, reference and information services, technical processing, circulation, outreach services, and administration. In an ideal situation, evaluation becomes a basic social and societal system of the library and a *culture of evaluation* permeates the library and all its functions and activities.

Rules for Understanding Systems

The following three basic rules for understanding systems are adapted from *The Last Whole Earth Catalog* (1974). They were originally intended to summarize, in a semi-facetious manner, the need to pay adequate attention to the ecology. Understanding and nourishing the ecology of a library is an essential function and an important focus for evaluation. Failure to accept and account for any of these rules can completely undermine any evaluation activity.

1. Everything is connected to everything else. The activities of the Anytown Public Library cannot be divorced from the activities of libraries in surrounding communities, from the activities of the Major Metropolitan Public Library, from the activities of the Regional University Library, or from any library with which the Anytown Public Library has even the most remote contact. Furthermore, the Anytown Public Library is directly linked to a wide range of other government offices, educational institutions, social service agencies, businesses, industries, and individual members of the public. Because these components all work together as a system, the administration and staff of the library are responsible for exploring and understanding those connections.

2. Everything has to go somewhere. If the library's administration, based on its own evaluation, decides not to offer a particular service at a determined level, some other entity or agency will be the recipient of the accompanying demand unmet by the library. If the library emphasizes a particular service at a determined level, some other entity or agency will experience a reduced demand for that service. In a worst-case scenario, the library may be marginalized by a decision to emphasize certain services and de-emphasize others. Although no library can be all things to all people, it is essential to understand that there is an intense need to evaluate need and demand for services and to evaluate their delivery.

3. There ain't no such thing as a free lunch (TANSTAAFL). Around the turn of the twentieth century, many bars and taverns advertised a "free lunch." The catch was that access to the free lunch was dependent on purchase of watered-down drinks. Library administrators and staff cannot and should not expect to benefit from any externally provided benefit at no local cost. The local cost of access to state-funded network services, for instance, may be reduced community appreciation for the direct services of the library. In some cases, expanded state funding for shared library resources may lead to reduced funding for local library resources.

Ranganathan's Five Laws

Indian library philosopher and educator S. R. Ranganathan (1964) posited five laws of library science as a guide for understanding and fostering the roles and purposes of the field. Those five laws are

1. Books are for use

2. Every reader its book

3. Every book its reader

4. Save the time of the reader

5. A library is a growing organism

Although Ranganathan concentrated on the book in his rules, he was in fact quite aware of the role to be played by other information resources, but consciously chose to use the term *book* in a generic sense.

Ranganathan's five laws are an excellent example of systems thinking and carry substantial implications for the need to evaluate libraries and their processes. If information resources are indeed for use, then there is a clear need to evaluate their use and determine both whether they are being used at all and if they are being used appropriately. The expression "every reader its (originally *his*) book" implies the need to evaluate the needs of individual patrons and of patron groups and to design library systems to meet those needs. Obversely, there is a need to proactively identify those patrons who can best make use of particular information resources and develop mechanisms for getting those resources to the patrons who can best use them. Saving the time of the patron is fundamental, although library systems have not always been designed with the patron's convenience in mind. It is the fifth law that most clearly relates Ranganathan's thinking to systems thinking. By describing the library as a growing organism, Ranganathan recognized that the library is not only a system but also a system with life. He also described the fate of an organism that ceases to grow.

Long after Ranganathan first formulated his five laws, Maurice Line (1979) presented an alternative view of the way things really are. Line's five laws are

1. Books are for collecting

2. Some readers their books

3. Some books their readers

4. Waste the time of the reader

5. A library is a growing mausoleum

There is a dark side to Line's humor that lies very close to home. Any observant, thoughtful, or simply aware librarian can think of many examples of situations and policies that are more closely aligned with Line's cynicism than with Ranganathan's idealism. Many honest librarians would have to admit that they have at one time or another been active participants in supporting the reality behind Line's facetiousness.

CHARACTERISTICS OF EVALUATION

Building a culture of evaluation is a deliberative process that requires thought, effort, planning, patience, and evaluation. It also requires a deep understanding of and appreciation for the fundamental characteristics of evaluation.

1. Evaluation results from design, not accident. Although assigning value is a basic human trait, true evaluation is a deliberately designed process. The success of the evaluation has its origin in the quality of the design. Carelessly planned and sloppily designed evaluation inevitably results in poor results that are of limited use. It is generally impossible to improve the quality of data once they are gathered, so making sure they are gathered properly and mean what they are believed to mean are essential steps in the design process.

2. Evaluation has a purpose. Effective evaluation is intrinsically goal oriented. If the purposes, goals, and objectives of evaluation are poorly defined, inadequately understood, or incorrectly communicated, the result will be a faulty evaluation.

3. Evaluation is about quality. Determining how well some process is carried out, how good some product is, how appreciated a service is, or how thoroughly a service outlet is used are all ways of assessing quality. Evaluation that does not address quality and that is not based in a desire to achieve high quality is sterile and fundamentally pointless.

4. Evaluation is more than measurement. Measurement may be part of evaluation, but that doesn't mean that measurement is a substitute for evaluation. Measurement must be tied to and derived from the design and purpose of evaluation. A university library with millions of volumes may ultimately be of less value to an undergraduate student with an undecided major than the local public library. A huge collection that contains multiple copies of aging titles may be inferior in quality to a library with an active weeding program.

5. Evaluation doesn't have to be big. A small, focused evaluation project that requires only a few days to complete in a single library can have as much immediate and long-term impact as a year-long study addressing a broad range of needs and based on data drawn from a nationwide survey. It is the explicit need and whether it is met through evaluation that determines the quality of the evaluation effort.

6. There is no one right way to evaluate. The need for evaluation is situational, as are the tools and resources available to carry out the evaluation and the skills of the individuals charged with carrying out the evaluation. Although it is appropriate and useful to seek models in the professional literature or by consulting with other librarians in other settings, imaginative librarians who develop their own ways of doing things carry out the some of the best evaluation projects. If the project has been carefully designed, if the purposes of the evaluation are well constructed and thoroughly understood, and if the tools, measures, and processes are appropriate to the need for evaluation, the evaluation project will yield useful results.

NURTURING THE EVALUATION HABIT

The Evaluation Action Plan

Building toward a culture of evaluation requires making evaluation a habit, making it more difficult not to evaluate than to evaluate. One approach to nurturing that habit is development of an Evaluation Action Plan to guide the evaluation process. An Evaluation Action Plan asks the following questions:

1. What's the problem?

2. Why am I doing this?

3. What *exactly* do I want to know?

4. Does the answer already exist?

5. How do I find out?

6. Who's involved?

7. What's this going to cost?

8. What will I do with the data?

9. Where do I go from here?

What's the Problem?

Evaluation is usually undertaken to solve some kind of problem; it is rare and justifiably unusual for anyone to begin an evaluation project solely for the enjoyment of the experience. Problems may begin as anomalous states of dissatisfaction, concern, or uncertainty. Conversely, they may come to the library's administration and staff as full-blown crises. It is important to thoroughly understand the problem and to recognize that the problem as it is originally presented or observed may not be the real problem. The problem may be stated as "the library doesn't offer enough parking" but really be a matter of staff members from the adjacent municipal office building finding it just a little more convenient to park in the library's lot rather in the lot officially designated for their use. Analyzing a problem is much like analyzing a reference question—the real problem may lie below the surface of the perceived problem.

It is also important to verify that there really is a problem. Most perceived problems turn out to be real problems that need to be evaluated and addressed. In some cases, however, the perception *is* the problem and the solution lies in assessing the perception and working to change it. The simple complaint "this library doesn't even have a copy of *The Autobiography of Miss Jane Pittman*" may reveal a collection gap, but may instead underlie a misperception that Ernest Gaines's renowned novel is a work of nonfiction.

Why Am I Doing This?

Evaluation of library services is carried out for a variety of purposes that derive from the contexts in which the library exists. The most prominent among these purposes are administrative decision making, public relations, and politics. Although these purposes can be discussed independently, the systems approach to understanding suggests a more holistic approach in which it is explicitly understood that evaluation may serve multiple purposes. The study conducted to determine how many patron computer workstations are needed may be useful in alerting the public to the library's ability to provide access to the Internet and may at the same time be used to support or defend an investment in computer technology.

Administrative Decision Making. Much of the focus of evaluation is making decisions regarding resource allocation, personnel training and evaluation, procedure development and revision, and planning. Evaluation projects carried out to meet these purposes tend to be very focused and concrete and may have very obvious expected outcomes.

Public Relations. Evaluation can play an important role in educating and persuading the public as well as explaining the library to parallel institutions such as schools and social service agencies. Evaluation as a public relations tool tends to focus on user satisfaction and may involve market surveys, patron surveys, and appeal marketing.

Politics. Libraries of every kind exist in a political arena; library administrators in particular must be sensitive to the political interactions of which they are an integral part. Evaluation can serve to justify and explain administrative decisions to governing bodies and higher level administrators.

What *Exactly* Do I Want to Know?

Determining precisely what results the evaluation is intended to generate is a matter of establishing perspective and refining the definition of the problem. Establishing a sense of perspective helps determine the specific models, methodologies, and tools that will be necessary for carrying out the evaluation. Some important perspective-oriented questions are

1. Do I want to assess the perceptions of the library, its services, or both? If so, do I want to look at patron perceptions, patron subgroup perceptions, perceptions of the general public, administrators' perceptions, governing body perceptions, or a combination?

2. Do I want to determine patterns of use of resources, services, or both?

3. Do I want to find out how much things cost? Am I interested in comparing costs of different ways of doing things to determine or improve efficiency?

4. Do I want to find out how effective library services are or how appropriately they are being exploited?

Question definition is the process of turning a vague understanding of a problem area into a question that can be answered. Vague questions lead to vague answers or, much worse, to answers that are deceptively specific and don't really address the true problem area. It is generally better to obtain a good answer to a small question than to produce a low quality answer to a big question. Some questions to ask during the question definition process are

1. Can this problem be solved? Can this question be answered?

2. Will the solution or answer be usable and useful?

3. Are there aspects of the problem that need to be clarified before proceeding? Is there a need to evaluate the problem prior to evaluating the process or service area in which the problem is perceived to be present?

4. What tools are likely to be available for answering the question or solving the problem? Are they the right tools?

Does the Answer Already Exist?

Librarians are—or should be—notorious for reinventing the same wheel over and over again. An essential task in carrying out an evaluation process is to determine whether the question has already been answered or the problem has already been solved.

(Very) Local History. The starting point for determining whether there is a preexisting answer or solution lies very close to home. The problem may have been addressed at a previous time in the same library, in another branch of a multipoint library system, or in a neighboring library system. Checking whatever records exist can provide, if not a reliable answer, at least an indication of how the question was explored previously. If there were

previous attempts, it is important to know what results they produced and to what extent the evaluation led to a successful solution. It may be the case that the data are too old to be of current use, but that the approach was reliable enough to be reproduced; this has the added value of providing comparative time-series data. It may also be the case that reliable results were produced but for some reason there was a failure to implement what was learned. These are very useful things to know prior to carrying out a new evaluation process.

Consulting the Literature. It has often been the lament of library and information science researchers that too much of what is published in the field are anecdotal accounts of "How we did it good in our library." Although the value of such reports is very focused, the reports are not without value, particularly if sufficient detail is provided to impart an understanding of how it was determined that doing things that way was truly good. It is impossible for every library to have a comprehensive collection of professional literature, but the advent of Web-based research and reference databases, document delivery services, and fax machines makes effective consultation of the professional literature much more available than ever before. An important part of any evaluation project is determining whether a useful solution has been published.

Polling the Field. If you have the problem, it is not unlikely that someone else has the problem or has had it in the past. In addition to the published literature, professional conferences and meetings have long served as a means of sharing approaches to problem solving. An outgrowth of the development of library-oriented e-mail-based discussion lists is the phenomenon of what is essentially a distributed network of experts. Sending a query to an appropriate discussion list can be a very effective way to determine the thinking of other professionals who have encountered a similar problem. These answers may not provide direct input into design of the evaluation project, but may suggest tips on what to do or not do, or may provide appropriate references to the professional literature.

Existing Data-Gathering Routines. Before launching a new way of gathering data, it is advisable to determine whether the needed data are already being gathered for some other purpose. Even if the required data are not being gathered, it may be possible to add them to existing data-gathering routines rather than inventing a new way to gather data.

How Do I Find Out?

Determining how to carry out the evaluation project is a matter of determining a methodology, establishing a procedure for implementing the methodology, and determining the extent to which the problem will be explored.

Methodology. The specific methodology for the evaluation project devolves from the perspective established for the evaluation effort. Certain methodologies lend themselves to certain perspectives. Focus groups, for instance, are very useful in determining patron perceptions, are of limited use in determining patterns of use, and are of extremely limited value in assessing efficiency or effectiveness.

Procedure. Determining the specific procedures and process of the evaluation project is a matter of examining the environment in which evaluation will take place and designing procedures that can be carried out in that environment without excessively interfering with the normal operations of the library or unacceptably compromising the results of the evaluation. To a certain extent, establishing procedures derives from the methodology selected, although procedural limitations may be imposed by the library's resource base. There is an aspect of establishing procedure, however, that is entirely a matter of situational logic and requires figuring out what makes sense for the specific project in a specific environment at a specific time.

Extent. The greatest determiner of the scope and extent of the evaluation project is the availability of resources to support the evaluation effort. This should not imply that, in the unlikely presence of unlimited resources, the scope of evaluation should be infinite. Determining the extent of the project should begin with the question "How far do we want to go?" Only after that question has been answered in an honest and satisfactory manner should the second question be posed: "How far can we go?"

Who's Involved?

The critical resource issue in evaluation is the availability of people to carry out the work. Human resources for evaluation may include some combination of administrators, regular staff, staff members hired specifically to carry out the evaluation, staff members hired to free regular staff members to engage in evaluation tasks, consultants, and volunteers. Finding the right combination is an essential part of the design and planning process. The question of who is to be involved can be looked at from three major perspectives.

Who Will Plan the Evaluation? Planning is everything. Without careful and effective planning, the evaluation project cannot succeed. An important and often overlooked principle is that planning is a process that continues throughout the life of the project. All too often, planning is viewed as something that occurs at the outset and concludes when evaluation begins. It is fundamental that planning should involve not just administrators, but representatives of all the groups who will be responsible for carrying out the evaluation as well as those groups who will feel the impact of the evaluation and its results.

Who Will Be Responsible for Evaluation? In the simplest of evaluation activities, the same individual or team carries out planning and execution. For larger, more complex projects, it is necessary to separate responsibility for planning from responsibility for execution. It is always desirable to retain some overlap between the group of people charged with planning and the group charged with execution. The planners need to receive continuous feedback on the process of carrying out evaluation tasks. Similarly, the action team needs to know the thinking of the planners.

Who Will Feel the Impact of Evaluation? The impact of evaluation is felt twice: once when the evaluation is being carried out and there may be a need for subtle adjustments in library operations, and again when the results of the evaluation are turned into formative action designed to modify those operations. The prime rule with regard to the impact of evaluation is advance notice—the people whose lives and work will be affected by the evaluation process and its outcomes need to know it is going to happen. It is best to keep in mind that a broad range of constituent groups may feel the impact—patrons, members of the nonpatron public, and staff in other units as well as the unit being evaluated will be affected in various ways. Anticipating the impact is always better than reacting to an unanticipated impact.

What's This Going to Cost?

As noted previously, evaluation isn't free. The costs of evaluation need to be anticipated and included in budget decisions. Evaluation costs fall into two basic categories: direct costs and indirect costs.

Direct Costs. Direct costs are tangible, obvious, and usually fairly easy to anticipate and budget. Although there will probably be some ancillary expenditures for materials and consumables required for the project, the dominant category of direct costs for evaluation is administrative and staff time. It is advisable to require staff to record time spent on special activities related to evaluation as a means of tracking evaluation costs. In some cases, it may be necessary to hire additional staff or a consultant.

Indirect Operating Costs. Indirect costs are expenditures that are necessary to the evaluation effort but that are not incurred solely in support of evaluation. These may include physical facilities costs, telecommunications, utilities, and the costs of other basic support services. Indirect costs are frequently difficult to identify precisely and may defy anticipation and budgeting. Because these expenditures are subsumed in the normal operating budget of the library, they are frequently more or less ignored in determining the cost of evaluation.

Indirect Human Costs. Although indirect operating costs may be ignored with impunity, ignoring indirect human costs is a perilous enterprise. Indirect human costs include the effects of service disruption and the impact of evaluation on staff morale.

When evaluation results in suspended, slowed, or disrupted service, there is a cost in goodwill and support for the library that must be anticipated and handled very carefully. Again, letting people know in advance that there will be or may be a disruption, and why, can go a long way toward avoiding incurring unacceptable levels of dissatisfaction with the evaluation process.

Staff morale can be tricky to assess and massage. Getting to know the staff is an essential part of the process, as is educating the staff. Some staff members may actually experience a boost in morale as a result of knowing that the area in which they work is important enough to be evaluated, but others may fear that the service or function evaluation is a personnel evaluation in disguise. The fundamental principle in conducting an evaluation that is not a personnel evaluation is making sure that staff members know that it is the service or function that is being evaluated, not them. This is especially important when the focus of evaluation is the quality of a service provided by staff.

What Will I Do with the Data?

Data Analysis. Data have no intrinsic value; they are only as good as the uses to which they are put. A detailed discussion of data analysis techniques is beyond the scope of this chapter, but it is essential to make sure that the analysis is both accurate and appropriate. Data analysis is the search for meaning, not an exercise in analytical eloquence or elegance. Qualitative data require examination, categorization, and synthesis. Quantitative data require tabulation, verification, and possibly statistical analysis. A rule of thumb in working with statistics is that the simplest, most straightforward analysis possible is frequently the most useful analysis.

Dissemination. The results of evaluation are of limited value if they are not distributed to the individuals and groups to whom they have the potential for being useful. Results may be useful to and even used by the people responsible for putting the results into action, the people who are affected by or involved in the evaluation process, and the administrations and staffs of other libraries. Dissemination may take a number of forms, including informal discussion at a routine staff meeting, a special meeting to present results, an article in a regular staff newsletter, a special news report, a detailed formal report, a presentation at a professional conference, or publication of a journal article. The goal is to get the results to the people who need them, want them, or would benefit from them in a timely and appropriate manner.

Action. The circle of the evaluation process is completed when change is implemented or when a decision is made that no change is necessary. A decision not to take action, when based on appropriate evaluation, is a positive action in and of itself. When taking action, it is important to remain aware of the nature and definition of the problem the evaluation process was designed to address and to retain close awareness of the results of the evaluation.

If correctly designed and implemented, the evaluation process should suggest targets for action, and staying close to those targets is a fundamental goal.

Where Do I Go from Here?

The last step in evaluation is evaluating the evaluation. What was learned about the problem? What was learned about other problems or areas of interest? What was learned about evaluation? What was learned about the library as a whole? What will the results of the evaluation do to influence the administration and operation of the library?

The most important potential outcome of a successful evaluation project is the completion of at least one step on the way to creating a culture of evaluation. When everything works as it should, when good results are rendered and positive action taken, when a positive attitude toward evaluation has been fostered, when people see that evaluation can make things better for them, the result may be an increased desire to engage in evaluation for the good of the library. When that happens, a culture of evaluation is truly in place and things will never be the same again.

RESOURCES

Churchman, C. West, 1968, *The Systems Approach*. New York: Delacorte Press.

The Last Whole Earth Catalog, 1974, Menlo Park, CA: Portola Institute.

Line, Maurice B., 1979, "Review of *Use of Library Materials: The University of Pittsburgh Study*," *College & Research Libraries* 40 (November): 557–58.

Ranganathan, S. R., 1964, *The Five Laws of Library Science*. Bombay: Asia House.

Measuring Organizational Effectiveness

Richard E. Rubin

EFFECTIVE ORGANIZATIONS

Effective organizations are the ones most likely to survive and prosper. It is easy to see, therefore, why measuring organizational effectiveness is crucial. Administrators, managers, and trustees all have significant stakes in determining whether their organizations are successful and why they are successful. Organizational effectiveness is not just the concern of those who work inside organizations, however, but is also important to consumers. When individuals select businesses or institutions to patronize, their decisions are often based on their evaluation of organizational effectiveness. People want to patronize organizations they believe are effective. The criteria for effectiveness used by consumers may, of course, differ in kind and in number from those used by individuals working inside the organization. For example, some patrons may use (or decline to use) a library simply because of its collection, its service, and its programs. A single unfriendly contact—one time an important item is not on the shelf, one long wait in line at the circulation desk—could substantially color a patron's view of the effectiveness of the library as a whole. The fact that there are many possible criteria for determining organizational effectiveness highlights a critical point: Measuring effectiveness depends, in large part, on point-of-view, on who is doing the judging. Librarians should be concerned about more than individual judgments, they must also be concerned with collective ones. It is the collective judgment of people connected to the library that forms the source of acceptance, stability, and prosperity for libraries.

Many researchers have expressed skepticism concerning whether it is possible to define and measure organizational effectiveness, but despite their concerns, interest in organizational effectiveness will not subside. Organizational effectiveness has been described as "the ultimate dependent variable" (Cameron and Whetten 1983a). That is, it is the standard by which almost all other measures are related. Specifically, it is critical to measure and analyze organizational effectiveness for the following reasons:

1. We want to know how well we are doing and to report our condition in an intelligible fashion to those who want or need to know.

2. We live in an age when public accountability and tight fiscal resources are a reality. We have many other competitors for limited resources, and there is little evidence that the public will be substantially increasing our available resources. Measuring organizational effectiveness provides an important rationale or justification for why resources should be allocated to libraries.

3. There is a considerable danger to organizations such as libraries if they are unable to measure and report performance. One of these dangers is that, in the absence of such information, citizens will find the most obvious and simplistic ways to assess organizational effectiveness (Cameron and Whetten 1983a). For example, research by D'Elia and Walsh (1985) reveals that patrons tend to evaluate libraries not on the quality or quantity of collections or helpfulness of staff, but on the condition of the physical facility and convenience of hours.

4. Library use is important to the library profession. A fundamental assumption of library management is that the organization can implement interventions that will increase use. Only by determining if the library is actually being used, and if not, why not, can the critical missions of libraries be achieved.

In sum, neither library administrators nor library patrons are going to suspend judgments regarding whether the library is effective or ineffective, no matter how difficult the task of measuring it is. Therefore, librarians need to find intelligent ways to determine how well the library is doing and to report the results clearly to the public.

THE SUBJECTIVE CHARACTER OF ORGANIZATIONAL EFFECTIVENESS

Like most organizational measures, it would be ideal if a scientific approach could be applied. It is generally easier if one can rely on measurable, quantitative, and easily definable factors to determine effectiveness. But management is as much an art as it is a science. Scientific approaches can help us manage and understand organizations, but libraries, like many other organizations, are also sociological and cultural institutions. They are value-laden institutions in which notions of social obligation and public good are intermingled with cost effectiveness and efficiency. Even in the private sector, the concept of organizational effectiveness is considered "inherently subjective" (Cameron and Whetten 1983a, 11). Recognizing this subjectivity requires in the evaluator a sense of modesty: that there is no "one best way" to measure organizational effectiveness; there are many ways and the evaluation itself depends heavily on who is doing the measuring and what measures are selected.

The selection of organizational effectiveness measures must therefore be seen as presupposing certain values and interests on the part of the evaluator. Each evaluation reflects these values and attitudes. In libraries, for example, choosing to survey only adult library users allows adults and library users more power than young people or nonusers to affect library decisions. Similarly, if librarians choose to evaluate by looking only at internal operations, greater influence is given to the views of employees than to the opinions of library users. In this sense, decisions concerning organizational effectiveness may tell us as much or more about those who conduct the evaluation as about the organization itself (Starbuck and Nystrom 1983). Failing to explicitly recognize these interests may result in distortion. This also highlights the need to be self-critical and reflective regarding measuring organizational effectiveness to ensure that values are not inappropriately imposed on the process. For example, the public library has often been accused of being an institution that caters to the better-educated and higher-income white middle class. Are our evaluation techniques primarily designed to assess this one set of interests?

CRITERIA FOR EFFECTIVENESS AT THE ORGANIZATIONAL LEVEL

When looking very generally at what is usually considered when measuring effectiveness at the organizational level, a wide variety of criterion have been used. Among the more common criteria are the following:

1. the extent to which goals are met,

2. the extent to which decision making is performed effectively and quality decisions are made,

3. the extent to which the organization maintains its survival,

4. the extent to which the organization meets the needs of its customers,

5. the extent to which the organization recruits and maintains a satisfactory labor force,

6. the extent to which the organization effectively directs staff,

7. the extent to which the organization exploits opportunities to grow, and

8. the extent to which the organizations treat staff and customers with respect (Cameron and Whetten 1983b).

An additional criterion is the extent to which the organization has a beneficial impact on society as a whole. This concept of trying to measure the impact on society is sometimes used to distinguish organizational effectiveness from *organizational success*. An organization is a success to the extent to which the organization satisfies the needs of society and improves it (Zammuto 1982). Obviously, for libraries this would be an appropriate, albeit elusive, measurement.

Because organizations can be viewed from multiple perspectives, there are multiple approaches and measures that can be adopted. It is best to use multiple approaches and determine if, in evaluating from different perspectives, the same basic results are being obtained. This is referred to as *triangulation*. Consider for example the multiple levels in the organization that can be subjected to evaluation and the types of measures that could be employed:

1. Individual level: To what extent does the organization create satisfaction, motivation, and commitment in the employees? To what extent are the individual goals of employees met?

2. Subunit level: To what extent do individual work groups perform effectively? To what extent are group goals obtained? To what extent is there group cohesiveness?

3. Unit level: To what extent do departments or branches meet goals? To what extent are these departments cohesive and adaptable to change?

4. Multiunit level: How effective is the coordination and communication between units? How cost effective is this coordination?

5. Organizational level: To what extent are organizational goals obtained? To what extent are customers satisfied? To what extent is the organization adaptable to change?

6. Population level: How does the organization's performance compare to other similar organizations? (Cameron and Whetten 1983b; Van De Ven and Ferry 1980).

The variety of levels and the many ways to measure effectiveness highlight the difference between what is referred to as *macro-organizational* criteria versus *micro-organizational criteria*. Macro-organizational criteria measure how effectively organizations provide for the community-at-large. They answer questions such as, "Is the organization serving its entire potential market and serving this market well?" In terms of a library, they ask, "Is the library serving all the potential users?" or "Is the library accomplishing its broader social goals?" Micro-organizational criteria focus on internal operations. They answer questions such as, "Are departments working efficiently?"; "Are qualified staff being recruited?"; and "Are employees satisfied and committed to the organization?" (Nord 1983).

MODELS OF EFFECTIVENESS

Over the years there has been much discussion and research regarding how organizational effectiveness can be measured and a variety of useful models have emerged. These include the *goal model*, the *critical constituencies model*, the *resource model*, the *human resource model*, the *natural or open systems model*, the *decision-process model*, and the *customer service model*. These models and the key questions they address are summarized in Table 2.1.

Table 2.1. Models of Effectiveness

Model	Key Question
Goal	Have the established goals of the library been met?
Critical Constituencies	Have the needs of constituents been met?
Resource	Have necessary resources been acquired?
Human Resource	Is the library able to attract, select, and retain quality employees?
Open Systems	Is the library able to maintain the system, adapt to threats, and survive?
Decision-Process	How are decisions made and evaluated?
Customer Service	How satisfied is the clientele with the library?

Goal Model

The goal model is the most popular model for organizations in the private and public sector. It is commonly used in libraries and the one model explicitly accepted by the Public Library Association through the development and promotion of its planning and goal-setting process. Several case studies in this book are grounded in the goal model. See, for instance, Miller's case study on total quality management (Case Study 2.1) or Radcliff and Schloman's discussion of using comparative data to set goals for reference services (Case Study 3.1).

In the goal-based model, the function of the organization is to accomplish the goals that have been established. The goal-based model is generally considered a rationalist model because it presumes that organizational goals can be clearly and rationally determined and that the organization can be organized in a rational way to accomplish these goals. It also assumes that the goals established are measurable and are shared and pursued by all members of the organization (Holland n.d.). The end result is what is called *goal optimization* or accomplishment of the goal.

Despite its widespread acceptance, there is considerable skepticism regarding this model: It is criticized for being simplistic. It is also criticized for producing "sweat shop" approaches to performance that can cause burnout as individuals are driven to meet goals that may be unrealistic given limited human and fiscal resources (Holland n.d.).

It is equally important to consider that an organization or department can accomplish a goal and still be perceived as ineffective by *others*. Goals can, for example, be set by many people or groups and may not even be known or disclosed to the organization. Consider the many different sources from which goals can arise:

1. The board and administration can set goals. This is a very common type of goal setting in libraries. Such goals are sometimes developed at retreats where few are present.

2. Goals can be set by staff or management. It may come as some disappointment to directors and board members, but from an operational perspective, it is the goals of managers that tend to influence organizational behavior on a day-to-day basis (Zammuto 1982). Despite earnest attempts to make goals and objectives in lower levels conform to the greater goals set by the "visionaries," preserving the status quo is particularly important, especially for middle managers. Goals that promote experimentation or reflect new and sometimes minority perspectives are typically avoided because they are unsettling to the organization and consequently threaten the security of the manager.

3. Various constituency groups, including those outside the organization can set goals. These goals may not even be known to the organization. Public institutions, like libraries, can be especially vulnerable because a particular constituency group may not explicitly reveal its goal until it is not accomplished. Disclosure of the unmet goal may first appear at a public board meeting or through a letter to the editor. Constituent judgments give social legitimacy to an organization (Zammuto 1982). If the goals of these constituents are not met, the organization's survival may be seriously threatened. Interestingly, goals established either implicitly or explicitly by outside constituents can be valid and important, but they might also be anathema to the values of the library. Groups agitating for special services to the undereducated and disadvantaged are examples of the former; groups agitating for censorship of library collections are an example of the latter. Interestingly, there is some evidence that constituency goals for public libraries may vary substantially

from the goals set internally by staff. The goal-setting process recommended for public libraries by the Public Library Association asks each library to identify three missions from eight predetermined ones. Research by D'Elia, Rodger, and Shearer reveals that public librarians often select missions for their libraries that are quite different from those chosen by the public (D'Elia and Rodger 1994; Shearer 1993). Librarians commonly set the provision of popular materials as a primary mission, whereas citizens identify educational materials as the public library's primary mission. These findings remind us that effectiveness judgments are a matter of perspective, and it is important for librarians to know which goals are accepted by the community as well as those accepted by the internal decision makers in the library.

Despite the ubiquity of goal setting in libraries, it is also important to recognize additional problems with using goal-based models:

1. Goals are sometimes hard to identify. This is true especially for social organizations, public organizations, or both in which goals are not easily expressed in quantifiable terms.

2. Goals change over time. In a dynamic social environment, demands on organizations may change substantially and quickly. This may result in significant changes in an organization's goals.

3. Goals are sometimes contradictory within the same organization or even among departments. It is easy when one reads the books on goal setting to say that all goals and objectives should be consistent; it is another thing for all units and employees to implement and understand goals in a consistent manner. This is the distinction between what is referred to as *formal* goals set by the organization and *operational goals*, which reflect the real behavior and attitudes of the employees (Holland n.d.).

4. Goals can be unrelated to or have an adverse impact on important constituencies. Goals are by their nature political as well as economic. They are choices providing positive benefits to some and depriving benefits to others. Goals will serve some constituencies but not others.

5. Sometimes goals are not relevant to the audience for which they are intended. Sometimes goals do not reflect constituency needs. Consider goals within a young adult department that emphasize books so strongly that the interest in audiovisual items and their benefits is largely ignored or inappropriately suppressed. The result might be less use of a library rather than more by the target audience.

6. Goals may reflect those who are powerful, rather than those who have the most need. Goals may be fashioned to reflect political and economic powers. Suffice it to say that institutions designed to serve broadly based constituencies must be mindful of their broader obligations. Sometimes serving the weakest segment of the community is an institution's most important obligation.

7. Goals assume a rational conception of the world. Goal setting is usually characterized as a rational process because goals are usually clear and consistent and usually have a set time established for completion. Goals of this type tend to force people into mind-sets that emphasize stability and control. Such a perspective discourages experimentation and flexibility, which are often critical for organizational effectiveness, especially in dynamic environments.

8. Goals may not focus on what is most important. With the tremendous domination of electronic technologies, there is a tendency to think of goals in primarily technological terms. Such an approach assumes that the resolving of technical problems represents achievement of true organizational goals. Librarians have been strongly focused on the implementation of technologies during the last two decades and this focus is unabated. Setting technological goals can easily lead to forgetting that technologies are means, not ends, and focusing on technological goals can lead us to de-emphasize the public and social goals of libraries. It is important for librarians to keep their social goals at the forefront and to understand technological goals as instrumental to the attainment of those greater goals.

Critical or Crucial Constituencies Model

Although the goal model is the most common, there are other models of considerable value. In the critical constituencies model, organizational effectiveness is measured by the extent to which the needs of critical constituencies are met. Each constituency has its own measure(s) of success and even for a given constituency the measures may change over time, especially in dynamic environments. The constituency model is quite appropriate for most libraries because they serve diverse populations and to serve them properly must delineate the various groups and plan collections and services to meet their needs. A variety of critical constituencies are addressed in case studies in this book, including legislators (Case Study 2.3 on quantitative reporting), employers (Case Study 2.2 on focus groups), and people with disabilities (Case Study 5.2 on access guidelines).

Constituencies are "persons acting in their own interest or as representatives of others and having some form of interdependency with the organization; constituents have needs to be fulfilled" (Seashore 1983, 55). These constituencies take on many forms, including the board and administration, middle management, staff, accrediting bodies, funding agencies, regulatory agencies, the general public or subgroups within the general public, and individuals or groups doing business with the organization.

The *critical* constituencies are usually the ones that shape the policies and practices of the organization the most. Such constituencies can be

1. the most numerous,

2. the most politically or economically powerful,

3. the most vocal, or

4. the most meaningful (e.g. children).

In reality, judgments concerning organizational effectiveness are usually seen from the perspectives of the *dominant* elite groups, who are usually perceived as the critical constituencies (Starbuck and Nystrom 1983). A great concern for public service institutions is the fact that many legitimate constituencies may be silent; these constituents tend to be less politically or economically powerful.

Not all critical constituencies are external. Library staff are a very important constituency, who by training and tradition promote and deliver services to external constituencies. Some theorists have suggested that the dominant constituencies within an organization, such as the library board determine organizational effectiveness, because these constituencies exercise the dominant power to determine the ends of the organization.

In order to use a critical constituency model effectively, the organization must engage in a variety of activities. These include

1. identifying the critical internal and external constituencies,

2. determining the resource and service needs of external constituencies,

3. identifying the needs of internal constituencies,

4. assessing the current ability of the organization to meet the needs of external constituencies and designing collections and services to meet them,

5. assessing the current ability of the organization to meet the needs of internal constituencies and making organizational changes to meet them, and

6. determining whether changes made for internal and external constituents are meeting their needs. Organizations must be especially mindful that the needs of internal and external constituents may conflict. Such conflicts can generate considerable tension.

Resource Model

The resource model views an organization as having as its central mission the acquisition of needed resources (Cameron and Whetten 1983a). This is not an unreasonable concept for public institutions, because their survival depends on resources. It also highlights a central aspect of resource effectiveness in public institutions: the source of the necessary fiscal resources.

For libraries, the source of funding is not, for the most part, the individuals who directly consume the product (library users), but the bodies that provide funds. Librarians look to legislators, mayors, county governments, or city councils for direct support. Although there is likely to be some relationship between the use of the library and funding, it is usually indirect and is substantially mediated by these political funding bodies. For this reason, measuring organizational effectiveness using the resource model means that substantial attention is paid to the relationship of the library to political units that provide funding. Smith (Case Study 2.3) provides an example that uses quantitative data in a persuasive, educational approach to decision making. Burton (Case Study 2.4) underscores the value of meaningful performance measures in explaining library services and garnering support from external constituencies.

Assessing organizational effectiveness under the resource model means

1. measuring the effectiveness of the process of obtaining and increasing fiscal resources,

2. measuring the degree to which influential funding sources (human or organizational) are positively disposed to the library,

3. measuring the degree to which the library is able to monitor threats to fiscal resources or the degree to which opportunities for new resources are exploited, and

4. measuring the degree to which a productive relationship is maintained with those supplying material resources such as books, audiovisual materials, computers, and supplies.

Human Resource Model

The human resource model is an offshoot of the resource model. Within the context of the human resource model, organizations are considered effective "when they attract, select and retain diverse kinds of people who are able and willing to comprehend what an organization's goals should be and to behave in ways that push the organization toward the future"(Schneider 1983, 30). The human resource model provides an important framework for several of the case studies described in this casebook. Miller (Case Study 2.1) emphasizes the importance of staff participation in administration and goal setting. Radcliff and Schloman (Case Study 3.1) utilize perceptions of patrons and staff in assessing reference services. Gatten and Radcliff (Case Study 3.2) use unobtrusive testing to evaluate the effectiveness of and need for training in interpersonal communication and questioning techniques.

Effectiveness is measured by the success of the organization in effectively carrying out human resource practices. To this end, effectiveness measures include

1. measuring the employee turnover rate and reasons for leaving,

2. measuring levels of job satisfaction and worker commitment among employees,

3. measuring the success of the hiring system to attract productive workers, and

4. measuring the employees' degree of belief that the reward system is fair and that there are positive effects to the display of personal motivation and ability.

Natural or Open Systems Model

This model has been extremely popular since the 1960s. It perceives the organization as similar to a natural system—a living organism. It is part of the General Systems Model, a much larger model developed in the 1960s. The organization is conceived metaphorically as a living thing. This model views living organisms as constantly interacting with the environment, making adaptations, and responding to threats in the environment. The purpose of living organisms is to survive; so it is with organizations. This is different from conventional approaches to understanding organizations in which their purpose is viewed as the maximization of profit. From the open systems perspective, although maximization of profit is a desirable end, the true purpose of the organization is to survive. Sensitivity to environmental change is evident in Froehlich's attention to search engines (Case Study 5.1) and Lilly and Mitchell's attention to services for people with disabilities (Case Study 5.2).

Many things may threaten libraries: funding deprivation, failures on the part of materials and service suppliers, low use by the public, and legal regulations. The problem is complicated because, in this view, many of the threats may not be fully disclosed. That is, just as with living organizations, sometimes the things that threaten us come as a big surprise with the result being a need for quick action. This concept is sometimes referred to as *limited* or *bounded rationality* in that we have only an obscured view of the threats that can face us.

The effectiveness of the organization is measured by its ability to maintain the system, adapt to threats, and survive. For public institutions, the concept of survival is somewhat different. Libraries, like many other public organizations, operate much like monopolies. Their effectiveness or ineffectiveness may not substantially affect income, at least not directly. In this sense, inefficient organizations do not necessarily fail; libraries themselves seldom go bankrupt or liquidate. Nonetheless, survival in the sense of being able to maintain an adequate level of services and materials is a real problem for libraries and their effectiveness can be measured by their adaptability to ensure such levels.

Assessing effectiveness requires measuring how the library adapts to threats in its environment. One attempts to identify the forces in the environment that could damage the library and explores how the library adapts to anticipate and deal with problems. This could be accomplished by

1. measuring the organization's ability to fill positions quickly and with qualified personnel,

2. measuring the organization's ability to create a positive public image among its users,

3. measuring the organization's ability to react productively to crises and promote programs and services successfully,

4. measuring the administration's success in creating among funding bodies a positive attitude toward the library, and

5. measuring the library's effectiveness in dealing with suppliers.

Decision-Process Model

Organizations develop their own methods for collecting, organizing, disseminating, processing, and using information. "An effective organization is perceived as one that optimizes the processes for getting, storing, retrieving, allocating, manipulating, interpreting and discarding information" (Seashore 1983, 60).

Measuring organizational effectiveness in this context focuses on how communications occur and decisions are made. Decision quality becomes the crucial factor. Among the possible sources of evaluation are

1. measuring levels of participation or levels of group involvement in making decisions, and

2. measuring the extent to which the decision processes and rules produce good consequences.

The iterative process of data gathering, decision making, and outcome testing is reflected in Miller's repeated use of employee surveys (Case Study 2.1), Smith's tracking of the impact and use of an educational brochure (Case Study 2.3), Radcliff and Schloman's repetition of a standardized reference effectiveness method (Case Study 3.1), and Halliday's use of list checking to examine the effectiveness of collection development policies and procedures (Case Study 4.2).

Customer Service Model

In the customer service model, the measure of effectiveness is the extent to which customers' needs are satisfied. This is sometimes referred to as the "consumer sovereignty" model because consumers' preferences are seen as controlling the decisions of the organization (Nord 1983). Evaluating customer attitudes is a complex process. One model suggests that the perception of service quality by customers is based on the following five factors:

1. Tangibles: appearance of physical facilities, equipment, personnel, and communication materials

2. Reliability: ability to perform the promised service dependably and accurately

3. Responsiveness: willingness to help customers and provide prompt service

4. Assurance: knowledge and courtesy of employees and their ability to inspire trust and confidence

5. Empathy: caring, individualized attention provided to customers (Parasuraman, Berry, and Zeithaml 1991, 338).

Based on these factors, measurement of customer satisfaction can be accomplished in many ways. Some methodologies, such as focus groups (Verny and Van Fleet, Case Study 2.2) ask patrons directly about their experiences and satisfaction levels. Others use proxies to assess likely levels of satisfaction (Gatten and Radcliff, Case Study 3.2). The basic perceptions of library service that should be examined include

1. the customer's view of the attractiveness of physical facilities and equipment,

2. the customer's view of the helpfulness of staff and informational materials, and

3. the customer's view of the dependability and quality of library services.

SUMMARY

All responsible librarians strive to be organizationally effective, but there is no one way to measure organizational effectiveness. Library administrators should view organizational analysis not as a one-time activity but as an ongoing multidimensional process. Although the goal-setting model recommended by the Public Library Association can be useful, it should not be seen as a complete approach. Much depends on the purposes of the evaluation and the perspective of those conducting it. Before deciding on a particular approach or set of approaches one must address a variety of issues. These include, but are not limited, to the following:

1. What is the purpose of the evaluation?

2. Whose point(s)-of-view is critical?

3. What functions are being evaluated?

4. What levels of the organization are being evaluated?

5. How will the results of the evaluation be used?

6. How much time, money, and staff are available to conduct the evaluation?

7. What type of information is needed to conduct the evaluation?

8. Against what standard can results be assessed?

9. Who will conduct the evaluation?

10. What are the possible sources of bias in the evaluation?

By approaching organizational effectiveness from many perspectives, it is possible to get a more accurate picture of the true performance of the institution. This, in turn, permits the library to deal more realistically with the problems and challenges facing it, and to plan constructively in the dynamic environment in which libraries now struggle to survive and prosper.

RESOURCES

Cameron, Kim S., and David A. Whetten, 1983a, "Organizational Effectiveness: One Model or Several?" pp. 1–24 in *Organizational Effectiveness: A Comparison of Multiple Models*, eds. Kim S. Cameron and David A. Whetten. New York: Academic Press.

———, 1983b, "Some Conclusions About Organizational Effectiveness," pp. 261–77 in *Organizational Effectiveness: A Comparison of Multiple Models*, eds. Kim S. Cameron and David A. Whetten. New York: Academic Press.

D'Elia, George, and Eleanor Jo Rodger, 1994, "Public Opinion About the Roles of the Public Library in the Community: The Results of a Recent Gallup Poll," *Public Libraries* 33 (January/February): 23–28.

D'Elia, George D., and Sandra Walsh, 1985, "Patrons' Uses and Evaluations of Library Services: A Comparison Across Five Public Libraries," *Library and Information Science Research* 7 (January): 3–30.

Holland, Thomas P., n.d., *Organizational Effectiveness in the Human Services*. Cleveland, OH: Case Western Reserve University, Mandel Center.

Nord, Walter R., 1983, "A Political-Economic Perspective on Organizational Effectiveness," pp. 95–133 in *Organizational Effectiveness: A Comparison of Multiple Models*, eds. Kim S. Cameron and David A. Whetten. New York: Academic Press.

Parasuraman, A., Leonard L. Berry, and Valerie A. Zeithaml, 1991, "Perceived Service Quality As a Customer-Based Performance Measure: An Empirical Examination of Organizational Barriers Using an Extended Service Quality Model," *Human Resource Management* 30 (Fall): 335–64.

Schneider, Benjamin, 1983, "An Interactionist Perspective on Organizational Effectiveness," pp. 27–54 in *Organizational Effectiveness: A Comparison of Multiple Models*, eds. Kim S. Cameron and David A. Whetten. New York: Academic Press.

Seashore, Stanley E., 1983, "A Framework for an Integrated Model of Organizational Effectiveness," pp. 55–70 in *Organizational Effectiveness: A Comparison of Multiple Models*, eds. Kim S. Cameron and David A. Whetten. New York: Academic Press.

Shearer, Kenneth, 1993, "Confusing What Is Most Wanted with What Is Most Used: A Crisis in Public Library Priorities Today," *Public Libraries* 32 (July/August): 193–97.

Starbuck, William H., and Paul C. Nystrom, 1983, "Pursuing Organizational Effectiveness That Is Ambiguously Specified," pp. 135–61 in *Organizational Effectiveness: A Comparison of Multiple Models*, eds. Kim S. Cameron and David A. Whetten. New York: Academic Press.

Van De Ven, Andrew H., and Diane L. Ferry, 1980, *Measuring and Assessing Organizations*. New York: John Wiley.

Zammuto, Raymond F., 1982, *Assessing Organizational Effectiveness*. Albany, NY: State University of New York Press.

Method @ A Glance: Total Quality Management

Purpose: Improving overall organizational effectiveness

Description: Total Quality Management (TQM) is a management style in which processes are examined and refined with the goal of improving the performance of an organization.

Strengths: Process oriented, customer focused, staff empowering, team centered, systematic, ongoing

Use: As part of strategic planning

Data Needed: Perceptions, opinions, observed behaviors, performance statistics

Sources of Data: Interviews, meetings, focus groups, staff satisfaction surveys, existing internal documents and procedures, procedures tailored to the specific data-gathering need

Organizational Model(s): Goal, Critical Constituencies, Human Resources, Open Systems, Decision-Process, Customer Service

Procedure:

1. Engage in management activities that build staff trust.

2. Train staff in the processes and procedures of Total Quality Management.

3. Build teams to work on implementation of quality initiatives.

4. Employ appropriate assessment and measurement tools to gather, analyze, and understand data.

5. Establish and move toward recognizable targets for improvement of quality.

Case @ A Glance:
Implementing Total Quality Management

Purpose:	Changing the management and organizational climate at the Westlake Porter Public Library
Description:	A comprehensive Total Quality Management (TQM) project begun in 1993 was the focus for five years of activity involving all library staff members.
Use:	To shift from a traditional organizational culture to a quality organization that focuses on customers, continuously improving processes
Sources of Data:	1. Internal employee attitude surveys conducted in 1992 and 1998
	2. TQM literature
	3. Feedback from training sessions and an intensive Staff Day
	4. Feedback from teams appointed to carry out quality initiatives
	5. Quantitative data gathered through use of a "TQ Toolkit"
	6. External data such as ranking in Hennen's American Public Library Report (HAPLR)
Procedure:	1. Employee attitude survey distributed and analyzed
	2. TQ Team appointed to develop procedures
	3. Training session for all library staff conducted focusing on individual operating styles
	4. Training session for supervisory staff conducted focusing on communication and management styles
	5. Staff Day for all library staff conducted
	6. Teams appointed to address issues identified by the employee attitude survey
	7. Predefined TQ Toolkit applied
	8. Targets for quality improvement established
	9. Second employee attitude survey distributed and analyzed

CASE STUDY

2.1

Implementing Total Quality Management

Paula J. Miller

SETTING

Westlake Porter Public Library is located in and serves a western suburb of Cleveland, Ohio. Porter is a medium-sized library with a collection of about 130,000 books and an additional 30,000 audiovisual items, periodical subscriptions, electronic resources, and other print materials. Westlake's population of just more than 31,000 (1998) is expected to grow to 40,000 over the next one to two decades, while the number of registered borrowers has grown from 36,000 (1992) to more than 42,000 (1998) due to additional users from surrounding communities. Porter's operating budget of about $3.5 million is comprised of approximately 35 to 40 percent in state funding and about 55 to 60 percent in local property tax dollars each year. When this project began in 1993, the staff size was 38.0 FTE. In 1998, 85 regular and 12 substitute positions constituted a dedicated staff of 48.5 FTE.

IMPETUS

In 1992, the timing was right for introducing a new management model at Westlake Porter Public Library. The organizational culture of the library was one of distrust, blaming, and punishment. The organizational structure was very narrow and strictly hierarchical. Communication was closed and secretive. Decision making was a privilege granted to only a few individuals and the resultant decisions seemed arbitrary to other employees. Customer relations focused on protecting the library's collection and facility, so procedures and rules punished the innocent and the guilty when perceived infractions occurred, creating situations that were frequently strained and confrontational. All of this combined into a model of negative interaction that obstructed effective internal relations and that jaundiced, if not sabotaged, effective service to the customers. In fact, individual stories about the library's lack of accountability and responsiveness to the community were surfacing in private conversations and public meetings outside the library, frequently accompanied by comments such as, "I won't ever go back." Internally, staff morale was at an all-time low. Externally, the library had lost credibility within the community, as evidenced by an early 1993 operating levy that passed with only a 50.3 percent yes vote.

This rather strict, punitive organizational culture was fairly commonplace in many businesses and organizations, not just in this library, for many years. Medium-sized to larger, bureaucracy-laden organizations were particularly prone to creating and fostering this type of environment in an attempt to standardize service. Although the reasoning was understandable, the side effects became injurious to the organization. This was certainly an ineffective model for good public service and *not* a model the library wanted to continue to support. In fact, in the early 1990s, popular as well as scholarly literature and management gurus began to emerge encouraging businesses and organizations nationwide to replace old, hierarchical organizational structures with new management systems based on empowerment and teamwork. Many organizations were beginning to embrace new management tenets, while still grappling with *how* to effectively transform themselves.

In the latter half of 1992, the director of Westlake Porter Library retired, and a new director (this author) was hired. This turnover in leadership presented opportune timing for a change initiative, and the need for one was evident within the first few months. The board and the employees were aware that the existing situation was less than optimal and seemed primed to try something new. To fully assess staff attitudes and morale and to determine which problem areas needed to be resolved first, an internal employee attitude survey was created and distributed. Survey questions solicited input on a variety of job satisfaction and morale issues, including opportunity for creativity, opportunity for input, level of challenge versus boredom in everyday work, amount and quality of communication, change orientation, sense of teamwork versus territorialism, and knowledge of "the big picture." The survey also asked for input on such issues as current policies, suggestions for improving customer service, and perceptions of fairness in budget and resource allocation.

Forty employees, 20 full-time and 20 part-time, completed the survey. The results were compiled and immediately communicated to the library board and the staff. Overall results as well as specific individual remarks within the survey reinforced the notion that a significant change effort was necessary and elucidated the fact that any effort would have to address two key areas.

First, some major customer service issues, policies, and procedures needed to be evaluated and then aligned with the mission of the library. These issues required fairly immediate resolution to improve the library's fragile relationship with the community.

Second, a more gradual, long-term transformation of the organizational culture, that is, how things got done, by whom, with whom, and how quickly, etc., needed to be initiated to improve job satisfaction and morale.

Because the situation demanded attention to people and process issues, to internal and external customers, to both feelings and facts, I suggested *Total Quality management* (TQ) as a process that might help us to assess the problems and then determine reasonable and appropriate solutions. The beauty of TQ and the primary reason it seemed to fit our existing need was that although Total Quality emphasizes data analysis to assess organizational effectiveness, its overriding tenets also constantly remind us that we should not get so lost in the numbers that we forget the people issues. After an introduction to Total Quality basic tenets, the staff and the board agreed. Thus it was in 1993, Westlake Porter Public Library began to implement TQ, with the objective of leaving behind a hierarchical, restriction-laden environment and achieving instead an organizational culture in which decisions would be grounded in facts, in which the operating environment would be built on valuing individual employees and facilitating teamwork, and in which innovation and change would be the norm.

METHOD

Preparatory Activities and Preliminary Decisions

A TQ team was appointed early in 1993. The team consisted of seven employees, including the director (myself) and the assistant director. Of the other five members, two were part-time and three were full-time. Two were professionals, and three were not. One was a supervisor, and the other four were not. Each of the five was from a different department in the library. A diverse array of operating styles and personalities was represented on the team. This overall balance in the team was purposeful and necessary. If the TQ effort was to be successful, it needed to involve *everyone*, and it needed to be led, from its inception, by front-line as well as supervisory and administrative staff.

The role and objectives set for the TQ Team were fourfold:

1. to learn about, ask questions of, and internalize TQ concepts (*become experts*);

2. to lead the entire staff in an examination of the TQ concept (*become trainers*);

3. to facilitate a total organizational commitment to quality service at Porter Library (*become mentors*); and

4. to facilitate incorporation of quality service into the strategic planning process (*become leaders*).

TQ was reaching the height of its popularity at this time, so there were a number of Total Quality leaders, definitions, and templates from which to choose. The team adopted as a working definition: "Total Quality adds value for customers by continuously improving processes." Paramount in that definition were three values: customer service, continuous evaluation, and process improvement. To each value, we affixed a primary message or concept. First, we consciously interpreted customers to include both internal and external customers and aggressively preached this interpretation to staff. Every department and employee needed to understand that the other departments and employees were also their customers and should be treated as such. Second, continuous evaluation would automatically bring with it continual change. Third, this process improvement meant finding and fixing problems and would focus on fixing the process rather than blaming the person.

Through readings and training during the first six months of its existence, our team narrowed down our TQ focus primarily to W. Edwards Deming's 14 Points in general, but we also began to identify what was most crucial to our own organization and refined our focus even further. Our goal was to become a quality organization that

1. focuses on customers,

2. continuously improves processes,

3. uses the knowledge and skills of all staff,

4. prevents mistakes,

5. uses facts to make decisions,

6. uses statistical and analytical tools to measure success,

7. uses feedback to evaluate success, and

8. adds value.

By examining this list of eight descriptors, one can see that Total Quality addresses two *sides*, that is, uses two approaches, to achieving effective business operations. One aspect is the behavioral or *soft* side of TQ, which addresses people and environment issues in the workplace. The second is the statistical or *hard* side of TQ, which introduces tools and techniques for data analysis to obtain objective and appropriate measurements. One of the most important, "right" things our team did early in the implementation process was to focus on the soft side of TQ first. Our rationale for doing so was an overwhelming sense of urgency to begin to address the organizational culture, or internal customer issues, first. If we could not work well together, how could we expect to give good customer service to the public? If we remained internally dysfunctional, how could we expect to improve anything else?

The choice to focus on the soft or people issues first proved to be a fortuitous one, as we later discovered. A number of other libraries around us were interested in pursuing Total Quality, but chose to focus on a specific project or problem to resolve, jumping right in to using the evaluation tools and focusing on the numbers first. In discussions with individuals from these libraries, it seemed that those TQ efforts either failed or experienced limited success. To our knowledge, no other TQ effort around us succeeded as ours did, nor did any other library around us experience the full staff support for the effort that ours maintained.

The second "right" decision we made early in this process was to avoid approaching TQ in too formulaic a fashion. We did not want to be so constrained or worried about implementing Deming's 14 Points, in order from 1 to 14, for instance, that Total Quality became an inflexible and time-consuming chore rather than a useful problem-solving tool or an effective operations mode. Thus, we made a conscious decision *not* to implement all the steps and *not* to utilize all the tools available right away.

The third "right" decision we made spawned an additional, unexpected level of intricacy to our initiative, for we could locate no other library that could serve as a model: We decided to incorporate and utilize the tools and techniques of Total Quality in our long-range planning process. No long-range plan existed for Porter Library in 1993. A strategic plan, by its very nature, however, would obviously address and assuage some of the staff concerns that had surfaced in the internal survey such as clarifying library priorities, rendering decision making less arbitrary, and providing direction for the organization. The plan would certainly also clarify objectives for effective services to the public and contribute order and continuity to the steps for achieving those objectives. If we were to become a Total Quality organization, it made sense to apply Total Quality tenets and tools to the root of the organization's future activities, that is, to incorporate Total Quality measurements and evaluation techniques into the planning process as well as into the strategic plan itself.

The Steps to Implementation:
Trust → Training → Teams → Tools → Targets

The timing was right. We laid the preparatory groundwork. We began the process of implementing and internalizing TQ, not realizing until much later that the steps we took actually seemed to fall into five phases: trust, training, teams, targets, and tools. The first three phases dealt with people (soft side) issues, whereas the final two focused on the numbers (hard side) of TQ.

Trust

Deming's Point 7 is to "institute leadership" and his Point 8 is to "drive out fear." Our first challenge or step in implementing TQ was to establish enough trust in the leadership and in each other that fear of mistakes and of retaliation were totally obliterated. Our ultimate objective was to be so successful at establishing a positive, trusting environment that creativity and ideas could flourish and employees could feel empowered enough to implement those ideas. To reinforce a more positive internal environment and to begin to repair damaged and fragile morale, we emphasized the concept of internal customers. We needed to focus on internal relations first and then let improved external customer service follow, naturally.

During this phase, library leadership and the TQ team heavily reinforced our philosophy of not pointing fingers to place blame, replacing it with a mantra of blaming the process, not the person. We also emphasized the necessity of informed risk taking or experimentation and gave consent to make mistakes, to not always be right the first time.

Early Training

The concepts just described were stated and described in our first phase, but they were internalized during our second phase, *training*. Two early training components were provided very early in the process. They were key elements and set the stage for all activities and training to follow. Both were conducted internally, by the director, and were about two hours in length.

Operating Styles. Attendance at this first training component was required of all staff; sessions were repeated to allow every employee to attend. Basically, we provided an educational, but fun, exercise and discussion on individual operating styles—how people tend to approach situations and problems differently, depending on their individual personalities. Various tools are available to assess styles—the Meyers–Briggs Type Indicator, a variety of tools that categorize people into four quadrants, or more recently, enneagrams, for instance. Any of these tools would work. The very strong message in this training was that there is no wrong style or personality and that, in fact, there is also no one right operating style. In fact, the best ideas and solutions are generated by *teams* of individuals representing a *variety* of styles, utilizing the strengths of each in approaching the problem to come up with the best solution.

Communication and Management Styles. This second training component was specifically for supervisory staff of the library. This component focused on communication styles of managers, highlighting the advantages of open communication. This session also prepared supervisors for a team-oriented work environment through a discussion on the shift from traditional management roles and tasks to a more facilitative management style. This new model of management emphasizes trust over believing the worst, sharing information rather than guarding it, preferring team consensus and solutions to solving the problem alone, emphasizing process over task, using coaching skills rather than controlling ones, and serving as a catalyst to innovation rather than maintaining the status quo. All supervisors were required to complete pertinent background reading prior to this training to facilitate discussion of these issues.

Staff Day. By far the most significant training component, however, was the full Staff Day held in the summer of 1993. Our TQ initiative was approximately six months old and, up to this point, had primarily focused on training and preparing our TQ Team. The TQ team led a Staff Day full of activities and training components to officially kick off our full staff Total Quality initiative. There were three major components of the Staff Day training: 1) Internal customer service and creating a positive environment, 2) Paradigms and change, and 3) Empowerment and teamwork.

Internal Customer Service and "Eliminating Fear". The training component on internal customer service and positive environments reinforced everything that we had previously alluded to or discussed concerning showing trust and respect for each other and expecting the same from "the organization."

Paradigms and Continuous Change. To explain the concept of paradigms, we used a videocassette produced and narrated by futurist Joel Barker. The video effectively shows how paradigms, or mind-sets, are barriers to organizational innovation. They can stifle truly wonderful ideas and can hinder revolutionary organizational progress. This video made such an impact on library staff, in fact, that, for a while it became almost a cult phenomenon. The video has become part of our "Core Training" program for new employees, and we provide popcorn for viewers, allowing any "groupies" to watch it again, if they wish. I credit this powerful video with giving our employees the resolve to avoid organizational stagnation and the motivation to become more than just another public library.

At Staff Day, we followed up the paradigms video immediately with training to facilitate a better understanding of the change cycle. In this training segment, we emphasized that even "good" change causes stress, that change can be difficult to assimilate, and that complaining about it is a natural part of the adaptation process. We also emphasized that different individuals adapt to change, or go through the change cycle, at different rates, that is, that, at least where change was concerned, we shouldn't expect to all be on the same page at the same time. Our final training message was that employees should begin to expect fairly constant change at Porter Library, because change was a natural partner to continuous improvement.

Empowerment and Teamwork. The training component on empowerment encouraged front-line and individual decision making. We acknowledged the knowledge and skills of all staff members and articulated library administration's sincere commitment to utilize those talents better. An inverted organizational structure, which pushed decision making as close to the customer as possible, was unveiled and instituted. Staff members were encouraged to begin taking more control over the procedures that affected them the most. A second empowerment issue stressed in the training, however, was that decisions and actions by empowered staff should not be arbitrary, but should still be made and taken responsibly. To that end, we included an interactive exercise designed to generate a list of factors that are important to consider when making a decision. The list is still valid and available today to help employees to consider all aspects of a problem and to ensure selection of the best alternative available to them at the time (Table 2.1.1).

Table 2.1.1. Responsible Empowerment: The WPPL Model

Decision-making Questions and Considerations
What is the cost? ($, +/- PR, time, other)
What is the big picture?
How reliable is the information I have? Do I need more?
How does this affect other departments, teams, areas?
Is safety or security an issue?
What is the long-term as well as the short-term impact?
What is the *real* problem/issue from the customer's perspective? From our perspective?
Is time a factor?
Is there any *good* reason we shouldn't do this?
If I *can't* do what is being asked, what can I do?

The Staff Day training component on teamwork built upon the concepts that had been introduced in the operating styles training. If diverse individual operating styles bring different strengths and concerns to the table, then a team of employees working together on a particular problem will bring even more potential alternatives and a greater likelihood that the resultant solution will be effective. The teamwork component encouraged staff to discard and ban "killer phrases," such as, "We've never done it that way," "We tried that," etc.

Additional training for staff later that year and in ensuing years included bringing in a consultant to provide an overview of Total Quality for all employees; bringing in a consultant to train and prepare the TQ team in facilitation skills and team dynamics; providing training on creativity for all staff; and providing training for all staff in several techniques for measurement and evaluation.

Teams

Deming's Point 9 is "break down barriers" and Point 12 is "remove barriers to pride." The Staff Day training component on teamwork set the stage for working in teams on a variety of projects. By the end of 1993, five teams were established to deal with issues that were identified as major concerns in the staff survey: building constraints, policies, performance appraisal, materials selection, and awards and recognition. Six additional teams were established for strategic planning, one for each overarching goal in the plan. All teams were cross-functional and multidimensional, with part-time as well as full-time representation, intermixed department representation, and diverse operating styles. To ensure active involvement in the creation of a planning document that would guide the library's initiatives for the next five years, and to reinforce experience with the Total Quality process, every employee working 20 or more hours a week was *required* to be on a strategic planning team, regardless of position in the library. Involvement of other staff, for example, part-timers working less than 20 hours per week, was voluntary. Individuals were assigned to teams, to ensure balance of team makeup, but employees could indicate their areas of interest ahead of time, and those preferences were taken into consideration.

After bringing in a consultant to provide training in team dynamics, facilitation skills, and several Total Quality measurement tools, TQ team members were ready to serve as team leaders for the strategic planning process. The library used the American Library Association's (ALA) strategic planning process, but added a twist. We folded in the Total Quality data-gathering and analysis techniques. For instance, we did an environmental scan, as recommended by the ALA planning process, of course, but then used Total Quality methods to sort through, analyze, and prioritize that data. The overall goals for the plan had just been generated and approved by the Board of Trustees. Total Quality techniques, including multivoting, affinity groupings, and a Pareto analysis, were used at board meetings to reach consensus on the plan's final goals.

Tools

If the only tool you have is a hammer,
everything starts to look like a nail.

Abraham Maslow

Abraham Maslow's words suggest that employees need to be skilled in a multitude of measurement and analysis techniques, so as not to inadvertently arrive at the same solution—or an inappropriate solution—every time a problem arises. In other words, employees needs to have at their disposal a problem-solving toolbox from which they can select the most appropriate tool for analysis. Again, the TQ team served as the experts and trainers, developing a required half-day training session for all library staff. Requiring everyone to attend the tools training was one of the keys to successful implementation of TQ: Everyone needed to know how to use at least a few basic tools. In the month following the training session, we put those new skills to the test. We required each department to use at least one of the tools in solving a problem or enhancing a service, thereby making the new skills immediately relevant (Table 2.1.2). We made this task easier by providing each department with readily accessible resources, in the form of a "TQ Toolkit," complete with Post-its®, dot stickers, markers, and easel pads.

Table 2.1.2. TQ Tools: WPPL's First Experiences

Dept. Team	Problem/service	Tool(s) Used
Reference	CD-ROM selection	Decision matrix
Finance	Meeting approval and reimbursement	Flowchart
Circulation	Registration codes	Brainstorming Multivoting
Administration	To LAN or not to LAN	Force-field analysis Mindmapping
Tech. Services	Reduction of new materials backlog	Flowchart Brainstorming Decision matrix
Board of Trustees	Goals for the strategic plan	Brainstorming Multivoting Affinity groupings Pareto chart

The second key to success in this "TQ Tooltime" training session was to make it manageable rather than overwhelming. Because this was the first exposure the general staff would have to the "hard side" of TQ, the team opted to introduce a limited number of tools, selecting the five they felt staff would find most useful and use most frequently—brainstorming, flowchart, fishbone diagram, Pareto chart, and decision matrix. The trainers also addressed the issue of comfort level with numbers and math, for example, we acknowledged the fact that many people have "math phobia," but pointed out that with the proper training and tools, no one need fear numbers, and that, to the contrary in fact, "numbers are our friends."

The introductory comments to the "TQ Tooltime" explained why data and objective analysis are important. Most frequently, organizations make decisions based on such factors as who argues the loudest, somebody's gut feeling, who has the most political pull, who holds out the longest, or who controls the resources. Data (any concrete statistics, information, or output), however, helps people understand, analyze, and evaluate a process or service objectively. The main purpose in data collection is to collect, organize, and present the numbers in such a way that individuals who may disagree can look at those numbers and begin to agree.

The final key to success with the "TQ Tooltime" training was to make it fun. The team used "favorite donuts" as the topic for the Pareto exercise, for instance. The director's introductory segment was videotaped in front of a basement tool counter, complete with hardhat and tool belt. To illustrate how to create and use a decision matrix, each group created a matrix to reach a consensus on where the entire staff would go if an all-expenses-paid (imaginary, of course) group vacation was suddenly available.

In ensuing months, supplemental measurement and evaluation tools were introduced. Additional tools for idea generation included refinements of brainstorming techniques (nominal grouping and multivoting), brainwriting, mindmapping, force-field analysis, fishbone diagrams, and *The Five Whys* (Senge 1994) root cause analysis technique. Tools for measurement and collecting data included a variety of charts as well as surveys and focus groups. Tools for consensus building and for prioritizing alternatives included affinity diagrams, Pareto charts, and decision matrices. Tools for goal setting, project management, and evaluation included the PDCA (Plan-Do-Check-Act) cycle, Gantt charts, and benchmarking.

Targets

Our early "targets" for the TQ effort numbered just three, and they were fairly broad and general:

1. to change the corporate culture to one that would facilitate change, foster empowerment, and facilitate teamwork;

2. to set some reasonable and some stretch organizational goals through benchmarking; and

3. to incorporate measurable objectives into the strategic plan to better monitor progress and effectiveness of library services.

Setting measurable objectives followed easily on the heels of the tools training. With the strategic planning teams in full swing, measurable objectives were formulated and incorporated into the strategic plan. Once the strategic plan was completed, one-year action plans were also created each year, accompanied by a Gantt chart (timeline), to monitor deadlines and progress.

And finally, to compare where the library currently was in terms of what was actually possible for a library of our size, we began to benchmark ourselves against other libraries. Using library statistics collected and distributed through the state, along with national data available from the Public Library Data Service's annual publication, we could begin to easily benchmark such standard library measurements as collection turnover, circulation per capita, cost per circulation, and circulation per FTE, to name a few. Benchmarking not only allowed us to determine whether our statistical outcomes were in line with other public libraries, but it also allowed us to set objectives for reaching the upper quartiles of these measurements for libraries of similar size. Benchmarking has become a crucial part of Porter Library's annual self-assessment.

It seems only appropriate, at this juncture, to also say a few words about awards and recognition. Recognizing employees' efforts and celebrating successes in reaching targeted goals is an important part of any Total Quality effort, or of any successful organization, for that matter. Beginning with our debut year, we instituted an annual awards and recognition program. The program was, in fact, developed and implemented by one of the first teams established at Porter. We have refined our awards program annually, to the point that it is frequently requested by other libraries to use as a model. Current awards range from fairly standard ones like longevity, to awards for "Bright Ideas," to our "Beyond the Walls" award for increasing the library's visibility in the community. Informal recognition, however, is just as important as formal awards: We print out birthday and hire-date anniversary cards for each staff member, and we hold quarterly "Cake and Coffee" anniversary celebrations with the director. Notes and cards expressing thanks as well as informal, fun awards for completing big projects are also distributed and genuinely appreciated.

FINDINGS

The internal impact of implementing a Total Quality effort at Westlake Porter Public Library has been phenomenal. Some of the major changes and innovations that have been implemented over the last few years include

1. renaming ourselves (from Porter to Westlake Porter),

2. changing our logo to better identify with the community,

3. eliminating annual performance appraisals in favor of a continuous feedback process,

4. establishing a "Core Training Program" that requires every new employee to complete more than 10 training components during the initial two years of employment (offerings rotate biannually), and

5. initiating a development and competencies program that reinforces organizational values and goals while providing a means for long-term employees to bump up a grade on the salary scale, through completion of specific training and activity requirements.

TQ's focus on training and on employee involvement has also resulted in the creation of several annual development opportunities for staff—an annual Planning Day, an annual Leadership Day, quarterly Brownbag ThinkTanks, semiannual Professional Issues Forums, and an annual State of the Library general staff meeting.

More specifically, attending to and nurturing the soft side tenets of Total Quality has, indeed, resulted in an organization that is innovation and change oriented. A can-do culture has replaced a can't-do attitude. The process has generated a happier, more informed, more involved staff. This, in turn, has resulted in organizational continuity through consensus and stronger staff commitment to the organization.

In the fall of 1998, the internal staff survey completed in 1992 by all staff was revived, revamped, and redistributed. A number of questions were left exactly the same as in 1992 to provide a direct comparison and accurately evaluate progress. The results show that although there are still areas that need to be addressed, significant improvement has occurred on most internal staff issues (Table 2.1.3). Although the percentage of positive responses increased in *all* areas from 1992 to 1998, progress in some areas was less than hoped for and certainly still less than acceptable. A few of the lower percentage responses are actually inconsistent with some of the higher ratings elsewhere in the survey. Part of the reason may be reasonably attributed to the timing of the survey. At the time the survey was being completed in 1998, the library had had to delay an expansion or renovation project by several months due to external circumstances. Space constraints and frustrated expectations had likely begun to impact on library services and internal working conditions and relationships.

Table 2.1.3. Employee Satisfaction & Morale: Westlake Porter Public Library Employee Survey Results

1992	Topic or Question Percent of Positive Responses (Excellent or Good)	1998
74%	Satisfied with working here?	95%
65%	Opportunity for creativity?	85%
64%	Opportunity for input?	87%
55%	Getting enough development and training?	86%
55%	Feel free to problem-solve on your own?	75%
76%	Good communication in your department?	96%
74%	Department works well as a team?	98%
37%	Staff morale okay?	81%
74%	Adequately challenged?	86%
51%	Organizational structure appropriate?	71%
83%	Feel appreciated?	96%
41%	Future opportunities here?	48%
47%	Feel well-informed?	77%
18%	Feel organization has a common goal?	43%

Finally, in terms of results, our early focus on internal customer service has, as anticipated, resulted in outstanding external customer service. Our service response has gone from reactive (being surprised by the problem) to proactive (anticipating the problem) to creative (preventing the problem by adding value). In direct contrast to its 1992 image, Westlake Porter Library has developed a reputation in the community for excellent customer service, as evidenced by an increase in positive patron comments. Everywhere our employees go in the community—the dental office, the dry cleaners, the school—people rave about the service at Westlake Porter Library. Several customers in the library have imparted to me such comments as, "It's a pleasure coming here; you can tell the staff really enjoys working with each other." The library has also been cited in the local newspaper as being a model of a "community-responsive" organization. Our family-focused Summer Reading Program was one of the first in the area to incorporate an adult component, and it has been extremely popular. Ours was one of the first libraries in the area to circulate CD-ROMs. The library added "midnight madness" hours during exam week and prior to the federal tax deadline.

This external impact of our TQ effort is also evident in increases in library usage levels and community support (Table 2.1.4). Most impressive of these changes is that circulation increased more than 50 percent in the six years since implementation of TQ began—a timeframe during which many other public libraries were experiencing stabilization of, if not decreasing, circulation levels.

Table 2.1.4. WPPL Critical Numbers: A Comparison

Measurement Area	1992	1998	Percent Change
Circulation	572,836	897,110	+57%
Visits	339,976	395,690	+16%
Registered Borrowers	34,551	42,353	+23%
Circulation per Capita	21.2	28.9	+36%
Reference Questions	91,936	117,832	+28%
Collection Turnover	5.1	5.6	+10%
"Yes" Vote Support	51%	59%	0.08

In January 1999, using a variety of weighted factors, Thomas J. Hennen published the results of his newly developed ranking system in an article in *American Libraries*, entitled "Go Ahead, Name Them: America's Best Public Libraries." Westlake Porter Public Library was ranked 3 in the midsized population category (serving 10,000–99,999). It was no accident that Westlake Porter Library was ranked in the "Top Ten." The library had specifically targeted a number of the evaluative measures used by Hennen in our strategic plan for improvement. The library's "Top Ten" ranking was, for us, an acknowledgment of the success of the library's Total Quality initiative. It was a credit to all of the dedicated, hardworking employees of the library who contributed to that ranking through their excellent customer service, to each other, *and* to the public. It was a testament to our forward-looking library board's willingness to allow the staff to innovate and to let the library break new ground with programs and services, internally and externally.

INTERPRETATION

Implementing Total Quality was the right choice for Westlake Porter Public Library. Our experiences can serve as a model to other libraries wishing to pursue a similar course—whether it be instituting a bona fide Total Quality effort, or pursuing a modified team-based orientation to management, or learning and beginning to use some of the measurement tools extolled by TQ. Each library, however, should select its own areas of emphasis and should not be afraid to modify the process to address what best suits its own particular organizational culture.

Interested libraries should also be aware that implementing TQ or any similar initiative brings with it some caveats. It takes a lot of time—in training, in team meetings, in making sure that everyone is fully informed every step of the way. It takes a lot of time—for the transition to take place. It takes a tremendous energy commitment from top management and from leaders at every level within the organization, particularly in the early phases. Role confusion, especially, due to moving from a hierarchical to a team-based organizational structure, can complicate the process. And, it takes a financial commitment and investment in training, resources, and personnel.

ACTIONS

Though we no longer frequently refer to our mode of operation as Total Quality necessarily, everything that the library started as a part of that effort remains and has become strengthened today. First, the team approach to management and problem solving has been maintained. Though some teams are disbanded upon completion of their projects, new teams are created as needed, and new team assignments are made annually.

Second, the library continues its ongoing commitment to training and staff development by prioritizing funds for this function, by doing a training-needs assessment regularly, and by maintaining a Training Team to attend to those needs. Third, we continue to focus on objective data collection and "the numbers" to ensure that decisions are based on facts. Fourth and finally, the library has maintained the commitment to encouraging individual creativity and fostering organizational innovation.

Word has spread about Westlake Porter Public Library's successes in these areas, especially locally. Various team members have been asked to present programs to other groups or libraries or, more specifically, to provide information about what we are doing right to achieve the levels of customer service and support that we have.

EVALUATION

The future of Total Quality, not just in Westlake Porter Public Library, but in general, is an interesting issue. Touted as not a fad at the height of its popularity, it has become a casualty of our management trend of the month business society, nonetheless. It is interesting that Total Quality encompasses so many of the other current management trends, issues, and buzzwords.

A Learning Organization

Westlake Porter Public Library is truly a learning organization as a result of our Total Quality initiative's considerable emphasis on training. In fact, our goal has been to become the learning organization at the center of Westlake's learning community and this goal has already heavily influenced the building design for upcoming expansion and renovation of the facility.

A Systems Approach to Management

Because of Total Quality's emphasis on the soft as well as the hard side issues, in conjunction with its emphasis on checks and balances such as the PDCA (Plan-Do-Check-Act) cycle, Westlake Porter Library is using a systems approach to organizational effectiveness. We continue to try to bring all aspects of the organization's operation into alignment with each other. Every job description, as an example, is being revised to include the mission statement of the library, clarifying how this particular job helps the library to meet its mission.

An Open-Book Management and Knowledge Management

Communication at all levels, in all directions, is crucial for a Total Quality organization, and Westlake Porter Library rapidly became, indeed, an open-book organization. Implementation of empowerment and teamwork reinforced the value of informed, knowledgeable staff to us long ago. The more staff know, the better their decisions, their work with each other, and their interactions with the public will be.

Work or Life Issues

Our emphasis on trust and respect within the organization has placed us at the forefront of examining and resolving work or life issues, an increasing concern for businesses today. Westlake Porter Library initiated a well-received Wellness Team and program in 1996, for instance. Around the same time, we planned and offered our first annual Employee/Family Day, when family members of staff—children, parents, favorite sisters—could visit the employee, learn about that specific job, and have a behind-the-scenes look at library operations. We also have adopted a philosophy of making work truly fun for both employees and the public. For example, we have announced jokes over the public announcement system during National Humor Month. We announce updated Cleveland Indians scores during playoff games. In early 1999, when we moved to a temporary site to facilitate construction, we held a staff contest to generate "Burma Shave" type sayings. The signs helped direct the public to our new temporary location. Staff in our Brownbag ThinkTank programs generated many of these clever ideas. We have, in fact, become so creative and unorthodox in our approach to services and solutions that I sometimes like to refer to us as the Southwest Airlines of the public library world.

Westlake Porter Public Library's Total Quality initiative is now six years old. For us, it has been a truly successful effort in every way. It has strongly reinforced to us that one cannot deal strictly with numbers or statistics in a vacuum, that is, every statistical analysis must also consider and address the people issues that surround the numbers.

Total Quality has helped and enabled us to identify and create an infrastructure of values—customer service, respect for employees, appreciation of diverse operating styles, open and honest communications—that will guide us for many years to come. It has helped us to develop an organizational skill set—innovation, fact-based decision making, change management, continuous evaluation and improvement, team-based problem solving—that any business would do well to emulate. We have internalized these values and skills to the extent that we no longer think of them as unusual, nor do we refer to them as specifically Total Quality issues. Newer staff, in fact, are not always immediately aware that we even consider ourselves a Total Quality organization. The bottom line for us, however, is employees who enjoy coming to work—and customers who rave about our service (and our employees). Whether we continue to refer to it as Total Quality or not is irrelevant. Total Quality was a total success at Westlake Porter Public Library.

RESOURCES

Aggarwal, Sumer, 1993, "A Quick Guide to Total Quality Management," *Business Horizons* 36 (May/June): 66–68.

Amabile, Teresa M., 1998, "How To Kill Creativity," *Harvard Business Review* 76 (September/October): 77–87.

Ashar, Hanna, and Sharon Geiger, 1998, "Using the Baldrige Criteria to Assess Quality in Libraries," *Library Administration & Management* 12 (Summer): 147–55.

Atkinson, Philip E., 1990, *Creating Culture Change: The Key to Successful Total Quality Management.* Bedford, UK: IFS.

Barker, Joel A., 1990, *Discovering the Future: The Business of Paradigms.* Burnsville, MN: ChartHouse International Learning Corporation. Videocassette.

Brache, Alan, and Geary Rummler, 1997, "Managing an Organization as a System," *Training* 34 (February): 68–74.

Carson, Kerry David, Paula Phillips Carson, and Joyce Schouest Phillips, 1997, *The ABCs of Collaborative Change: The Manager's Guide to Library Renewal.* Chicago: American Library Association.

Chatterjee, Sangit, and Mustafa Yilmaz, 1993, "Quality Confusion: Too Many Gurus, Not Enough Disciples," *Business Horizons* 36 (May/June): 15–18.

De Geus, Arie, 1997, "The Living Company," *Harvard Business Review* 75 (March/April): 51–59.

Deming, W. Edwards, 1985, "Transformation of Western Style of Management," *Interface* 15 (May/June): 6–11.

"The Enlightened Manager's Guidebook," 1998, *Inc.* 19 (October): 45–51.

Harari, Oren, and Linda Mukai, 1990, "A New Decade Demands a New Breed of Manager," *Management Review* 79 (August): 20–25.

Hennen, Thomas J., Jr., 1999, "Go Ahead, Name Them: America's Best Public Libraries," *American Libraries* 30 (January): 72–76.

Houghton, James R., 1993, "It's Time for a New Management System," *USA Today* 121 (March): 62–63.

Mackey, Terry, and Kitty Mackey, 1992, "Think Quality! The Deming Approach Does Work in Libraries," *Library Journal* 117 (May 15): 57–61.

Maslow, Abraham H., with Deborah Stephens and Gary Heil, 1998, *Maslow on Management*. New York: John Wiley.

Mears, Peter, 1993, "How to Stop Talking About, and Begin Progress Toward, Total Quality Management," *Business Horizons* 36 (May/June): 11–14.

Muir, Holly J., 1995, "Benchmarking: What Can It Do for Libraries?" *Library Administration & Management* 9 (Spring): 103–6.

O'Neil, Rosanna M., 1994, *Total Quality Management in Libraries: A Sourcebook*. Englewood, CO: Libraries Unlimited.

Orenstein, David, 1999, "Developing Quality Managers and Quality Management: The Challenge to Leadership in Library Organizations," *Library Administration & Management* 13 (Winter): 44–51.

Peischl, Thomas M., 1995, "Benchmarking: A Process for Improvement," *Library Administration & Management* 9 (Spring): 99–105.

Peitz, G. S., and E. F. Moherek, 1993, "Front-line Leaders: A Balance Between People and Systems," *HR Focus* 70 (May): 17.

Riggs, Donald E., 1993, "Managing Quality: TQM in Libraries," *Library Administration & Management* 7 (Spring): 73–78.

Senge, Peter M., 1994, *The Fifth Discipline Fieldbook: Strategies and Tools for Building a Learning Organization*. New York: Doubleday.

Sweeney, Richard, 1997, "Leadership Skills in the Reengineered Library: Empowerment and Value Added Trend Implications for Library Leaders," *Library Administration & Management* 11 (Winter): 30–41.

Thompson, Kenneth R., 1998, "Confronting the Paradoxes in a Total Quality Environment," *Organizational Dynamics* 26 (Winter): 62–74.

Method @ A Glance: Focus Groups

Purpose:	Gaining a rich understanding of constituent perceptions
Description:	Focus groups are a method for eliciting in-depth opinions and perceptions from representative individuals.
Strengths:	Interactive, in-depth, spontaneous, serendipitous
Use:	As part of service evaluation, constituent education and awareness, and strategic planning
Data Needed:	Perceptions, opinions
Sources of Data:	Representative constituents
Organizational Model(s):	Critical Constituencies, Customer Service
Procedure:	

1. Define the problem or area of interest.
2. Identify the audience or constituent group.
3. Select a neutral moderator.
4. Formulate questions.
5. Select participants to represent the constituent group.
6. Conduct focus group sessions.
7. Interpret data.
8. Generate a report.

Case @ A Glance: Conducting Focus Groups

Purpose:
: Assessing the need for professional library and information science education for the state of Ohio and the role of the Kent State University School of Library and Information Science in delivering such education

Description:
: The State Library of Ohio conducted three focus group sessions to be used in conjunction with other data sources for program assessment and planning.

Use:
: To augment quantitative data as part of the School's program planning and assessment activities in conjunction with a university graduate program review and review for accreditation by the American Library Association

Sources of Data:
: Feedback from participants in three focus group sessions

Procedure:
: 1. Need for feedback not available from routine sources recognized
  2. State Library of Ohio identified as facilitator for focus group sessions
  3. Primary groups of constituents identified
  4. Facilitator/moderators selected from the development staff of the State Library
  5. Schedule of questions developed
  6. Representative individuals identified
  7. Focus group sessions conducted
  8. Data recorded and examined for trends
  9. An oral report presented to the School at a public forum
  10. Results incorporated into reports prepared for the School's university and accreditation reviews

CASE STUDY

2.2

Conducting Focus Groups

Roger Verny and Connie Van Fleet

CONTEXT

In April 1997, the director of the Kent State University School of Library and Information Science (KSU/SLIS) requested that the State Library of Ohio conduct a series of focus groups targeting the need for professional library and information science education for the state and the role of the School in delivering such education.

The School had surveyed graduating students on a regular basis and had worked with the University's Division of Research and Graduate Studies to gather data on the perceptions of current students and the most recent five years' alumni. Although those sources of data were useful in assessment and planning, they missed a major constituent group of the School—Ohio's professional library and information science community. The focus group method was seen as an effective and cost-efficient method of gathering qualitative data. The State Library was an excellent source for skilled, knowledgeable, and neutral moderators.

DEFINITION

Focus groups gather together people who possess certain characteristics into a series of groups to provide qualitative data through focused discussion led by a neutral moderator. Focus groups allow for greater interaction among participants, more in-depth exploration of opinions and perceptions, and recognition of more spontaneous and unanticipated perceptions than other methods such as mail or telephone surveys.

Advantages of Focus Groups

1. Focus groups are interactive. This method allows the researcher to probe into a topic through dialogue with participants.

2. Focus groups are easily understood by those conducting the focus group and those participating.

3. Focus groups are relatively low cost.

4. Focus groups provide results quickly.

Limitations of Focus Groups

1. The researcher has limited control. Groups are often unpredictable.

2. Other participants influence responses. A respondent usually fills out a survey in isolation; you get that person's response to your question. With focus groups, everyone hears what others say, and respondents are susceptible to group dynamics.

3. Data are more difficult to analyze. Each response is important and attempts to categorize and tally should be avoided. The researcher must discern trends without losing the richness of individual perspectives. A combination of methodologies, those that yield qualitative and quantitative data, may be most effective.

4. Because data are gathered from a relatively small number of respondents, one must be careful when generalizing to larger populations.

5. A trained facilitator is necessary to conduct a focus group successfully, keep things under control, to moderate discussion.

6. Organization may be difficult, as it is dependent on people attending.

Use of Focus Groups

Focus groups can effectively be used

1. to get opinions from a knowledgeable stakeholder group,

2. to investigate complex behaviors or motivations: why people do or do not use a service; satisfaction or expectations,

3. to obtain feedback when there is a gap between the administrators and the target audience, and

4. to build rapport with community and staff.

Focus groups should not be used

1. when participants cannot freely express opinions,

2. when participants are not knowledgeable about the topic,

3. when quantitative or statistical data are desired: avoid any tendency to ask for "a show of hands" or in any other way attempt to quantify or tally responses,

4. to resolve a conflict: a focus group is not designed to gain consensus,

5. to make a decision by consensus: the purpose of the focus group is to gather information to aid in decision making, not to arrive at the decision, and

6. to change attitudes of participants.

Examples of effective use of focus groups can be found in Table 2.2.1.

Table 2.2.1. Examples of Use of Focus Groups

Baker, Sharon L. 1991. "Improving Business Services Through the Use of Focus Groups." *RQ* 30 (Spring): 377–85.

Connaway, Lynn Silipigni. 1997. "Online Catalogs from the Users' Perspective: The Use of Focus Group Interviews." *College & Research Libraries* 58 (September): 403–20.

Massey-Burzio, Virginia. 1998. "From the Other Side of the Reference Desk: A Focus Group Study." *The Journal of Academic Librarianship* 24, no. 3 (May): 208–15.

Ozinga, Connie Jo. 1998. "Focus Groups View Public Libraries." *The Unabashed Librarian* no. 108: 4.

Rose, Pamela M. 1998. "A Focus Group Approach to Assessing Technostress at the Reference Desk." *Reference and User Services Quarterly* 37, no. 4 (1998): 311–17.

PROCESS MODEL

The process model for the focus group follows eight steps

1. problem definition,

2. audience identification,

3. moderator selection,

4. question formulation,

5. participant selection,

6. focus group sessions,

7. data interpretation, and

8. report generation.

Problem Definition

In the broadest terms, what do you want to know? What is the purpose of the focus group? What types of information are desired? Who wants the information? Why conduct a focus group?

In this case, the School of Library and Information Science identified the problem in its request to the State Library. The School required feedback from the professional community to be used in conjunction with other data sources for program assessment and planning. More specifically, the School was interested in satisfaction with the program and suggestions for improvement. The focus group method was selected because it would target the specific constituents in a cost-effective manner. At the same time, it would allow for fresh perspectives and interactive communication. Surveys often tend to limit responses to those that have been anticipated by the questioner.

Audience Identification

Who is the ultimate audience for the program or idea being discussed? Can sets of individuals who represent this audience be identified? Will they be willing and able to provide the desired information?

The professional library and information science community of the state comprises the ultimate consumers of the educational program in that it hires the School's graduates and uses research produced by the faculty. Four primary groups of constituents were identified: school librarians, academic librarians, public librarians, and special librarians/information professionals. Individuals were identified as belonging to and being representative of these sets through membership in various professional organizations, through past experience, and through nomination. As the School provides a generalist program, it was necessary to ensure that perspectives from all of the constituent groups were represented.

Moderator Selection

What does the moderator do? Should an internal or external facilitator be used? What characteristics should the moderator possess?

The moderator is responsible for guiding discussion and recording responses. It is essential that the moderator be knowledgeable enough about the topic to lead discussion, but unbiased in approach. Ensuring that all participants are given the opportunity to voice opinions—even unpopular ones—without fear of ridicule within the group or fear of retaliation is critical. The moderator must be able to strike a balance between free discussion and a free-for-all.

The director of the School requested that the State Library of Ohio conduct the focus groups. The State Library then formed a team of facilitators, comprised of the deputy state librarian and two library development consultants whose primary interactions had been with the specific constituencies named. The team was not only knowledgeable about librarianship in general, but was also familiar with the individual practitioners within the state. The focus group participants and the School perceived the facilitators as having substantial credibility.

Question Formulation

What kinds of questions should be asked? How should they be phrased?

Open-ended questions using straightforward, audience-appropriate language should be developed to address specific aspects of the problem statement. Typically, a variety of questions are developed and provide a smooth sequence: opening questions, introductory questions, transition questions, key questions, ending questions, a summary question, and a final question. The questions for the KSU/SLIS project were designed around key aspects of the School's responsibility: preparation for the first professional position, research, and continuing education.

The opening or introductory question in the KSU/SLIS project was a very general one: "When hiring for entry-level professional positions, what makes a candidate attractive to you?" The question then moved to a related question, more specific to Kent State: "What course or curriculum changes should be made to make the KSU graduate more attractive to employers?" The next question provided another opportunity to address curriculum change, but was broader to allow for a wider range of response, including administrative matters, visibility, and recruitment: "For your nondegreed staff who are interested in obtaining an MLS while still working, what would you suggest to the KSU program to make itself attractive to these nontraditional students?" Two additional questions related to specific initiatives currently underway within the state were also included: "What role can alternative instructional-delivery systems play in reaching nontraditional students?" and "What can Kent State do to recruit and retain minority students to the program and the library profession in Ohio?"

Research activity was addressed by two questions. The first question was based on opinion and personal experience: "How can research done by the Kent State Program help you do your job?" This was followed by "How can the Ohio library community and KSU partner in the area of applied research?"—a question that asked for specific applications and strategies.

The final topic-specific question concerned continuing education: "What can Kent State contribute to helping staff keep current after obtaining the MLS?"

The sessions ended with a summary question: "What one message would you like to send to Kent State?" In different groups, this question was paraphrased as "What last words do you have for KSU?" and "What message would you like to send to Dr. Wallace [the director]?" A list of questions used in the Kent State University focus groups is included in Table 2.2.2.

Participant Selection

How many people should be in a group? How should they be selected? How do you get them to participate?

Focus groups are normally comprised of 8 to 12 people. With fewer than eight, the dialogue becomes stilted; with more than 12, people don't have a chance to say what they want. A series of smaller groups is preferable to one large group. The group should be homogenous in its representation of a particular audience segment, but diverse enough to offer a variety of opinions. The sample should be selected to match the objectives of the research. That is, participants should be chosen because they can provide some insight relevant to the problem statement. As with nearly all research methodologies, incentives can vary from a small token of appreciation to a large prize or cash payment to satisfaction in having one's opinion heard.

Table 2.2.2. Example: Question Protocol Kent State University School of Library and Information Science

---

Satisfaction with KSU Graduates

Graduate Education Role:

"When hiring for entry level professional positions, what makes a candidate attractive to you?"

"What course or curriculum changes should be made to make the KSU graduate more attractive to employers?"

"For your nondegreed staff who are interested in obtaining an MLS while still working, what would you suggest to the KSU program to make itself attractive to these nontraditional students?"

"What role can alternative instructional delivery systems play in reaching nontraditional students?"

"What can Kent State do to recruit and retain minority students to the program and the library profession in Ohio?"

Research Role:

"How can research done by the Kent State Program help you do your job?"

"How can the Ohio library community and KSU partner in the area of applied research?"

Continuing Education Role:

"What can Kent State contribute to helping staff keep current after obtaining the MLS?"

"If Ohio librarians were required to be certified, what role could Kent State play in the certification or re-certification process?"

Last words:

"What one message would you like to send to Kent State?"

Four focus groups (public libraries, academic libraries, school libraries, and special libraries) were created. Names of participants were gathered from association rosters, past experience with the State Library of Ohio, and nominations from the School of Library and Information Science. Letters were sent to 17 potential participants for each of the four groups. Groups were convened at the State Library. The academic and special librarians were combined for a group of 13. There were 11 participants in the public libraries group, and 5 in the school libraries group. All of the school library media specialists worked in public schools. Other than lunch, no tangible incentives were provided. Participants from all groups expressed their appreciation at having been asked to participate and encouraged future interaction.

Focus Group Sessions

Sessions were held on two consecutive days at a hotel centrally located in Columbus. Because of travel time for some participants, sessions were held midday, with lunch provided by the State Library. Rooms were set up with comfortable chairs arranged in a circle, with a flip chart for the moderator. Sessions were also audiotaped (with permission of all participants). No attempts were made to identify individuals on the tapes or charts. Each session began with a discussion of ground rules. Moderators assured participants of anonymity. The value of each person's opinion was reiterated and participation of each individual encouraged. Participants were reminded that the purpose was to gather a variety of perspectives and ideas and not to reach decisions or consensus. Sessions lasted approximately two hours. Moderators worked from the basic question protocol, but varied focus or wording depending on the group's responses.

Data Interpretation

What do the data mean? How can they be analyzed?

The data from focus groups are very rich in that they provide in-depth, creative, unique responses. As with many qualitative methodologies, however, the data are not readily generalizable. There are no inferential statistical tests that suggest that the opinions of the focus group are reflective of those of the entire library and information science professional community. Nevertheless, the responses may be examined to determine if there are common trends and suggestions among the groups in the series and may suggest areas for future study and exploration. Focus groups may be used to explore issues in depth raised by other methodologies, such as surveys or use studies, or may be used to generate questions or variables that can be explored more widely through those methods.

Report Generation

What should be in the final report?

Typically, the decision to use the focus group methodology includes a realization that the final report will include words, not numbers or tables. In most cases, it is appropriate to provide raw data in the form of the original audiotapes (if they were made) and transcriptions of comments recorded on flip charts, as well as a summary outlining method, procedure, and key trends. Examples of transcriptions from the School of Library and Information Science study are included in Table 2.2.3.

Two of the State Library of Ohio team presented findings to the School of Library and Information Science faculty, administration, students, and other interested parties in an open forum at the Kent State University. After a brief overview of method and question protocol, responses of each of the focus group sessions were presented. The director of the School received all raw data (explanation of procedure, copies of the question protocol, all tapes, transcriptions of flip chart records) and a copy of the presentation handout.

Table 2.2.3. Example: Transcriptions from Flip Charts—Final Question

School Library Media Specialists: "What last words do you have for KSU?"
- School librarians need to be represented at all levels.
- Need to be pro-active (part of management course)
- Thank you, Dr. Wallace, for asking us.
- Would like to see copies of all input from focus groups.
- Can get it on several list serves if have permission
- "People with special need" for a course in library science
- With new SchoolNet focus, need help with distance learning—an immediate need.
- Special issues with distance learning need to be addressed.
- Call and ask to visit school—talk to people face-to-face.
- Post questions for input on listserv/OELMA listserv
- KSU develop MLS strand of studies for school librarians without repeating all courses already took that aren't necessarily pertinent and make it accessible. Talk with State Dept. of Ed so administrators see value and need for this.
- Include fee waivers
- Practicing school librarians in program—1 yr. Visiting school librarian teaching in program not just workshops! MLS
- Outstanding continuing education program. If continue to serve as role models need to be on cutting edge of technology and literature.
- KSU be as politically active as possible in state and federal government as library advocate also working with school boards.
- Be a driving force in creating/encouraging multi-type library cooperation, i.e., school/public.
- Accessible (geographic/monetary), timely courses on timely issues—as times change.
- Consider (strongly) development of doctoral program—none in Ohio—at least coop with a doctoral program
- Thank you for the opportunity

Public Librarians: "What message would you like to send to Dr. Wallace?"
- Market librarianship—posters, videos, etc.
- Communicate with practicing librarians
- Network/OLC/SLO
- Network statewide agencies
- Why not an undergraduate program in library science?
- How can we graduate more people of color from the program?
- Involve working librarians
- Guide students carefully through program
- You're doing a lot of great things, keep up the good work!
- Work to attract a diverse student body
- Remember the public sector—connect with the library community
- Visits—develop an active list of people willing to take calls, visits, etc.
- Mentoring: involve a base of mentors
- Guest lectures, visits from "real world"
- Library "student teaching"
- Work to make the MLS degree mean something
- Keep talking to this group...we're willing and happy to help

Academic/ Special Librarians: "What last words do you have for KSU?"
- Be more visible
- Be more statewide—visible and interactive
- Don't be seduced into becoming technology trade school
- Diversification of program—Not made these known if doing many things
- Working cooperatively with other entities
- Personnel doesn't know what librarians do—Have to make skills known
- Comments applicable to all library school programs
- Continue to do good job
- Connection between theory and practice—what to do and why

HOW WERE THE DATA USED?

The responses from the professional community supported and reinforced annual survey data from graduating students, a survey of the five previous years' alumni, input from the School's advisory council, enrollment trend data, and several other sources of planning information. The combination of diverse sources and types of data provided a wealth of information for all of the School's basic planning activities, including curriculum revision, strategic planning and annual goal setting, and in preparation of the program presentation for the School's accreditation by the American Library Association.

PLANNING YOUR OWN FOCUS GROUP STUDY

Focus groups can be valuable mechanisms when used appropriately. Library managers who are interested in this methodology should first re-read the sections "Advantages of Focus Groups," "Limitations of Focus Groups," and "Use of Focus Groups" to decide whether the focus group methodology is appropriate to the context. This case study provides a brief outline and example of appropriate use. For more in-depth information on focus groups, see the *Resources* section below.

RESOURCES

Greenbaum, Thomas L., 1988, *The Practical Handbook and Guide to Focus Group Research.* Lexington, MA: Lexington Books.

Krueger, Richard A., 1994, *Focus Groups: A Practical Guide for Applied Research*, 2d ed. Thousand Oaks, CA: Sage Publications.

Krueger, Richard A., 1998, *Focus Group Kit.* Thousand Oaks, CA: Sage Publications.

> Vol. 1 Morgan, David L., 1998, *The Focus Group Guidebook.* Thousand Oaks, CA: Sage Publications.

> Vol. 2 Morgan, David L., 1997, *Planning Focus Groups.* Thousand Oaks, CA: Sage Publications.

> Vol. 3 Krueger, Richard A., 1998, *Developing Questions for Focus Groups.* Thousand Oaks, CA: Sage Publications.

> Vol. 4 Krueger, Richard A,. 1997, *Moderating Focus Groups.* Thousand Oaks, CA: Sage Publications.

> Vol. 5 Krueger, Richard A., 1997, *Involving Community Members in Focus Groups.* Thousand Oaks, CA: Sage Publications.

> Vol. 6 Krueger, Richard A., 1998, *Analyzing and Reporting Focus Groups.* Thousand Oaks, CA: Sage Publications.

Stewart, David W., and Prem N. Shamdasani, 1990, *Focus Groups: Theory and Practice.* Thousand Oaks, CA: Sage Publications.

Method @ A Glance: Using Quantitative Data

Purpose:
Summarizing and comparing critical characteristics across libraries and over time

Description:
Quantitative data analysis is a means of summarizing and synthesizing information in numeric form.

Strengths:
Capable of summarizing large bodies of data, precise, consistent, objective, replicable, amenable to comparison, externally valid, analytically sophisticated

Use:
As part of service evaluation, administrative decision making, constituent education and awareness, and strategic planning

Data Needed:
Factual, numeric information from a variety of library and nonlibrary sources

Sources of Data:
Federal, state, and local library reports and public documents.

Organizational Model(s):
Critical Constituencies, Resource, Human Resource, Decision-Process, Customer Service

Procedure:
1. Determine the purpose of the project.
2. Identify the target audience.
3. Select appropriate library data.
4. Select meaningful context data.
5. Determine mode of presentation.
6. Prepare and distribute presentation.

Case @ A Glance:
Gathering and Presenting Comparative Data

Purpose:	Producing a pamphlet with the dual purpose of 1) describing the volume of use in Texas academic, public, and school libraries, and 2) indicating the extent of underfunding in Texas libraries
Description:	The Public Relations Committee of the Texas Library Association (TLA) gathered data from library and nonlibrary sources for presentation in a miniature brochure in preparation for the 1997 state legislative session.
Use:	To present persuasive data to a critical constituency in an attractive and easily understood format
Sources of Data:	Major state and national library statistical reports, the Texas Education Agency, World Wide Web sites for popular amusements in the state of Texas

Procedure:

1. TLA Legislative Day identified as a target event

2. Format (miniature pamphlet) selected

3. Aproach (general public) identified

4. Content emphasis (volume of use of Texas libraries) clarified

5. Library data elements selected

6. Library data located and compiled

7. Nonlibrary data located and compiled

8. Brochure prepared

9. Brochure distributed at TLA Legislative Day

10. Use of brochure tracked through advances in library support and use of the brochure in the press

CASE STUDY

2.3

Gathering and Presenting Comparative Data

Mark L. Smith

IMPETUS

The Public Relations Committee of the Texas Library Association (TLA) first conceived the idea of a small pamphlet presenting statistical data about Texas libraries. Founded in 1902 and now with over 8,000 members from the school, public, and academic library communities, TLA is one of the oldest state-based library associations in the United States, and the largest. The Public Relations (PR) Committee of TLA is charged with "raising the stature and image of libraries and librarians" and also takes seriously its role to "support legislative and other advocacy efforts." In preparation for the 1997 legislative session (the Texas Legislature convenes every other January), the PR Committee decided to produce a pamphlet with a dual purpose:

1. to describe the volume of use in Texas academic, public, and school libraries, and

2. to indicate the extent of underfunding in Texas libraries.

Members of the committee felt that the pamphlet should present not only library data, but also data from nonlibrary sources that would put library use and expenditures in contexts that could be understood by the general public.

The committee and staff recognized the inherent challenge of any publication of this sort: to balance the accomplishments and benefits of libraries with a description of their critical needs. Texas libraries are chronically underfunded; however, no public official wants to support a losing cause. It was imperative to show the funding crisis without making libraries appear pathetic. And indeed they are not pathetic, but are thriving institutions that have become amazingly adept at producing startling levels of service for modest investments. This, too, is a point that we were cautious not to overstate, lest legislators and others conclude that libraries can continue to "get by" on available funds.

The committee chair, Jan Moltzan, a library activist and the retired director of the Texas Center for the Book (housed in Texas at the Dallas Public Library), communicated to me the committee's desire to create this document and to have it ready for the

1997 TLA Legislative Day. This event is held every other year in February (during the biennial session of the Texas Legislature) and allows librarians and library supporters from across the state the opportunity to travel to Austin, the state capital, to lobby state senators and representatives on library issues.

It was our intention to assemble a set of data that would "cut to the chase"— that is, to present in a very limited space only those data elements that most directly and eloquently built our case. We were mindful that we live in the "sound bite" age in which time to read is scarce and the competition for the public's attention is fierce. We knew that we had to choose our data carefully and present only a handful of statements that were attention getting and each of which would carry important information.

FINDING LIBRARY DATA

Useful data abound. Data from within and without the library world that can be fashioned into an argument for increased support for libraries are relatively easy to find and to present. Much data can be found on the World Wide Web, analyzed using standard spreadsheet software or a calculator, and presented in documents designed in word processing or desktop publishing software. This is precisely how the Texas Library Association produced "Libraries—A Capital Investment" (Figure 2.3.1). This tiny publication, which TLA staff and members researched and produced in a relatively short period of time, has been a remarkably effective means of generating publicity and awareness for Texas libraries.

Finding data from library sources is easy if you know where to look. As the former state data coordinator for Texas public library data to the National Center for Education Statistics of the U.S. Department of Education, I knew where to look for public and academic library data. And although I was not exactly sure where to find the school library data I needed, I at least knew the appropriate state agency with which to start.

First, however, I went after the data that were easiest to find, Texas public library data, which are collected by the Texas State Library and Archives Commission. At the time—January 1997—the most recently published print volume was the *1994 Texas Public Library Statistics*.

When it comes to data gathered by government agencies, there is an unavoidable lag between collection and print publication of data. However, it is often possible to find data more recent than the last published information either by contacting the agency directly or by visiting the agency's Web page where data are often available in electronic format in advance of print publication. I knew there were more recent data that had been collected but not yet published. I called the State Library and requested the 1995 data. (The 1996 data had only just begun to be collected at that point.) The State Library sent the entire database by e-mail attachment and I was able to take the data sets into Microsoft® Excel and perform the calculations necessary to give me most of the public library usage and expenditure data presented in the pamphlet.

I also requested from the State Library other public library data that I wanted to include and that the agency collects in separate surveys. These include persons attending literacy programs and the number of children participating in the summer reading programs. As with any other government agency, it is worthwhile to get to know the State Library staff members (usually in the Library Development Division or corresponding unit) who may have access to statistics that you need but that are not yet published or may not be collected for publication. I happened to know that the Texas State Library and Archives Commission is also responsible for collecting academic library data (like other states, Texas participates in the national collection of academic library data in the Post-

Secondary Education Data Survey, or IPEDS). The Texas State Library releases these data online at (http://www.tsl.state.tx.us/LD/AcademicLibraries1997/cover.html.) and in a biennial publication, the *Texas Academic Library Statistics*. I had the most recently released volume of these data in my office and was able to extract the academic library data I needed from that publication.

Texas Libraries

The national average for public library expenditures is $21.27 per capita.

Texas spent an average of $12.89 per capita for public library service in 1997.

For a family of four, that's library service <u>for a year</u> for only $51.56. It would cost about $120 for the same family to attend Six Flags Over Texas <u>for one day</u>--even if they didn't buy any snacks or souvenirs while they were there!

Texans make over 100 million visits to libraries each year--that's enough attendance to fill The Ballpark in Arlington to capacity for the next <u>2,100 home games</u>!

Texas Library Association

For more information, contact:

The Texas Library Association
3355 Bee Cave Road, Suite 401
Austin, TX 78746
512/328-1518
fax: 512/328-8852
http://www.txla.org

This publication was paid for by the TLA Public Relations Fund.

Libraries—A Capital Investment

"Read for Your Life"

School Libraries

Texas has 4,736 school librarians serving a total of 3,828,975 students and 476,877 school personnel on over 6,600 campuses in 1,043 districts.

Each school librarian in Texas serves an average of nearly 900 students and over 100 staff.

Texas school librarians spend 75% of their time teaching students how to find and to evaluate information; the other 25% is spent gathering and organizing library resources.

School libraries spent just $11.77 per pupil for books in 1996-97.

The average expenditure for school libraries is only $82 per student, or 50% of the $164 per student spent for guidance counseling services.

School libraries account for only about 1.7% of total school district expenditures.

Public libraries

Texans borrowed over 77 million items from Texas public libraries in 1997, of which about 34% were children's materials.

Texans borrowed an average of 4.2 items per person from public libraries in 1997. At average book prices, that's a value of about $100, or an 8-to-1 return on their investment of $12.89 per capita for library service.

Literacy programs in Texas public libraries helped nearly 90,000 Texans learn to read in 1997, and over 400,000 children participated in summer reading club programs in Texas public libraries in 1998.

The state of Texas provides only 26 cents per capita for public libraries and is one of only 13 states that provides no direct aid to libraries.

Academic Libraries

Texas college and university librarians answered over 8.4 million reference questions in 1997, eight times the total annual attendance at UT football games.

College libraries receive only about 2 cents of every dollar spent on higher education.

If the cost of gas had risen as fast as the cost of academic library materials in the last 15 years, gas would now cost $4 per gallon.

In a typical week over 1 million students and faculty visit college and university libraries.in Texas.

Figure 2.3.1. "Libraries—A Capital Investment"

From The Texas Library Association. (512) 328-1518.

The school statistics are a bit more difficult to obtain. Although state education agencies collect mountains of K through 12 school data, they do not usually survey school libraries as separate entities, and what library statistics are collected are usually subsumed within campus and district data. Some useful information on the library is collected, however, and again, it helps to have a friend in the agency. My contact at the Texas Education Agency (TEA) is Gloria McClanahan, a librarian, TLA member, and the administrator of a statewide school-library, resource-sharing project. Gloria is always willing to help me find the needle of library data in the haystack of education statistics collected by her agency. She provided me with the most current data available for school library expenditures (virtually no data is collected on school library usage, at least in Texas). I might have been able to locate these numbers on the Texas Education Agency Web page (http://www.tea.state.tx.us), but it would have taken hours and ultimately been inconclusive. If you are trying to find school library data for your state, find the Gloria McClanahan at your state education agency and get to know her or him.

Before moving on from school data, a parenthetical issue should be noted here. Statisticians make a distinction between *descriptive* and *analytical* statistics. For the purposes of this pamphlet, and for most uses to which we would put statistics for library publicity, lobbying, and management purposes, descriptive statistics are sufficient, that is, simply using numbers to describe the status of libraries and library service. Education data, on the other hand, hold the key to much more profound analysis and understanding of the impact of library service, especially in the schools. Researchers such as Keith Lance of the Library Research Service at the Colorado State Library have been able to use these data to show the relationship between library service and academic achievement. To be reliable and authoritative, however, these analytical conclusions depend upon a sophisticated and rigorous process of statistical method. Unless you have the training and the time to devote to deriving analytical findings from huge data sets, it is probably advisable to stick to descriptive statistics, which can also yield powerful insights.

Our approach in creating "Libraries—A Capital Investment" was decidedly descriptive, and we needed one additional element of library data to complete the picture of how Texas libraries compare to libraries in other states. Statistical information about every public library in the United States is collected and published in print and electronic form by the National Center for Education Statistics (NCES) through a collaborative project known as the Federal State Cooperative Service for Public Library Statistics, or FSCS. The FSCS data represent a subset of the data collected annually by states. These data are forwarded to the NCES by the states and published in a print volume called *Public Libraries in the United States* and online at the NCES Web site (http://nces.ed.gov/surveys /libraries/public). This survey is one of several library surveys conducted by the NCES, the complete data files for which are available on the NCES Web site.

From these sources, I was able to complete the picture of how Texas public libraries compare to those in other states. It is not a pretty picture: Texas ranks 46th in the United States in total per capita expenditures for libraries, spending only $12.89 per capita compared to the U.S. average of $21.27. From a different NCES project, the *State Library Agencies* survey, we learned that at 26 cents per capita, the state of Texas ranks 36th among the 44 states that appropriate aid to public libraries, and that Texas is one of only 13 states that does not appropriate funds for direct aid to public libraries. (These data are the most current statistics that are used in the updated version of our pamphlet.) A list of sources of data used in compiling "Libraries—A Capital Investment" is provided in Figure 2.3.2.

Bowker Annual: Library and Book Trade Almanac. New York: R.R. Bowker Co. (annual).

Bureau of Labor Statistics Web site: http://stats.bls.gov/datahome.htm.

Public Libraries in the United States. National Center for Education Statistics, U.S. Department of Education. Wash, D.C.: U.S. Department of Education (annual). Also available online at http://nces.ed.gov/surveys/libraries/public.

Six Flags Over Texas Web site: http://www.themeparks.com/sixflags/sftexasfacts.htm.

State Library Agencies. National Center for Education Statistics, U.S. Department of Education. Wash, D.C.: U.S. Department of Education (annual). Also available online at http://nces.ed.gov/surveys/libraries/public.

Texas Academic Library Statistics. Library Development Division, Texas State Library and Archives Commission. Austin: Texas State Library and Archives Commission (biennial). Also available online at http://www.tsl.state.tx.us/LD /AcademicLibraries1997/cover.html.

Texas Education Agency Web site: http://www.tea.state.tx.us/.

Texas Public Library Statistics. Library Development Division, Texas State Library and Archives Commission. Austin: Texas State Library and Archives Commission (annual).

Texas Rangers Web site: http://www.texasrangers.com/.

University of Texas Men's Athletics Web site: http://www.utexas.edu/athletics/masterplan /tx_stadium.html.

Figure 2.3.2. Sources Used in Compiling "Libraries—A Capital Investment"

From The Texas Library Association. (512) 328-1518.

SELECTING NONLIBRARY DATA

The TLA Public Relations Committee and staff wanted to use this small publication to make an important point about Texas libraries: that they return a huge benefit on a very small investment. To adequately convey the scope of that investment and return, we knew that it was important to express the numbers in relation to popular consumer goods and services. One of the few a priori advantages we have in arguing for library services is that libraries are a perceived good. The public already believes that libraries are a valuable asset, but what is harder for the public to grasp is that the investment in libraries is dwarfed by what is spent for other activities in the public and private sector most of which, although entertaining, are not always of the same potential educational and cultural benefit as libraries. It is also surprising for many people to learn—even some within the library world—the extent to which libraries are used, often much more heavily than these other popular services.

With these thoughts in mind, we went looking for the data to demonstrate this comparison in usage and funding.

To put in perspective the per capita expenditure of $12.89 for public library service, we stated that:

> For a family of four, that's library service *for a year* for only
> $51.56. It would cost about $120 for the same family to attend
> Six Flags® Over Texas *for one day*—even if they didn't buy
> any snacks or souvenirs while they were there!

The price of tickets at this popular amusement park is easily obtained through the Six Flags Web site (http://www.themeparks.com/sixflags/sftexasfacts.htm). Then all we had to do was the math to show that a year's unlimited library service costs less than half of what the same family would spend for a day at an amusement park. We chose an amusement park to further heighten the effect of comparing an educational service to a purely entertainment service.

> Texans make over 100 million visits to libraries each year–
> that's enough attendance to fill The Ballpark in Arlington to
> capacity for the next *2,100 home games*!

Once we had the seating capacity of the Texas Rangers' Ballpark at Arlington (49,166) from the team's Web page (http://www.texasrangers.com/), it was a simple matter to divide the total library visits (a significant underestimation because school library visits are unknown, but public and academic total well over 100 million) by the stadium capacity. The result surprised even us and caught the attention of several reporters who called about this item. A point that was not lost on readers is that Texas Governor George W. Bush was, at the time, a part owner of the Texas Rangers.

> Texas college and university librarians answered over 8.4
> million reference questions . . . eight times the total annual
> attendance at UT football games.

For this, of course, we used the same basic strategy as the baseball item; however, we used actual attendance figures obtained from the University of Texas Web site: (http://www.utexas.edu/athletics/masterplan/tx_stadium.html) as the comparison statistic (this site seems no longer to have actual attendance figures per game, but only stadium capacity figures).

> If the cost of gas had risen as fast as the cost of academic
> library materials in the last 15 years, gas would now cost $4
> per gallon.

To relate the runaway cost of academic library materials to everyday experience, we needed to equate it with an everyday expenditure. Every librarian knows that the *Bowker Annual: Library and Book Trade Almanac* publishes extensive data on book prices, including indexes and trends in prices over a number of years. When we had a percentage increase in 15 years, all we needed was the price of gasoline 15 years ago. Information on consumer prices and consumer price indexes are available from the Bureau of Labor Statistics of the U.S. Department of Labor and most are accessible via the agency's Web site (http://stats.bls.gov/datahome.htm).

CONCLUSION

Considering the modest costs in time and money, the benefits of the publication, "Libraries—A Capital Investment," have been remarkable. In addition to its initial use as an insert in TLA Legislative Day packets, it has also been distributed to countless city and county officials, library board members, and press members across Texas. Direct effects are hard to measure; however, TLA made some modest gains for libraries in the last session of the Texas Legislature, including increased funding for the TexShare academic library consortium and the creation of new legislation to permit the formation of public library districts. The pamphlet has also been useful in building support among city officials. Efforts to inform these influential decision makers have resulted in the support of the Texas Municipal League for library issues in the 1999 legislative session, including the creation of a Texas Public Library Fund to provide first-ever direct aid for Texas public libraries.

The public relations uses of the pamphlet have been easier to track. In the most notable case, a reporter for the *Austin American-Statesman* picked up a copy of the pamphlet at the Texas Book Festival in November 1997 and used data in the article as the basis of a lengthy article about the state of libraries in Texas ("Falling a Page Behind," *Austin American-Statesman*, Sunday, December 7, 1997). More recently, figures included in a copy distributed at the 1998 Texas Book Festival, appeared in a letter to the editor of the *Dallas Morning News*, indicating the unexpected effects that can arise from putting the data into circulation.

Such a publication can never be the sole publicity for library issues and "Libraries—A Capital Investment" is one of many publications that the Texas Library Association uses to raise awareness of Texas libraries. TLA has recently completed production on a costly television public service announcement that aired on Texas television stations during 1999. But such high-profile publicity cannot convey the depth of detail possible with a tiny publication containing a few well-chosen and powerful statistics.

RESOURCES

Smith, Mark L., 1996a, *Collecting and Using Public Library Statistics: A How-To-Do-It Manual for Librarians*. New York: Neal-Schuman.

Method @ A Glance: Standard Measures

Purpose:	Ensuring consistency and thoroughness of measurement of library services within and across libraries
Description:	Application of standard measures is a technique that allows local libraries to gather data that are comparable across time and across libraries. Such data may be used within a library for benchmarking and trend analysis or to compare the library's performance with that of peer libraries.
Strengths:	Capable of summarizing large bodies of data, precise, consistent, objective, replicable, amenable to comparison, externally valid, analytically sophisticated
Use:	As part of performance evaluation, constituent education and awareness, external reporting, and strategic planning
Data Needed:	Professional standards; data specified by standards
Sources of Data:	Professional associations, other governing bodies, existing internal documents and procedures, procedures tailored to the specific data-gathering need
Organizational Model(s):	Critical Constituencies, Resource, Decision-Processing, Customer Service

Procedure:

1. Identify assessment needs and goals.

2. Identify required/desired standards and measures.

3. Design and implement data gathering procedures.

4. Determine appropriate bases for comparison, including past performance and contemporary peer performance.

5. Tabulate and interpret data.

6. Evaluate data in appropriate contexts.

7. Make decisions regarding performance and goals.

8. Implement changes.

Case @ A Glance: Measuring Library Services

Purpose:

Developing a set of meaningful measures, consistent procedures, and understandable guidelines for assessment of Ohio public library services

Description:

A broad-based project to revise Ohio's public library performance measures resulted in redefined, field-tested measures and new data reporting procedures.

Use:

To improve the quality of statistical data reported to the State Library of Ohio and to encourage meaningful gathering, compilation, and use of statistical data at the local library level

Sources of Data:

Public library planning documents, American National Standards Institute, Federal State Cooperative System, library and information science literature, special task forces appointed by the Ohio Library Council, public forums at Ohio Library Council conferences and meetings.

Procedure:

1. Project coordinator appointed

2. Steering committee established

3. Project goals articulated

4. Task forces formed

5. Project consultant hired

6. Criteria for measures established

7. Subject area task forces convened

8. Basic measures and data gathering procedures designed and developed

9. Meetings held to foster cooperation

10. Measures and procedures field tested

11. Procedures revised and manual finalized

12. Librarians throughout the state trained

13. Revision procedures designed and implemented

CASE STUDY

2.4

Measuring Library Services

Jay Burton

THE MEASUREMENT CONUNDRUM

Picture this. It's your turn to work the weekend and it's a busy Saturday afternoon. The phone is ringing nonstop, every study table is filled, the library is filled with people, and you and your colleagues on the reference desk are answering questions one after another. It's never been so busy and yet monthly statistics indicate that circulation is at best level with last year and at worst, dropping. The director is making the rounds and stops by. Shaking her head she looks around and says, "How can statistics indicate that we're not busy? Look at this!"

SETTING

Ohio's Public Libraries

Ohio public libraries are among the best supported in the country, with an average per capita income (from all sources) of $41.40, well above the national average for public library support (*Statistics of Ohio Libraries* 1996). More than 69 per cent of library income is derived from the state's Library and Local Government Support Fund (LLGSF). There are 250 tax-supported Ohio public library systems with a total of 450 service outlets, serving a state population of 11,150,506 (*Statistics of Ohio Libraries* 1996). In 1995 Ohio public libraries held over 41 million volumes and were responsible for over 133 million circulations. Every public library is a member of the state-funded Ohio Public Library Information Network (OPLIN), which provides support for telecommunications costs and access to a selected group of commercial database subscriptions as well as the Internet.

Like most states, however, averages do not tell the whole story. Ohio's libraries vary greatly in terms of the number of people each library serves, the size of the library or system, the amount of funding, the administrative structure, and resources such as number of staff, size of collection, and level of automation.

IMPETUS FOR THE MEASUREMENT PROJECT

As the busy librarian in the opening scenario observed, we seem to be busier than ever, but we don't have an effective way to assess the level of our activities or to make them known to our constituents. In Ohio, there were already two state-level procedures in place. Each public library is required to file an annual statistical report with the State Library of Ohio. It includes questions generated within the state, but is based largely on Federal State Cooperative System elements. The Standards Task Force, Ohio Library Development Committee of the Ohio Library Council, recommends a set of standards that combines output measures and policy guidelines. Reporting is on a voluntary basis. Regional groups and Ohio Library Council (OLC) chapters reported to OLC that concerns about measurement and reporting were arising in discussions throughout the state. Among issues and trends that were frequently mentioned were

1. Lack of confidence in comparative data. Library administrators felt that there was a great deal of inconsistency in the way that measures were being gathered and reported. As a result, they could not be confident about the state level data for benchmarking or other comparative techniques. They wanted to be sure that they had "good" data to report for budget presentations and public relations. In addition, they were concerned that the figures used to allocate state monies within their counties were not truly comparable, as libraries were defining the elements and gathering the data differently.

2. The need to demonstrate the full range of library activities. Questions were raised about continued reliance on circulation as a primary measure of use. Community-based planning required attention to resource intensive activities such as programming and outreach services to groups and individuals.

3. Impact of electronic information delivery. Librarians expressed concern that provision of online and remote services would create a decline in circulation and reference measures, creating a false impression that library services are no longer in demand. Whether or not such a decline actually appears, there is an obvious and critical need to measure use of new delivery mechanisms in their own right if librarians are to provide a complete and compelling picture of library activity and to plan effectively.

The Measuring Library Services project was based on a shared concern that existing measures were not always used, gathered, or reported consistently. Additionally, it was felt that it was time to take into account the significant changes in the resources and services being offered in public libraries, with particular regard to the impact technology has played.

Perhaps the most important aspect of Measuring Library Services project was in providing libraries with compelling arguments and good strong reasons for going to all this effort. Some of these reasons are

1. As public funding grows tighter and tighter, public libraries must increasingly demonstrate their worth in order to maintain and increase funding levels. Accurate and uniform information assists in demonstrating to local, state, and community leaders that libraries use public funds

effectively. Measures must be clearly defined and consistent procedures applied for true comparisons.

2. Information gained from Measuring Library Services will provide the public with a clear vision of what libraries do and their importance to the community. The problem is not that we are doing less; it is that we are engaged in different types of activities, from electronic information delivery to literacy training and outreach.

3. Information gathered through this project will assist libraries in evaluating existing library services and developing new services.

4. Documented usage of the increasing use of electronic resources will allow libraries to plan for the effective use of technology and reflect use of library resources much more accurately than continuing to rely on circulation as the primary measure.

5. Information gained through measuring various services provides an individual library with ways to evaluate the effectiveness of specific library services. This information can be used for allocating resources for various library operations, including collection development, staffing, and programming.

6. And for Ohio public libraries, and maybe for you too—participation in the Measuring Library Services project demonstrates that public libraries understand the importance and benefits of cooperation on a statewide level.

PROCEDURE

The Measuring Library Service project is truly a collaborative effort. The Ohio Library Council, in partnership with the State Library of Ohio, conducted a two-phase project on measurement of library services. With funding coming from two Library Service & Technology Act (LSTA) grants, Phase I was conducted from July through September 1996. Phase II took place from June 1997 through September 1998.The major steps we followed during the course of the project were

1. Appointed project coordinator. Frances Haley, executive director, Ohio Library Council, who organized workflow, coordinated activities, and obtained grant support, coordinated the project.

2. Established a steering committee. The first step of the Measuring Library Services project was to identify a steering committee of five librarians representing different size public libraries from various areas around Ohio and four representatives from the State Library of Ohio staff. They were invited to participate by the State Library and Ohio Library Council. Individuals from this group were responsible for developing the initial goals and objectives of the Measuring Library Services project, chairing the task forces, conducting and planning additional steering committee sessions, and preparing and presenting the final report of recommendations from each task force.

3. Articulated goals for project. Three goals emerged from the initial planning meetings:

    Goal 1:   Identified and defined the library services to be measured.

    Goal 2:   Recommended methods of measurement.

    Goal 3:   Recommended procedures for implementing and reporting these new measures of service.

    Using these goals as a starting point, four task forces were formed. Three were to address major subject areas: 1) circulation, 2) reference, and 3) programming and outreach. A fourth task force was identified to address implementation issues.

4. Identified project consultant. The project consultant's role was to attend all task force meetings; to offer consistency, coordination, and information about national trends and evaluation research; and to identify other groups and organize interaction with them. Further, the consultant represented the task force at state and regional library conferences, organized the groups' work into a final report, and developed recommendations for further activities.

5. Established criteria for measures. The subject-area task forces were each given a set of criteria to use in developing a set of measures. The guidelines stipulated that to be included, a measure had to be

    a. *Meaningful.* Measures had to be self-evidently relevant to lay people and governing boards and be useful in management processes. The guiding question was not, "What *can* we measure?" but "What *should* we measure?"

    b. *Standardized.* Nationally recognized definitions and procedures were used when these were available.

    c. *Easily gathered.* Only measures supported by data that could be easily and consistently gathered in even the smallest library were selected.

    d. *Quantitative.* Counts or tallies are more easily gathered and numeric data lend themselves more readily to comparison. Counts can be used as the basis for more complex quantitative measures or to point to areas where more qualitative studies might be desired at the local level.

6. Convened subject-area task forces. The next step was to identify members of the Ohio public library community to serve on the task forces. Every attempt was made to ensure that the members represented libraries of a variety of sizes, geographic regions, and resource bases. Each task force was co-chaired by a public librarian and a State Library of Ohio consultant. Each of the subject-area groups was given the charge to meet, discuss, and produce a set of recommended measures, appropriate definitions, and recommended data-gathering procedures appropriate to their assigned subject areas. Task force chairs were responsible for making meeting arrangements and setting the agenda of task force sessions.

7. Developed and defined basic measures and data-gathering procedures. Each of the task forces brainstormed and decided on basic measures. Defining measures clearly and unambiguously was difficult. All of the task forces were aware of widespread confusion about and idiosyncratic applications of even the most basic definitions (*circulation*, for instance). To facilitate the work of the task forces

   a. Standardized definitions were provided when available from the national literature and served as the starting point for further refinement.

   b. A general outline for each measure was developed from the work of the various task forces and provided to all to guide their work. Each task force used several elements in an attempt to ensure clarity and consistent definition. First, the measure was defined, and the data-gathering procedure was explained. Counting rules were provided for each measure, as well as examples and self-quizzes. Forms were included where appropriate. (See Appendix 2.4.1.)

   Overlap and gaps in the perceived areas of concern of each task force soon appeared from the discussions. As a result of these discussions, the circulation task force quickly redefined itself as *access services*. In particular, the impact of electronic communication technology and digital formats for library materials soon surfaced in all groups. Ultimately, six subject areas were defined and categorized in the training manual: 1) Use of materials, 2) Use of electronic resources, 3) Reference services, 4) Library programs, 5) Outreach services, 6) Marketing (See Figure 2.4.1 for Table of Contents). These six areas of measurement were designed to be used together to provide complete a view of library services. Together, they constituted the foundation for all the work of the project participants and demonstrate the level of library activity that should and can be measured.

8. Fostered cooperation with other groups. Concurrent with the work of the task forces, meetings were held with representatives of groups with parallel or overlapping interests. Among these were the executive director of the Ohio Public Library Information Network, State Library of Ohio's data coordinator, and chair of the Ohio Library Council's Public Library Standards Task Force. Public presentations and open forums were held at the Ohio Library Council's state and regional conferences. As a result of these meetings, OPLIN utilized the task forces' recommendations for statistical reporting in selecting database vendors and the director of OPLIN was asked to be a part of the electronic measures task force formed in Phase II of the project. Additionally, some questions on the State Library of Ohio report form were revised and others eliminated. The State Library of Ohio streamlined the reporting part of the process by introducing online state reporting and access as recommended in Phase I of the project. An example of the project can be found at http://winslo.state.oh.us/publib/libdir.html. Click on *Directory of Ohio Public Libraries* to see the specific statistics page.

CONTENTS

Figure 2.4.1. Measuring Library Services 1998: A Joint Project of the State Library of Ohio and the Ohio Library Council—Contents

From The Ohio Library Council. (614) 221-9057.

9. Field tested measures and procedures. A preliminary training manual with organizational guidelines was provided to nine field test libraries that tested the procedures and reported back to either task force chairs or the project consultant. The libraries ranged from a small, single outlet library to a major county library system, which tested the measures at the main library and over 20 branches.

10. Revised procedures and finalized manual. Procedures and forms were revised as suggested. Some procedures (such as using patron sign-up logs to measure computer use) were eliminated. References to the Ohio Public Library Standards were incorporated. Manuals were sent to every library outlet in the state.

11. Conducted training. Project implementation began in January 1999 after providing a series of eight project workshops in October and November of 1998. These workshops provided librarians with an opportunity to receive a copy of the implementation manual, read and review it as a group, ask and answer questions, and generally get a feel for the project and how to proceed.

12. Used a "grace" year to test the measures, data-gathering and reporting procedures, and to allow librarians time to adjust to a sometimes new way of looking at things. Nineteen ninety-nine was a trial year for use and reporting of the measures. Plans are to provide a mechanism for librarians to report on how the Measuring Library Services measures and manual have helped or hindered their statistical information gathering and what can be done to improve not only the recommended measures, but integrate them into the annual State Library of Ohio report. Analysis and evaluation will indicate the manner in which the project will move ahead and the extent to which the measures will be incorporated into the required State Library of Ohio annual report.

13. Continued refining and defining services and measures as services develop and change. The project defined preferred measures and their definitions and reporting procedures, but strongly recommended relying on automated counting processes for consistent and comparable measures. When the project first began, there was no available way to measure use of the Internet from the user (library) end. Mechanisms remain cumbersome; individual software products do not employ standard definitions or processes. Although some librarians want to know specific sites visited for organizational and collection-development purposes, others fear the introduction of filtering or the loss of patron confidentiality that may accompany such software. OPLIN is training librarians in the available administrative reporting systems for electronic access offered through the state system, and work continues in trying to recognize and accommodate varying definitions and counting methods used by different vendors and in different local environments.

Throughout the project, the goal has been to simplify statewide reporting and provide a standard for gathering, reporting, and using the recommended measures set forth in the Measuring Library Services project. The challenge ahead is to encourage librarians to integrate this process and use these measures to identify, gather, and report library service statistics.

HOW DO YOU DO IT?

The Ohio Measuring Library Services project described in this chapter began three years ago and is an ongoing process. Two grants and considerable volunteer effort have supported it. We presented the results, with emphasis on measuring electronic services, at the American Library Association Annual Conference in 1999 and received considerable interest. We hope that you can build on the project's processes and outcome in your own library and state. Here's how:

1. First, read *Measuring Library Services 1998*, available from the Ohio Library Council, 35 E. Gay Street, Suite 305, Columbus, Ohio 43215, 614-221-9057 (voice), 614-221-6234 (fax), http://www.olc.org. For other questions please feel free to contact Jay Burton, Head, Library Programs & Development Division, State Library of Ohio, 65 South Front Street #506, Columbus, Ohio 43215, Telephone: 614-466-5511, FAX: 614-728-2788, e-mail: jburton@winslo.state.oh.us.

2. Assemble a planning team of staff most affected or most familiar with the services being measured.

3. Determine which measures the local library can use.

4. Outline local procedures for gathering and reporting measures requiring actual annual totals and those based on samples.

5. Schedule sample periods. Data for each measure based on sampling are gathered during two sampling periods, each one week in duration. Each week should be a "typical" one, with no holidays or extraordinary events. Ohio selected February and October as our typical months.

6. Refine the procedures for local data gathering.

7. Prepare for staff training. Determine what information will be presented and who will be presenting it.

8. Provide staff training. Be enthusiastic and positive. Tell staff why gathering data is important. Let them know how the data will be used and the potential impact on staff and resources. Help them recognize the important part they play in ensuring accurate and consistent results.

9. Collect and summarize data related to the pertinent measure(s). Concentrate on procedural details making sure the process is followed all the way through.

10. Report results to the staff, library board, or both.

11. Meet to review results and procedures and revise process.

12. Have a party to celebrate a job well done and successful project—then plan for next year.

AND FINALLY . . .

We feel we can identify several factors that have led to the success of this project: a systematic approach, use of existing measures and procedures, local adaptation, field testing and revision, and an emphasis on awareness and training activities. Key, however, has been the atmosphere of collaboration and cooperation. Through the cooperation of the State Library of Ohio, Ohio Library Council, the Center for the Study of Librarianship at the Kent State University School of Library and Information Science, and the work of the many Ohio librarians who contributed to the work of this project, we have begun the task of developing a comprehensive, useful system for measuring public library service. There is still a great deal of work to be done, but by working together to develop an accurate and comprehensive understanding of current and future library service, we can create a vision of the public library of the future and a plan for making that vision a reality.

RESOURCES

American Library Association, 1995, *ALA Handbook of Organization, 1995/96*. Chicago: American Library Association.

American National Standards Institute, Inc., 1983, *American National Standard for Library and Information Sciences and Related Publishing Practices—Library Statistics*. ANSI Z39.7-1983. New York: American National Standards Institute, Inc.

Baker, Sharon L., and F. W. Lancaster, 1991, *The Measurement and Evaluation of Library Services*, 2d ed. Arlington, VA: Information Resources Press.

Binkely, Dave, and Tom Eadie, 1989, *Wisconsin–Ohio Reference Evaluation at the University of Waterloo*. CALCUL Occasional Paper Series No. 3. Ottawa: Canadian Association of College and University Libraries.

Brown, Barbara J., 1992, *Programming for Librarians: A How-To-Do-It Manual*. New York: Neal-Schuman.

Cullen, Rowena, 1992, "Evaluation and Performance Measurement in Reference Services," *New Zealand Libraries* 47 (March): 11–15.

Curran, Charles, and Philip M. Clark, 1989, "Implications of Tying State Aid to Performance Measures," *Public Libraries* 28 (November/December): 348–54.

Emerson, Katherine, 1984, "Definitions for Planning and Evaluating Reference Services," pp. 63–79 in *Evaluation of Reference Services*, eds. Bill Katz and Ruth A. Fraley. New York: Haworth Press.

Goldhor, Herbert, 1987, "An Analysis of Available Data on the Number of Public Library Reference Questions," *RQ* 27 (Winter): 195–201.

Haley, Frances, and Connie Van Fleet, 1996, *Measuring Library Services: A Joint Project of The Ohio Library Council and The State Library of Ohio: Final Report*. Columbus: Ohio Library Council.

Hallman, Clark N., 1981, "Designing Optical Mark Forms for Reference Statistics," *RQ* 20 (Spring): 257–64.

Heim, Kathleen M., 1982, "Stimulation," pp. 120–53 in *The Service Imperative for Libraries,* ed. Gail A. Schlachter. Littleton, CO: Libraries Unlimited.

Hernon, Peter, 1987, "Utility Measures, Not Performance Measures, for Library Reference Service?" *RQ* 26 (Summer): 449–59.

Kesselman, Martin, and Sarah Barbara Watstein, 1987, "The Measurement of Reference and Information Services," *The Journal of Academic Librarianship* 13 (March): 24–30.

Lynch, Mary Jo, 1983, "Measurement of Public Library Activity: The Search for Practical Methods," *Wilson Library Bulletin* 57 (January): 388–93.

National Center for Higher Education Management Systems, Dennis Jones, Project Director, 1977, *Library Statistical Data Base: Formats and Definitions.* Boulder, CO: National Center for Higher Education Management Systems.

Palmour, Vernon E., Marcia C. Bellassai, and Nancy V. DeWath, 1980, *A Planning Process for Public Libraries.* Chicago: American Library Association.

Public Library Management Forum Standards Review Committee, Illinois Library Association, 1996, *Serving Our Public: Standards for Illinois Public Libraries.* Springfield: Illinois Library Association.

"Report on the Library and Information Services Policy Forum on Impact of Information Technology and Special Programming on Library Services to Special Populations," 1996, funded by the National Center for Education Statistics and Co-sponsored by the U.S. National Commission on Libraries and Information Science with the Cooperation of the Office of Library Programs and the National Institute on Postsecondary Education, Libraries, and Lifelong Learning. Alexandria, Virginia. May 20-21, 1996.

Rubin, Richard, 1986, *In-House Use of Materials in Public Libraries.* Urbana, IL: University of Illinois, Graduate School of Library and Information Science.

Smith, Mark L., 1996a, *Collecting and Using Public Library Statistics: A How-To-Do-It Manual for Librarians.* New York: Neal-Schuman.

Smith, Mark L., 1996b, "Using Statistics To Increase Public Library Budgets," *The Bottom Line: Managing Library Finances* 9, no. 3: 4–13.

Standards Task Force, Ohio Library Development Committee, Ohio Library Council, Mary Pat Essman, chair, 1996, "Standards for Public Library Service in Ohio. Draft Document for Discussion. 12 August 1996." Columbus: Ohio Library Council.

Statistics of Ohio Libraries 1996, 1996, Columbus: State Library of Ohio.

Trotta, Marcia, 1993, *Managing Library Outreach Programs: A How-To-Do-It Manual for Librarians.* New York: Neal-Schuman.

Van Fleet, Connie, 1998, *Measuring Library Services 1998*: *A Joint Project of the State Library of Ohio and the Ohio Library Council. Manual and Training Guide.* Columbus: Ohio Library Council. The manual and training guide includes sections on the need for measurement, relationship of the recommended measures to the Ohio Public Library Standards and the Federal State Cooperative System measures, forms and checklists. The sections devoted to measures include definitions, planning and implementation procedures, counting rules, and examples. Copies of *Measuring Library Services 1998* are available from the Ohio Library Council.

Van Fleet, Connie, and Frances Haley, 1997, "Clarity, Consistency, and Currency: A Report on the Ohio 'Measuring Library Services' Project," *Advances in Library Administration and Organization* 15: 35–62. This article summarizes the contents of the Phase I final report for a national audience.

Van House, Nancy A. et al., 1987, *Output Measures for Public Libraries: A Manual of Standardized Procedures*, 2d ed. Chicago: American Library Association.

Appendix 2.4.1

Measuring Library Services 1998: A Joint Project of The State Library of Ohio and the Ohio Library Council—Reference and Other Questions

REFERENCE AND OTHER QUESTIONS

Measures

Reference Questions

total number of reference questions

Total = (February one week sample + October one week sample) x 26

Other Questions

total number of questions not defined as reference questions

Total = (February one week sample + October one week sample) x 26

Definitions

Reference Question

"an information contact that involves the use, recommendation, or instruction in the use of one or more information sources, or knowledge of such sources, by a member of the library staff. Information sources include: (1) print and non-print materials; (2) machine-readable databases; (3) the library's own bibliographic records, excluding circulation records; (4) other libraries and institutions; and (5) persons both inside and outside the library." (American National Standard for Library and Information Sciences and Related Publishing Practices, 1983). An information contact between staff and patron may take several forms: in-person, telephone, mail (letter), electronic mail (e-mail), or FAX.

Other Question

any question not properly categorized as a reference question. Policy, mechanical, directional, and administrative questions are counted under "other" questions.

Related Standards

Service Standard: All Ohio residents should:

C.1:   receive correct answers to their questions, with 80% of those questions answered by the end of the business day.

Management Guidelines: Ohio libraries are encouraged to:

C.1.1:   provide remote access to as many services as possible.

C.1.2:   provide reference and information services using reference sources including subject specialists, on-line services, and access to other resources through networks and referrals.

C.1.3:   provide active customer service by giving prompt, friendly and accurate assistance.

Procedures

Base: Sample

Report: Annual total from two sample periods (One week sample + One week sample) x 26

Forms: Daily Reference Tally Sheet

Weekly Question Log

Who: Staff at all public service desks and supervisors

Method: Select one week in February and one week in October. Use the "Daily Reference Tally Sheet" to record the number of reference and "other" questions. Staff should mark desk tally sheets each time either a reference or "other" question is asked.

Compile the daily totals to a weekly total using the "Weekly Question Log."

Reference question total = (February one week sample + October one week sample) x 26

Other question total = (February one week sample + October one week sample) x 26

Report only the annual total as calculated. **Do not report actual annual totals even if such data are available.**

DAILY REFERENCE TALLY SHEET

Library/department: _____ *Haley Library* _____ Date: __6/15/98__

Make a hashmark (/) in the appropriate category each time a question is asked.

Reference Questions

"an information contact that involves the use, recommendation, or instruction in the use of one or more information sources, or knowledge of such sources, by a member of the library staff," in-person, telephone, mail (letter), electronic mail (E-mail), or FAX. (ANSI Standard, 1983)

//// //// ////

Other Questions

all questions not properly categorized as reference questions. Policy, mechanical, directional, and administrative questions are counted under "other" questions.

//// //// //// ////

WEEKLY QUESTION LOG

Week of _____ *June 15* _____

Reference Questions

Day/Desk	*Ref*	*Circ*	*Info*	*Bus*					Total
Monday	35	10	10	20					75
Tuesday	10	15	20	25					70
Wednesday	10	10	20	10					50
Thursday	10	10	10	20					50
Friday	50	30	50	50					180
Saturday	150	50	70	60					330
Sunday	100	30	50	50					230
Desk totals	365	155	230	235					
Total Reference									985

Other Questions

Day/Desk	*Ref*	*Circ*	*Info*	*Bus*					Total
Monday	40	50	5	5					90
Tuesday	20	55	10	19					104
Wednesday	20	43	12	11					86
Thursday	10	22	8	13					53
Friday	16	10	11	17					54
Saturday	56	70	19	20					165
Sunday	40	60	20	20					140
Desk totals	222	330	85	100					
Total Other									742

Preparation: Send memo to management team members about the survey.

Review the measures, counting rules, and examples.

Complete the "Reference or Other?" exercise in the Test Yourself section.

Duplicate and distribute the Daily Question Tally Sheet and the Weekly Question Log.

Counting Rules

Count all questions, regardless of whether they are asked at the reference desk or at another location in the library. A question that is referred from one location/desk to another should be counted by both.

Count each question, not the number of patrons aasking questions. If a patron asks more than one question, count each question separately.

Distinctions between reference and other questions can be determined using the lists of examples in "How to Count Reference Questions" and "How to Count Other Questions"

Reference Question Examples

Listed below are types of questions and examples that are counted as reference questions.

General and ready-reference questions: "I need information on applying for a small business loan." "How do you spell 'plethora'?" "What is the address and phone number for the American Border Collie Association?"

Information and/or resource queries: "I need information on applying for a small business loan." "Can you help me find a book on starting an aquarium?" "Where do I get something to read about coaching youth soccer?"

Homework and/or school related questions: "I have to do a report on a famous American inventor. Can you help me?" "My teacher wants me to write a paper on the state symbols of Ohio." "Do you have anything about how to study for the GED?"

Research and in-depth questions: "Can you find a chart or something that has the past ten years Gross National Product figures for the United States?" "I need to compare a current presidential speech with the Gettysburg Address." "Where can I get a list of the casualty figures for these World War II battles?"

Reader's Advisory: "I love Stephen King books. Can you recommend any other authors similar to him?" "Can you recommend any good mysteries with female sleuths?"

Referrals: "Where could I go to arrange for a reading tutor?" "Do any organizations in town have information on businesses?"

Instruction: "How can I look up articles on the Olympics?" "How do I use the online catalog?" "Can you help me use this computer?" "How do I use the OPLIN Internet Computer?"

Technology Assistance & Instruction: "Can you help me log on to the Internet?"

"Other" Question Examples

Some questions are not properly categorized as reference questions. Policy, mechanical, directional, and administrative questions are counted under "other" questions. All questions that do not fit the reference question definition should be counted as "other."

Questions of Rules and Policies: "Are you open on Sundays?" "Do you allow caged birds in the library?" "How much are fines?"

Mechanical Questions on the Use of Machines: "How do you make a copy?" "Will you show me how to print this article?"

Directional Questions: "Where are the restrooms?" "Can you show me where the 633s are?" "Where are the videos?"

Administrative Questions: "How many books do I have checked out?" "Are you holding *The Sparrow* for me?"

TEST YOURSELF
REFERENCE OR OTHER?

1. What is the capital of Alaska?
   Reference question. Requires use of ready reference source.

2. Does anyone in town have information on activities for older adults?
   Reference question. Provides information using community resources, whether in library, through database, or referral.

3. Where are the books on photography?
   Reference question. Requires use of library catalog or staff expertise to locate materials.

4. I need information for a report on the Western Reserve for my Ohio history class.
   Reference question. Requires use of library resources and staff expertise.

5.   What books do I have checked out?
     Other question. Definition of reference question specifically excludes circulation records. In essence, this is examining a patron record for his or her personal use and convenience. It is administrative information.

6.   I need information on the library's policy on buying books for children.
     Other question. This is a question of library policy and as such comes under the heading of "other."

7.   How do you print this article?
     Other question. This is a purely mechanical question dealing with a straightforward mechanical process not dealing with a search for information.

8.   Where are the 645s?
     Other question. The patron has already done the intellectual work of finding a call number. Staff is merely providing physical location.

9.   Do you have any more books like this one? (A Barbara Cartland novel)
     Reference question. This is a readers' advisory question that requires knowledge of the librarian or staff member.

10. Does the library have a book called *Shoeless Joe*?
     Reference question. This question requires use of the library catalog or staff knowledge.

11. How much are library fines?
     Other question. This is a library policy question.

12. Who are Ohio's U.S. Senators?
     Reference question. Requires use of library resources.

13. Can you show me how to search the Internet for genealogy information?
     Reference question. This request requires the staff member to provide bibliographic instruction in this resource, not just mechanical direction. The question is about searching for information, not operating equipment.

14. Can you fix the printer?
     Other question. While this may require some staff expertise, the problem requires a mechanical solution.

15. Where are the videos on learning sign language?
     Reference question. This patron's question cannot be answered with a simple directional response. He/she needs to locate videos about a specific topic, and this will require use of the library's catalog or staff expertise beyond a knowledge of the physical layout of the library.

16. I love mysteries. Are there any other people who write like Dick Francis?
     Reference question. This is a readers' advisory question that requires staff knowledge of readers's advisory tools and mystery authors.

17. I need information on planning a wedding.
     Reference question. Answering this question involves use of a number of library resources.

18. What does YA mean? I saw it next to a number on a book I looked up in the catalog.
     Reference question. The patron is asking the meaning of the classification, so this would be a reference question, as it falls in the category of bibliographic instruction. Had the patron asked, "Where are the YAs?" this would be a directional, or "other" question.

19. Where are the paperbacks?
     Other question. The answer requires only a location.

20. Does anyone offer childbirth classes for first time parents?
     Reference question. Answering this question involves use of library resources, a community database, or referral.

Evaluating Reference and Information Services

Kathryn Dana Watson

INTRODUCTION

How well do libraries address the reference needs of their constituents? What are the best methods of determining the quality of these services? These questions have been the subject of many research studies and reports over the years. Although no one methodology emerges as appropriate for all evaluation projects, overall procedures to be followed are generally consistent. Recent publications provide direction in linking evaluation methods with that facet of reference services under study. We have access to past discussions and research that provide us with background to examine our own purposes, methodologies, and expected use of evaluation results. Additionally, these previous studies offer models for our own evaluations. As each library and community is unique, local needs shape the evaluation of reference and information services. Yet, evaluators can take advantage of the experiences and contributions of others in the profession.

THE LITERATURE

An abundance of literature is available pertaining to all aspects of reference and information services evaluation. Included here is a sampling of reviews of the literature, thematic issues of journals, key monographs, and a specific manual to provide guidance to appropriate instruments for reference and information services evaluation.

The Reference Assessment Manual attempts "to provide practicing librarians, reference managers, and researchers with access to a wide range of evaluation instruments useful in assessing reference service effectiveness" (1995, v). Its annotated bibliography provides access to the literature of reference evaluation. The "Summaries of Instruments" section describes and reviews specific evaluation instruments. Instruments are also linked to the overview chapters on specific aspects of reference services.

Von Seggern's (1987) guide to publications concerning reference assessment methodology and instruments selectively lists Reviews of Reference Evaluation Literature, Annotated Assessment Components (an annotated bibliography in categories of: Answering Success, Accuracy, Quality; Cost and Task Analysis; Interview and Communication; Enumeration and/or Classification of Reference Questions; Reference Collections; Staff Availability; Use and Nonuse of Reference Services), and Related Concerns.

Two theme issues of *The Reference Librarian* address evaluation of reference and information services. In 1984, "Evaluation of Reference Services" examined the process from multiple perspectives (Katz and Fraley). More recently, the 1992 special issue "Assessment and Accountability in Reference Work," looked at methodologies, the library environment, assessment, the human factor, reference evaluation, and connections with the rest of the library (Blandy, Martin, and Strife). Baker and Lancaster's (1991) *The Measurement and Evaluation of Library Services*, includes evaluative studies of reference services and describes techniques, patterns, and practical applications for libraries.

EVALUATION

If reference services are defined as personal assistance given to library users by library staff (Rothstein 1961), then reference evaluation is the examination of such assistance. Evaluation is an ongoing activity, part of the planning process, which assesses the effectiveness of current procedures and provides data that can help set direction for future activities. The overall goal, of course, is to improve service. Evaluation can be targeted to different components of reference services. Measurements of the accuracy of responses, the processes involved, instruction in the use of the library, user and librarian satisfaction with transactions, and efficiency are all service areas typically evaluated. An initial evaluation may establish a benchmark with which to later compare data or to match with established standards. Common evaluation approaches include comparing results with defined goals, established criteria, or both.

Useful criteria with which to compare results include the Reference and Adult Services Division (RASD), Reference and User Services Association (RUSA) guidelines, "Information Services for Information Consumers: Guidelines for Providers" ("Information Services" 1990). Adopted by the RASD Board of Directors in June 1990, this document addresses information services from the perspectives of services, resources, access, personnel, evaluation, and ethics. For personnel evaluation, the "Guidelines for Behavioral Performance of Reference and Information Services Professionals," approved in January 1996 by the RASD Board of Directors, identifies observable behavioral attributes in such areas as approachability, interest, listening/inquiring, searching, and follow-up activities ("Guidelines" 1996). Other criteria have been developed by individual libraries and reported in the literature. These guidelines form the basis for Gatten and Radcliff's testing of the effectiveness of reference instruction (Case Study 3.2).

Comparing evaluation results to defined goals and objectives assesses the degree to which goals are achieved. Reference services involve numerous activities: answering questions in person, via telephone or e-mail, instructing users in accessing the library's resources, and assisting with patron searches and performing online searches for patrons among others. To effectively evaluate these processes using the goal comparison approach, evaluators need to identify the previously determined goals and objectives for the designated aspects of reference service, and then complete the total evaluative process. This involves determining parameters of studies, choosing the most appropriate methodologies and administering them effectively, analyzing the findings, and implementing changes to improve service.

Criteria and goal-referenced approaches provide differing points of view. "Goal-based internal evaluations are a product of management theory. Such evaluations usually begin by identifying organization goals, and then seek to define operational measures that can be used in evaluating the library's success in meeting these goals" (Pierce 1984, 10). The success of this approach is dependent on a positive relationship between the needs of the organization and the ideals of service rooted in professionalism. "Professionalism, based on an appeal to goals and standards established by groups external to the organization, is relevant to such evaluations only insofar as the authority structure of the local institution chooses to support professional over other organizational goals" (Pierce 1984, 11). Quantitative evaluations are commonly used in this process but may not be completely effective in determining progress toward reaching goals. Numbers of reference transactions as a total do not truly reflect the actual experiences of the librarian and user. Using established criteria assumes the library manager and staff accept the guidelines or standards as applicable to their library and as representative of a level of professional service to which they aspire.

PROCEDURES

According to Bunge, most authors "agree that evaluation of reference services should be guided by the reference service's overall philosophy, mission, goals, and objectives" (1994, 197). He provides suggestions on how to achieve these goals and objectives in an earlier article (1984). Manuals from American Library Association (ALA) divisions, *Output Measures for Public Libraries* (Van House et al. 1989) and *Measuring Academic Library Performance* (Van House et al. 1990) certainly follow this goal-oriented model. Bunge, in helping librarians determine if they have reached their targets, developed a set of questions to guide the process:

1. What do we want to know about?

2. Where do we want to be?

3. How will we know if we are getting there?

4. How close are we?

5. So what?

6. What next? (1994, 198)

He elaborated on each of these steps and suggested standards, studies, and statistics useful for those contemplating or engaged in some phase of evaluation.

When evaluating reference and information services, library managers want to know about successful answering of reference questions, costs and tasks involved with reference services, the reference interview and its accompanying search strategy, and personnel performance, among others. (Another area of concern, of course, is maintaining a quality reference collection and that aspect is addressed Case Study 4.1, "Using Qualitative Criteria to Evaluate Reference Resources.") Determination of the quality of these services can be obtained through a number of methods outlined in this chapter, including obtrusive (Radcliff and Schloman, Case Study 3.1) and unobtrusive study (Gatten and Radcliff, Case Study 3.2), expert judgment (Kahn, Case Study 4.1), and librarian or patron reports (Burton, Case Study 2.4 and Froehlich, Case Study 5.1). The methodology and tools depend on the individual library and the purpose of the evaluation—the "What do we want to know?" question.

Defining the purpose of the research is the first of four basic steps to effective studies of reference services described by Whitlatch (1992, 17). Believing the research must have potential to impact decision making, she asked, "Will the study provide information useful in improving library services?" Other steps included clearly listing the goals and objectives of the study and the required information, selecting methodologies directly related to the objectives of the study, and collecting and analyzing the data. *The*

Reference Assessment Manual added another to this list: communicating the results of the assessment (1995, viii). Those involved in evaluation need to be made aware of the results.

GENERAL METHODOLOGIES

"Good measures are valid, reliable, practical and useful" (Van House 1990, 14). Each of these components contributes to the success of the evaluation. A valid measure accurately reflects that which it is meant to measure. For example, if the accuracy of responses to reference queries is under study, compiling answers about perceived satisfaction of library services is not a valid measure. A reliable instrument is known to be stable and predictable. It is pretested, includes an adequate sample size, and uses good techniques. Items are always counted in the same consistent way. A practical measure gathers data in the most straight-forward manner possible and a useful measure provides data for decision making.

Evaluation processes include subjective and objective methods and approaches. Although the emphasis tends to be on objective (quantitative) methods, the subjective (qualitative) approach can provide a balance to the evaluation (Katz 1997, 257). In fact, a combination of quantitative and qualitative methods is recommended to more fully answer questions. Quantitative methods are typically those that provide statistical data or work with known quantities. The quantities may be manipulated or changed and the variations measured. These methods answer questions of "what" and "how many?" and are straight-forward to use (see Smith, Case Study 2.3, Burton, Case Study 2.4, and Froehlich, Case Study 5.1). Qualitative methods such as observation, interviews, and case studies are able to gather complex data and provide insight into the "why" questions and in assessing quality concerns (see Verny and Van Fleet, Case Study 2.2 and Gatten and Radcliff, Case Study 3.2). These methods result in descriptive reports and categorization of responses but are site specific and not broadly applicable.

Quantitative Studies

Quantitative studies gather statistical data and use known quantities as a way to look at the impact a change in one component might bring about. For example, a library manager could look at the number of reference questions answered in terms of different times of the day, numbers of staff available, location, or amount of time available. The advan-tage of this approach is the ability to control the environment to allow the effect brought about by the change in one variable to be measured. A cause and effect relationship can then be established. This approach does not address the complexity of social interactions that might impact service but can provide useful data for hiring questions and other service decisions. As a methodology, objective or quantitative studies are easier to administer and more common than qualitative ones.

Qualitative Studies

Qualitative studies, in such forms as surveys, observations, interviews, and case studies, are able to examine complex factors in the social interactions inherent in reference and information services. Because these are unique studies, however, findings cannot be generally applied to a larger group. The quantity of raw data gathered is likely to be large and, because it is descriptive data, more difficult to categorize. A major concern is to see the measurement is done without evaluator bias—that there is objectivity to the study. This ability to examine "real-world" aspects of reference services provides insight into the multiple human factors involved.

Obtrusive—Unobtrusive Studies

Evaluative methods used in reference and information services can include obtrusive and unobtrusive approaches. Obtrusive methods, the more common of the two in examining the reference process, refer to those in which the library staff know some type of evaluation is being performed. It could be a survey of users, for example. Unobtrusive techniques are those in which library staff are unaware a study is underway. Often this technique is used to examine a component of the reference transaction in personnel evaluation. The objective is to ensure that normal behaviors are being studied. A combination of the methods is often used to evaluate reference transaction outcomes.

SPECIFIC METHODOLOGIES

Selecting a specific methodology depends on the purpose of the evaluation, its expected uses, and the community under study. *The Reference Assessment Manual* (1995) can be most helpful in assisting with the selection of an appropriate methodology. It provides summaries of instruments useful to assess reference service effectiveness for both public and academic libraries. Chapters include information about users and questions, the reference process, human resources (but not reference personnel performance management), and results. An extensive annotated bibliography is an integral part of this manual. The instruments included have been tested and used in library situations. Because the "design and administration of an effective evaluative tool is difficult and time-consuming" (Green 1988, 168), managers might profitably seek out tested instruments. Specific methodologies commonly employed are surveys, interviews, sampling, observation, and case studies.

Surveys are efforts to gather information about different aspects of services in a variety of library settings. These usually take the form of questionnaires given to a portion of the library community. Survey instruments are helpful in determining opinions and attitudes about facets of library and information services including effectiveness; they are not, however, useful in describing why a library system is functioning effectively. Surveys need to be carefully constructed and administered. A survey questionnaire needs to be pretested and designed to prevent problems of question interpretation, bias, reading ability, and other completion errors (Green 1988, 169). Problems of including infrequent library users in samples and low return rate on surveys may impact results. Suggestions and strategies for effective design of surveys are readily available in the library literature (Whitlatch 1992). Because effective surveys are difficult and time consuming to design, library managers may wish to use an instrument that has already worked well in other settings or collaborate with more experienced librarians, researchers, or both. Radcliff and Schloman describe their use of the standardized Wisconsin–Ohio Reference Evaluation Program in Case Study 3.1.

Sampling refers to the selection of a random or targeted portion of the population to survey or include in a study. This technique is also useful for analyzing components of reference services, such as types of questions users ask. It can also be used to gather statistical data periodically, every month or several times a year. For example, tallies are often used to find out how many questions were asked, who asked the questions, and how questions were resolved. Questionnaires may be given to a sample of library users to obtain feedback at selected times of the day, week, month, or year. The advantage of sampling is it takes less time than if the data were continually collected or if the entire user population was contacted.

Interviews involve a personal interaction, often structured, between an evaluator and librarian or user. This is a time-intensive approach that results in more detailed data. The interviewees can include experts and focus groups as well as individuals. The very structured interview in which the same questions and instructions are repeated with different individuals or groups can provide reliable data. An unstructured interview is useful for exploratory studies and for determining the actual feelings of people. The advantages of the interview methodology lie with the presence of an interviewer who can sort fact from fiction, provide explanations, and identify opinions and bias. The interview may elicit information that would not be gathered in any other way. The main disadvantage, of course, is the time required. Lack of good communication between the interviewer and respondent, dislike of an oral process, or attempts to give the "right" answer can all skew the results. A possibility of interviewer bias and interpretation also exists. These small samples provide rich data but are not representative of the total population.

Observation is a methodology that notes factual conditions or behaviors through personal scrutiny. Used in both obtrusive and unobtrusive studies, observation studies need to be carefully structured to ensure accurate results and to minimize the influence of any human element. In reference services evaluation, observations are often used in studies that utilize anonymous researchers to ask typical questions of reference librarians and then record the results. Gatten and Radcliff (Case Study 3.2) describe an unobtrusive observation methodology for assessing reference behaviors. Self-observation is a variation in which journals and diaries report behaviors and conditions. Direct observation of reference transactions is difficult because the intrusion of the observer may alter the behavior of the user or librarian. As a methodology, observation yields a large amount of descriptive data that provides challenges of categorization, interpretation, and reporting. Although the observation technique can be a valuable partner to the survey method, the researcher needs to be aware of the potential for observer bias. In a variation, participative observation, the researcher carries out typical librarian duties in conjunction with the observation. In this situation the researcher has the difficult task of concurrently contributing to the flow of activities, developing a positive relationship with the librarians, and conducting the observation.

Case studies thoroughly describe a single situation through the utilization of a variety of methods: interviews, use of documents or records, and structured or unobtrusive observations. The case study provides an in-depth understanding of one particular group or organization, an understanding that cannot be applied to other groups or situations.

The most appropriate methodology matches the goals of the research with the strengths of a particular approach. Using more than one methodology or collecting data from more than one perspective can result in a better understanding of the service under study. For example, evaluating reference service staff and user perceptions of service may provide valuable insights. Combining a quantitative survey such as a questionnaire with qualitative observations could gather information about what the situation is and why that is so.

CONCLUSION

Reference service is the point of contact between librarians and their constituents. In order to provide excellent customer service, librarians continually seek ways of describing, explaining, and improving reference activities. The components of excellent reference service have been delineated in guidelines promulgated by the professional association

("Guidelines" 1996) and ways of evaluating these components have been described in a number of excellent publications (Katz 1997; Lancaster 1993; *Reference Assessment Manual* 1995). Selecting measures and methodologies most appropriate to the local environment, mission, and goals of the library is a matter of professional judgment and a key area of professional responsibility. Librarians and library staff benefit from an improved working environment, enhanced community support, and confidence resulting from informed decision making and implementation. Ultimately, however, it is patrons who must be the reason, focus, and ultimate beneficiaries of the evaluation process.

RESOURCES

Aluri, Rao, and Mary Reichel, 1994, "Performance Evaluation: A Deadly Disease?" *Journal of Academic Librarianship* 20 (July): 145–54.

Baker, Sharon, and F. W. Lancaster, 1991, *The Measurement and Evaluation of Library Services*, 2d ed. Arlington, VA: Information Resources Press.

Blandy, Susan, Lynne Martin, and Mary Strife, eds., 1992, "Assessment and Accountability in Reference Work," *The Reference Librarian* no. 38.

Brown, Janet, 1994, "Using Quality Concepts to Improve Reference Services," *College & Research Libraries* 55 (May): 211–19.

Bunge, Charles A., 1984, "Planning, Goals, and Objectives for the Reference Department," *RQ* 23 (Spring): 306–15.

———, 1990, "Factors Related to Output Measures for Reference Services in Public Libraries: Data from Thirty-Six Libraries," *Public Libraries* 29 (January/February): 42–47.

———, 1994, "Evaluating Reference Services and Reference Personnel: Questions and Answers from the Literature." *The Reference Librarian* 43: 195–207.

Crawford, Gregory, 1994, "A Conjoint Analysis of Reference Services," *College & Research Libraries* 55 (May): 257–67.

Evaluation of Reference and Adult Services Committee, Reference and Adult Services Division, American Library Association, comp. and ed., 1995, *The Reference Assessment Manual*. Ann Arbor, MI: Pierian Press.

Gorman, Kathleen, 1987, "Performance Evaluation in Reference Services in ARL Libraries," SPEC Kit 139. Washington, DC: Office of Management Studies, Association of Research Libraries.

Green, Louise Koller, 1988, "Assessing the Effectiveness of Reference Services: A Difficult But Necessary Process," *Catholic Library World* 59 (January/February): 168–71.

"Guidelines for Behavioral Performance of Reference and Information Services Professionals," 1996, *RQ* 36 (Winter): 200–203. Also available at http://www.ala.org/RUSA/.

Hernon, Peter, and Charles R. McClure, 1987, *Unobtrusive Testing and Library Reference Services*. Norwood, NJ: Ablex.

"Information Services for Information Consumers: Guidelines for Providers," 1990, *RQ* 30 (Winter): 262–65.

Katz, Bill, and Ruth A. Fraley, eds., 1984, "Evaluation of Reference Services," *The Reference Librarian* no. 11.

Katz, William A., 1997, "Reference Service Policies and Evaluation," *Introduction to Reference Work*, Vol. II. 7th ed. New York: McGraw-Hill.

Lancaster, F. W., 1993, *If You Want to Evaluate Your Library. . . .*, 2d ed. Urbana, IL: University of Illinois, Graduate School of Library and Information Science.

Larson, Carole, 1994, "Developing Behavioral Reference Desk Performance Standards," *RQ* 33 (Spring): 347–49.

Murfin, Marjorie E., and Jo Bell Whitlatch, eds., 1993, *Research in Reference Effectiveness: Proceedings of a Preconference Sponsored by the Research and Statistics Committee, Management and Operation of Public Services Division, American Library Association, San Francisco, California, June 26, 1992.* Chicago: Reference and Adult Services Division, American Library Association.

Phillips, Steven, 1993, *Evaluation.* London: Library Association.

Pierce, Sydney, 1984, "In Pursuit of the Possible: Evaluating Reference Services," *The Reference Librarian* 11 (Fall/Winter): 9–21.

Robbins, Jane, Holly Willett, Mary Jane Wiseman, and Douglas L. Zweizig, 1990, *Evaluation Strategies and Techniques for Public Library Children's Services: A Sourcebook.* Madison, WI: University of Wisconsin-Madison, School of Library and Information Studies.

Rothstein, Samuel, 1961, "Reference Service: The New Dimension in Librarianship," *College & Research Libraries* 22 (January): 12.

Tyckoson, David. 1992. "Wrong Questions, Wrong Answers: Behavioral vs. Factual Evaluation of References Service," *The Reference Librarian* 38: 151–74.

Van House, Nancy A., Mary Jo Lynch, Charles R. McClure, Douglas L. Zweizig, and Eleanor Jo Rodger, 1987, *Output Measures for Public Libraries: A Manual of Standardized Procedures,* 2d ed. Chicago: American Library Association.

Van House, Nancy A., Beth T. Weil, and Charles R. McClure. 1990. *Measuring Academic Library Performance: A Practical Approach.* Chicago: American Library Association.

Von Seggern, Marilyn, 1987, "Assessment of Reference Services," *RQ* 26 (Summer): 487–96.

Westbrook, Lynn, 1990, "Evaluating Reference: An Introductory Overview of Qualitative Methods," *Reference Services Review* 18 (Spring): 73–78.

Whitlatch, Jo Bell, 1992, "Reference Services: Research Methodologies for Assessment and Accountability," *The Reference Librarian* no. 38: 9–19.

Method @ A Glance: Standardized Survey

Purpose:	Summarizing perceptions, opinions, or other information gathered from a large number of constituents
Description:	Surveys are a technique for gathering a large number of responses and summarizing them in a quantitative manner for analysis.
Strengths:	Capable of summarizing large bodies of data, reliable, amenable to comparison, easy to administrate, externally valid, analytically sophisticated
Use:	As part of service evaluation, administrative decision making, and strategic planning
Data Needed:	Responses to preformulated questions
Sources of Data:	Representative constituents
Organizational Model(s):	Goal, Critical Constituencies, Resource, Human Resource, Decision-Process, Customer Service

Procedure:

1. Define the problem or area of interest.
2. Identify appropriate survey instrument.
3. Adapt instrument to local needs.
4. Identify target respondents.
5. Distribute survey instrument.
6. Collect completed surveys.
7. Tabulate and analyze data.
8. Interpret data.
9. Incorporate findings into practice.

Case @ A Glance: Using the Wisconsin–Ohio Reference Evaluation Program

Purpose:	Assessing the outcome of the reference transaction and identifying factors related to success or lack of success at the Kent State University main library reference desk
Description:	The Main Library Reference Department used the Wisconsin–Ohio Reference Evaluation Program (WOREP), which provides standardized surveys of staff and patrons, expert analysis of local findings, and comparative data from other libraries participating in the program.
Use:	To supplement quantitative measures such as numbers of transactions and to provide longitudinal data for the individual library as well as comparative data for similar libraries
Sources of Data:	Pairs of standardized questionnaires, WOREP administration
Procedure:	1. WOREP program selected
	2. WOREP instruction manual studied
	3. Service points selected
	4. Time frame for survey determined
	5. Survey forms purchased
	6. Survey times designated
	7. Survey forms and definitions revised for local application
	8. Staff trained
	9. Necessary supplies provided at service desk
	10. Survey forms collected and sent for data analysis
	11. WOREP reports interpreted and results assessed

CASE STUDY

3.1

Using the Wisconsin–Ohio Reference Evaluation Program

Carolyn J. Radcliff and Barbara F. Schloman

SETTING

Kent State University is a Carnegie II Research University in northeastern Ohio comprised of eight campuses. The Kent campus has nearly 17,000 full-time equivalent students. The libraries are a member of the Association of Research Libraries, the Center for Research Libraries, and OhioLINK. The collection numbers more than 2.3 million volumes with more than 10,000 serials. The budget is approximately $10.4 million and there is a total staff of 105, including 44 librarians. On the Kent campus there are six branch libraries in addition to the Main Library. The Main Library Reference Center is staffed 70 hours per week by eight reference librarians, along with staff from other departments (each staff member contributing a total of 4 hours per week) and graduate library school students (as a group working a total of 85 hours per week). This case study reviews the use of the Wisconsin–Ohio Reference Evaluation Program (WOREP) by the Main Library Reference Department three times over the course of six years.

TODAY'S REFERENCE ENVIRONMENT

Today's reference librarians are faced with incredible change and organizational pressures. The double impact of evolving information technology and the networked environment has created an increasingly complex setting for service. Information is prepared, packaged, and delivered in ways that blend the new and the old. Traditional organization and retrieval schemes are often found to be ineffective. Patrons regularly exhibit a "technological idolatry" that demands quick and easy access to online resources in full-text. In the midst of all this, it is frequently difficult to lead patrons to resources that meet their information needs.

Institutions are experiencing steady-state or shrinking budgets. Reallocation is the tool used to guide change. Libraries and reference departments are not immune to reallocation. This creates a heightened need for management information to justify the resources allocated for the provision of reference service. There is a need to know, perhaps as never before, what constitutes good service and how a given service measures up.

A growing commitment to customer service principles and dissatisfaction with research findings about reference success (or the relative lack thereof) is bringing pressure to improve service and to re-conceptualize reference service. According to Whitlatch (1998, 15), reference librarians should develop "effective and practical methods of substantially improving reference service in all of our libraries." She advocated constant assessment of reference processes and sources as a backdrop for new efforts at offering expert evaluation and advice to patrons.

The reference literature provides examples of various types of service assessments, including questionnaires and surveys, observation, focus groups, and self- or peer-evaluation (Murfin 1995). Unfortunately, there is little in this evaluation toolbox that serves as a standardized instrument for measuring or evaluating reference service. Kent State University chose the WOREP for use because it is such a tool.

BACKGROUND OF THE WOREP

Charles Bunge of the University of Wisconsin and Marjorie Murfin of Ohio State University developed the WOREP, in 1983. The prototype was tested by 18 libraries of varying sizes and located in all regions of the country. During more than 15 years, it has been used by more than 100 academic and 85 public libraries. The WOREP is designed to assess the outcome of the reference transaction and to identify factors related to success or lack of success. Its key features are

1. it demonstrates validity—items actually measure what is indicated,

2. it demonstrates reliability—it is possible to replicate results,

3. it uses the natural reference center setting,

4. it includes sufficient factors to suggest cause and effect relationships, and

5. it provides for comparability of data.

The WOREP is unique in that it does not rely solely on patron input, but also collects data from staff. Also, it does not limit evaluation to patron satisfaction, but also considers the success of the transaction. This is of particular interest given that many studies have found success rates in reference transactions that barely exceeded 50 percent, even though patrons consistently report high levels of satisfaction. On the practical side, the use of the WOREP is enhanced by the fact that it is relatively easy to implement.

A particular strength of the WOREP is its diagnostic nature: It is designed to collect information on numerous environmental factors, which are considered to be either input or process factors. Input factors relate to those elements that are part of the reference setting and include collections, staff skill and knowledge, subject strengths, types of staff, and types of questions. Process factors refer to those items that make up the transaction. Included here are communication effectiveness, time spent, technical problems, assistance by directing or searching with, and instruction.

USING THE WOREP

The WOREP survey is a two-part form—one part to be filled out by the librarian and the other by the patron. Each part of the form has the same unique number, allowing for comparison of the perceptions of the librarian and the patron. Following each reference transaction, the librarian asks the patron if that patron would be willing to participate in a survey. If the patron is willing, the librarian separates the two-part WOREP form and gives the patron portion to the patron. After completing the form, the patron deposits it in a box before leaving the reference area. Similarly, the librarian completes the corresponding form. At the end of the evaluation period, the forms are gathered together and completed parts mailed to the WOREP administrative site for data compilation and statistical analysis. Several weeks later the reference department receives a detailed report accompanied by interpretative comments from the WOREP administrators.

The report then needs to be thoroughly reviewed and analyzed by the reference department. This information allows the department to focus on strengths and weaknesses—such as *strong* on speedy assistance but *weak* on statistics questions. This information helps the staff target improvement efforts. The WOREP report also provides comparisons with the "top scoring library" and comparably sized libraries. Although this information can be interesting, self-affirming, or even damning, another potential use of the WOREP is for a library to use it as a benchmark against which future implementations can be measured.

METHOD

The experience at Kent State University can be used to illustrate WOREP procedures. Foremost among the initial considerations are administrative and staff understanding and acceptance of the evaluation process. Without general understanding and support for the project, administrators may regard the results of the survey as irrelevant or suspect and the resulting recommendations for improvement may receive inadequate attention. It is also important for those involved to recognize that a significant amount of time will be needed to analyze the results and develop those recommendations.

Similarly, staff members who will be participating in the study should be willingly engaged in the process. Involving staff early in the planning stages facilitates such engagement by ensuring common understanding of the project goals and procedures. The WOREP is designed as a total-service evaluation tool and is not used for the assessment of individual employee performance. Everyone must participate to ensure an accurate picture of the total service. Also, the project coordinator should acknowledge the impact the survey will have during extremely busy times because of the added time needed to ask for patron participation and should encourage staff to discuss how this can be minimized. For instance, if the traffic at the desk is busy at the time a transaction is completed, the librarian may elect to note on the form which question was represented and then complete the form later when time permits. Discussing possible concerns and knowing that the disruption will be of relatively short duration (usually one to two weeks) allow staff and the project coordinator to work through issues to everyone's satisfaction.

The instrument itself comes with an instruction manual for conducting the survey. The procedures include

1. Select the service points to be included. Libraries may choose to evaluate general reference desks or other service units or branches.

2. Determine when to conduct the survey. For maximum usefulness, periods that are considered typical should be targeted. At Kent, the survey is conducted during a regular semester, when classes are in full swing and the reference desk is the busiest. This does not yield information about reference performance during the summers and between semesters, but the regular term is the primary concern. If there are special conditions that temporarily affect reference service, such as remodeling, it is best to avoid surveying during those times. Although information gathered during such times may be helpful in determining how well reference staff perform under unusual circumstances, such information is of quite limited value once the special conditions no longer exist. The library determines the length of the testing period. The time needed to complete the survey will likely range from one to two weeks and is based on how many time periods representative of the total service are selected as survey periods and the number of forms the library decides to use.

3. Decide how many forms to buy. The WOREP administrators recommend no fewer than 50 forms for each service point. However, more forms may be needed to represent all service hours adequately. Also, larger samples provide more useful information mainly because some types of transactions occur infrequently. For example, to assess effectiveness in answering questions about science and technology, it may be necessary to distribute hundreds of forms in order to accumulate sufficient numbers of science and technology transactions. The budget may also influence the decision on how many forms to purchase. The 1999 cost of the forms was $1.25 each, plus $165.00 for the data analysis per service point. The first time Kent used the WOREP, 150 forms were ordered. However, for the two most recent occasions, 500 were ordered. Even this large number of forms did not produce meaningful results for all types of questions. In 1996, for example, out of 500 forms distributed only three responses concerned government documents questions. Three transactions were too few to draw conclusions about the effectiveness of service provided in this area.

4. Contact the WOREP administrators. Forms are available from Dr. Michael Havener, Director of the School of Library and Information Science, University of Rhode Island.

5. Designate survey times. Choose survey times that represent the service schedule by hours of the day and days of the week. If possible, set up the testing period so that all staff participate about equally. The instruction manual advises survey blocks of around three hours, along with some additional recommendations. The more closely the recommendations are followed, the more likely that survey results will be free from bias.

6. Train staff. Although the WOREP form is not difficult to complete, it is important that all participating staff are familiar with the form and fill it out in a consistent manner. The instruction manual gives detailed information about completing the forms. At Kent, librarians, paraprofessionals, and graduate assistants participated in the survey. Training sessions were held with each group. Particular attention was paid to ensuring a common interpretation was given to items on the survey. For example, it was necessary to make certain everyone understood the choice

"helping with CD-ROM" to include assisting a patron with any electronic resource.

7. Provide necessary supplies. Patrons and staff must use #2 pencils for the forms. Boxes for patrons to deposit completed forms should be conspicuously and conveniently placed.

8. Collect the forms and submit them for data analysis.

9. Carefully assess results. Develop recommendations. The returned report includes a statistical profile and a guided interpretation. The statistical profile provides a report on the library's performance by each survey item and also a comparison with the top-scoring library and comparably sized libraries. The guided interpretation is provided by the WOREP administrators to suggest interpretations of the data. However, the information reported must be scrutinized and understood within the context of the surveying library's environment. This analysis may include identifying strengths and weaknesses, developing recommendations for targeted improvement, and comparing performance with other libraries and among staff types.

10. Implement recommendations. To get the most from the investment of time, effort, and money spent, it is necessary to follow through on findings and recommendations. Steps 9 and 10 are often the most difficult ones but are essential for meaningful evaluation.

11. Consider using the WOREP in the future for comparison. By using the WOREP more than once, it is possible to benchmark performance and investigate the effects of changes. Kent's efforts in this area are described in the section on evaluation.

FINDINGS AND INTERPRETATION

The findings presented here are based on the third implementation of the WOREP at Kent State University. Out of approximately 480 surveys given to patrons, there were a total of 312 surveys with matched patron and library staff responses. The statistical profile, upon which this analysis is based, provides comparative information for 41 libraries of similar size (more than a million volumes), the top-scoring library, and the average of all the libraries participating in the survey. Although the survey was conducted to elicit performance measures for three types of staff (librarians, paraprofessionals, and graduate student assistants) in addition to the overall measure, this section concentrates on selected librarian results. Summary comments are provided for the other two staff types.

Patron Profile

Table 3.1.1 shows that most patrons who participated in the survey were undergraduates, as expected. Graduate students also made up a significant portion. Faculty, alumni, and community member representation was low. Arts/Humanities, Education, Social Sciences, and Business students made up most of the majors approaching the reference desk, with the remaining student majors spread across the other disciplines.

Table 3.1.1. Patron Profile

Patron Types: Percentage of All Participants	
Freshmen	18%
Sophomores	13%
Juniors	16%
Seniors	24%
Grad. Students	18%
Faculty	4%
Community	3%
Alumni	2%
Patron Subject Disciplines: Percentage of All Participants	
Arts and Humanities	25%
Education	19%
Business	17%
Social Sciences	11%
Medicine and Health	11%
Other	17%

Success Levels

WOREP developers define a success transaction as patrons reporting "they obtained just what was wanted and that they were completely satisfied with the information or materials suggested" (Bunge 1990). Success rates for Kent were high, with 67.3 percent of the sample *obtaining exactly what was wanted and being satisfied* (see Table 3.1.2). This compared well with other libraries that have used the WOREP: 56.1 percent for libraries of a similar size and 68.8 percent for the top-scoring library. If patrons who found *approximately* what was wanted and were satisfied are added, the scores again are comparable: 77.9 percent for the Kent sample, 68.7 percent for libraries of a similar size, and 78.1 percent for the top-scoring library. The percentages at Kent were high for all levels of staff, with very little difference among groups. All staff appeared to offer the patrons the information they needed to find answers to their questions most of the time.

Table 3.1.2. Patron Success Levels

	Kent-Overall	Kent-Librarians	Kent-Graduate Assistants	Kent-Para-professionals	Libraries of Similar Size	Top-Scoring Library
Number of surveys returned*	312	183	112	17	N/A	N/A
Percent of those who found exactly what was wanted and were satisfied	67.3%	67.8%	67.0%	64.7%	56.1%	68.8%
Percent who found exactly or approximately what was wanted and were satisfied	77.9%	78.1%	77.7%	76.5%	68.7%	78.1%

*excludes specific-book questions, which, according to the WOREP administrators, test availability of materials more than reference skill

Factors Associated with Less-Than-Successful Questions

Although the overall results demonstrate a high level of success, it is important to understand why some transactions are not successful. One strength of the WOREP is its ability to highlight factors that are associated with less-than-successful encounters. This information was gathered from patrons who indicated that they did not find exactly what was wanted. Table 3.1.3 lists a number of factors associated with lack of success. More detailed information, including how the factors compare in their impact on success rates, is provided in the statistical profile sent by the WOREP administrators.

Table 3.1.3. Selected Factors Associated with Less-Than-Successful Questions

Factor	No. of Occasions
Librarian reports one source used	26
Patron reports "not enough"	21
Direct and suggest only	19
1st or 2nd Subject: Business/Economics	13
Type of question: short answer facts	11
Type of question: multiple object	11
1st or 2nd Subject: literature	11
Time: 0–3 minutes	10
Librarian reports busy	10
Patron reports "librarian not knowledgeable"	10
Type of question: something, anything, everything	9
Type of question: criticism, interpretation, reviews, etc.	9
Patron reports "librarian didn't understand"	8
Patron reports "not enough help/explanation"	8
Patron reports "need more in-depth"	8
Patron reports "not relevant enough"	8

(Note: Librarians only)

Additional data on the factor of *direct and suggest only*, listed in Table 3.1.3, showed that higher success rates occurred when the librarian searched with the patron instead of merely directing the patron to a source. Of the 115 occasions during which the librarian searched, the patron obtained exactly what was wanted 72 percent of the time. On the 62 occasions when the librarian directed, patrons obtained what was needed only 60 percent of the time. One striking finding is that in 49 instances, librarians did not appear busy, yet they directed rather than searched with a success rate for patrons of 57 percent. A recommendation based on this data is that librarians increase the frequency of searching, thereby increasing the likelihood of success.

The full statistical profile offers another way of looking at this problem that is not reflected in Table 3.1.3—the factor of *directed rather than searched* was associated with 75 percent of the less-than-successful transactions, making it the single most important negative factor. Other factors include *reference staff too busy* (14 percent of less-than-successful transactions), *collection weak, outdated, or in another area* (7 percent), and *books off shelf* or *cataloging or processing problem* (4 percent).

The data provide further intriguing information about reference transactions. There is conspicuous disparity in patron and librarian perceptions of success. Of the 95 occasions when the librarian reported *found exactly*, patrons reported the same result only 73 times (76.8 percent agreement). Overall consensus on *found exactly*, *partly found*, or *not found* was 58 percent. Some disparity is expected because the ultimate outcome of the reference transaction is often unknown, but these results demonstrate a problematic lack of awareness on the part of the librarian. An appropriate recommendation for staff is to inquire more carefully as to whether or not the patron has what is needed and to be more diligent about encouraging the patron to return if necessary.

In another area, communication, patrons reported communication difficulty 9.8 percent of the time (18 instances). Looking at those 18 instances, librarians also reported difficulty 3 times (16.7 percent), signifying a low rate of detecting communication problems that were present for patrons. Librarians need to pay more attention to patron perceptions of the interaction.

Patron and Librarian Reports of Problems

Patrons were asked to indicate if they had experienced any problems in their reference transactions, regardless of whether or not the needed information was obtained. Results are shown in Table 3.1.4.

Table 3.1.4. Patron Reports of Problems

Service	Number of Occasions	Percent of All Questions
Librarians appeared only partly or not knowledgeable	13	7.1%
Librarians only part or did not understand what was wanted	10	5.5%
Not enough time given	8	4.4%
Not enough explanation or help given	8	4.4%
Explanations only partly or not clear	7	3.8%
Librarians only partly or not courteous	4	2.2%
Information or Materials		
Not enough	21	11.5%
Need more in-depth	8	4.4%
Not relevant enough	8	4.4%
Couldn't find information in source	5	2.7%
Too much	5	2.7%
Found nothing	2	1.1%
Want different viewpoint	2	1.1%
Not sure if information is correct	1	.5%
Want more simple	0	0

(Note: Librarians only)

The factors of *not enough* and possibly *librarian appeared only partly or not knowledgeable* are the only ones that occurred frequently enough to warrant attention. The first one (*not enough*) is addressed by the previous recommendation to find out whether patrons have what they need and encourage them to return as necessary. It is difficult to make a recommendation about the second factor (*partly or not knowledgeable*) because it deals with perception, not results, and may be a matter of personal style.

Librarians also reported on question problems, with the only significant items being *wants number of things* (7 percent of all questions), and *question complexity and specificity* (44 percent). Neither of those factors is associated with lack of patron success, however, so they apparently pose no problem.

Factors Associated with Obtaining Exactly What Was Wanted

The data provide rich information about additional factors associated with patron success, including difficulty level of question and type and aspect of question, as shown in Table 3.1.5. Results for question difficulty indicate an expected trend in higher success for easier questions. It is interesting to note that when librarians identify the questions as being *easy*, only 76 percent of the patrons are successful in finding the information they need. As the level of difficulty increases, success rates decrease (67 percent for medium and 18 percent for hard). Although this decrease is expected, it is appropriate to focus staff discussion on increasing success rates for *easy* questions and to recommend development of strategies for handling more difficult questions.

For information and planning purposes, Table 3.1.5 shows the types and aspects of questions asked and how successfully they were handled. Given the low success rate for business questions, it is reasonable that the department pursue staff development in business resources.

Patron Learning

In addition to success and satisfaction, the WOREP provides information about what a patron may have learned as a result of the reference transaction. Table 3.1.6 presents the results. As an academic library, Kent's service priorities include teaching students and others about information searching and retrieval in addition to providing answers to inquiries. The results in this section indicate that patrons believe learning is taking place.

Table 3.1.5. Factors Associated with Obtaining Exactly What Was Needed

Librarian Report of Difficulty Level of Question and Patron Success in Obtaining Exactly What Was Wanted	Number of Occasions	Of Those, Found Exactly	Percent
Easy	92	68	76%
Medium	79	53	67%
Hard	11	2	18%

Type of Question and Patron Success in Obtaining Exactly What Was Wanted	Number of Occasions	Of Those, Found Exactly	Percent
Short answer facts	26	15	57.7%
Facts and statistics	13	11	84.6%
Explanation of particular source or library	25	18	72.0%
Something, anything	46	37	80.0%
Certain type of source or materials	18	11	61.0%
Criticism, reviews	25	16	64.0%
Analysis, trends, pro/con, cause/effect, how-to-do-it, etc.	14	11	78.6%
Focus on aspect	17	10	58.8%

Aspect of Questions and Patron Success in Obtaining Exactly What Was Wanted	Number of Occasions	Of Those, Found Exactly	Percent
Statistical	10	7	70%
Biographical	11	6	55%
Historical	7	5	71%
Bibliographical	18	13	72%
Education	14	14	100%
Business	17	5	29%

(Note: Librarians only)

Table 3.1.6. Patron Learning

Patron Reports Learning New Sources	Number of Occasions	Percent
Two or more new sources	61	33.5%
One new source	95	52.0%
No new sources	26	14.0%
Patron Reports Learning Something About the Library	**Number of Occasions**	**Percent**
Yes	151	83.4%
Yes and partly	173	95.6%
No	8	4.4%

(Note: Librarians only)

ACTION

The Reference Department, including librarians, paraprofessionals, and graduate reference assistants, performs well in handling reference questions. Most patrons are satisfied most of the time, although there is room for improvement. The results and recommendations were shared with administrators to provide information about the quality of service provided, supplementing the more frequently reported quantitative measures. Recommendations include

1. More careful inquiry as to whether or not the patron has what is needed, and increased encouragement to return if needed.

2. Increasing the frequency of searching, thereby decreasing directing.

3. Increasing attention to patron perceptions of the interaction.

4. Continual discussion of reference service provision, specifically seeking even higher success rates with "easy" questions and improving performance on more difficult questions.

5. Staff development in business resources.

After this study was conducted, the department acted upon these recommendations with varying consistency. The greatest attention has been given to following up with patrons and to staff development, including business resources. In addition, service has been enhanced in ways not specifically called for by these recommendations, including increasing visibility and availability by having staff rove through the reference center.

EVALUATION

The WOREP is a useful tool for assessing traditional reference service. Kent's experience has been enhanced by the repeated use of the instrument; the study has been conducted three times since 1991. Using the same instrument makes it possible to compare results across the years. Such comparisons allow for assessing if changes have had any noticeable effect and make it possible to continue to pinpoint areas for improvement. Some changes are not necessarily planned (e.g., personnel changes, decreasing reference collection budgets), but their effects may still be seen by repeated use of the WOREP. Overall success rates over the years are presented in Table 3.1.7.

Table 3.1.7. Patron Success Levels over Six Years

	1991	1993	1996
Number of surveys returned*	62	57	183
Percent of those who found exactly what was wanted and were satisfied	59.7%	73.7%	67.8%
Percent who found exactly <u>or approximately</u> what was wanted and were satisfied	64.5%	80.7%	78.1%

(Note: Librarians only)

*excludes specific-book questions, which, according to the WOREP administrators, test availability of materials more than reference skill

It is possible to describe factors that have influenced the outcomes of reference service provided at Kent over the past several years and that explain some of the variation in success rates. In the years immediately prior to the first survey period, a number of retirements and other staff changes led to the loss of personnel with many years of reference experience. Newly hired staff had much less cumulative experience than those they replaced. Kent's first online library catalog was implemented during this time.

Between the first and second survey periods, probably the most influential change was a transformation of the Reference Center in terms of its physical layout. The reference desk was given a much more prominent position than before and other changes affected in a positive way the flow of staff and patrons within the area. Also, the number of electronic resources began to grow significantly during this time period.

The time between the second and third surveys included several more changes and an overall reduction to the staff roster. The Reference Center established an information desk and adjusted the staffing mix by increasing reliance on graduate students and introducing classified staff at the information desk. The classified staff were individuals whose "home" departments were elsewhere in the library and who worked about two hours per week in the Reference Center. Another significant change during this time was the migration to a second integrated library system for the online catalog and the introduction at Kent of the statewide library system, OhioLINK.

Exactly how these changes and others affected the quality of reference service as reflected in WOREP results is uncertain. Reference staff and administration continue to look at both internal and external factors and believe that promoting effective service and its evaluation is an ongoing commitment. The WOREP provides objective data on performance and helps to pinpoint areas for potential improvement. The WOREP will continue to be used, with the fourth survey already scheduled.

RESOURCES

Bunge, Charles A., 1990, "Factors Related to Output Measures for Reference Services in Public Libraries: Data from Thirty-Six Libraries," *Public Libraries* 29 (January/February): 42–47.

Murfin, Marjorie E., 1995, "Assessing Library Services: The Reference Component," pp. 1–15 in *The Reference Assessment Manual*, comp. and ed. Evaluation of Reference and Adult Services Committee, Reference and Adult Services Division, American Library Association. Ann Arbor, MI: Pierian Press.

Murfin, Marjorie E., and Charles A. Bunge, 1988, "Responsible Standards for Reference Service in Ohio Public Libraries," *Ohio Libraries* 1 (April/May): 11–13.

Murfin, Marjorie E., and Gary M. Gugelchuk, 1987, "Development and Testing of a Reference Transaction Assessment Instrument," *College and Research Libraries* 48 (July): 314–36.

Stalker, John C., and Marjorie E. Murfin, 1996, "Quality Reference Service: A Preliminary Study," *Journal of Academic Librarianship* 22 (November): 423–29.

Whitlatch, Jo Bell., 1998, "Enhancing the Quality of Reference Services for the 21st Century," *Reference & User Services Quarterly* 38 (Fall): 15–16

Method @ A Glance: Unobtrusive Observation

Purpose: Gathering naturalistic data on routine processes

Description: Unobtrusive observation is a method in which trained proxies act as patrons and record their experience with patron–librarian interaction in a normal library setting. At least one participant in the interaction is unaware of the observation process.

Strengths: Nondisruptive, nonreactive (does not influence normal behavior)

Use: As part of service evaluation and strategic planning; restrict to outcome (accuracy or satisfaction) or process (behavior) evaluation; *not appropriate for individual personnel evaluation*.

Data Needed: Recorded proxy observations

Sources of Data: Trained proxies

Organizational Model(s):   Human Resource, Customer Service

Procedure:
1. State goals and objectives.
2. Identify libraries or service points to be studied.
3. Develop an evaluation form to record observations.
4. Formulate procedure for proxy–librarian interaction.
5. Identify and train proxies.
6. Engage in transactions.
7. Collect and analyze data.
8. Interpret findings.
9. Make recommendations.
10. Implement recommendations.

Case @ A Glance: Assessing Reference Behaviors with Unobtrusive Testing

Purpose:	Assessing the effectiveness of staff reference training provided by the Ohio Reference Excellence Initiative
Description:	An unobtrusive study of interpersonal communication behaviors during reference interviews was conducted at representative libraries.
Use:	To assess the impact of a statewide reference staff training program
Sources of Data:	Proxy reports on observed verbal and nonverbal behaviors of reference staff
Procedure:	1. Study sites selected
	2. Evaluation form designed
	3. Questions devised that could naturally lead to a reference interview
	4. Students in a library and information science course assigned responsibility for serving as proxies
	5. Class session devoted to proxy training
	6. Proxy visits completed
	7. Data from evaluation forms entered into database and analyzed using statistical program
	8. Results interpreted to determine effectiveness of the training experience

CASE STUDY

3.2

Assessing Reference Behaviors with Unobtrusive Testing

Jeffrey N. Gatten and Carolyn J. Radcliff

INTRODUCTION

Many libraries offer professional development opportunities to their staff members as a way to ensure that employees have the knowledge and skills needed to carry out their duties. The value of such professional development efforts rests in large part on the likelihood that participants do, in fact, gain or refresh knowledge or skills that they will subsequently use on the job. A persistent question for those responsible for professional development is whether or not the efforts have this kind of value. In other words, when you send staff to workshops, how do you know if they remember and use what was taught? This study presents one method for answering that question, based on a series of workshops designed in part to teach behavioral standards for reference service.

BACKGROUND

Measurements of effective reference service most often concentrate on the factual accuracy of responses to inquiries. Numerous studies have been directed in this area and are well reported in the professional literature. However, fewer studies have attempted to examine the characteristics of librarian–patron interaction during the reference interview as a predictor of reference success. In many instances, success may depend on a librarian's interviewing skills, questioning and exchanging information with a patron in order to discern real information needs masked behind vague or unclear inquiries.

In an effort to furnish librarians with specific guidelines for assessing librarian–patron interactions, the Reference and Adult Services division of the American Library Association established in 1992 the Ad Hoc Committee on Behavioral Guidelines for Reference and Information Services. The committee published their guidelines in 1996 as "Guidelines for Behavioral Performance of Reference and Information Services Professionals," identifying five important categories of observable behaviors: approachability, interest, listening/inquiring, searching, and follow-up.

1. *Approachability*: According to the guidelines, the librarian's role is to "make the patron feel comfortable in a situation which may be perceived as intimidating, risky, confusing, and overwhelming." These behaviors include being poised and ready to engage the patron, establishing eye contact, acknowledging the patron with a smile, using a friendly greeting, acknowledging others waiting for service, remaining visible, and roving and offering assistance whenever possible.

2. *Interest:* Librarians should exhibit a high level of interest in a patron's information need by facing the patron, maintaining eye contact, establishing a comfortable physical span, confirming an understanding of the patron's needs, appearing unhurried, and focusing attention on the patron.

3. *Listening/Inquiring*: The reference interview should be an exchange of information in order to effectively determine information needs. Behaviors include use of an appropriate tone of voice, demonstrating cordial and encouraging communication, allowing the patron to completely state the information need, paraphrasing the need back to the patron, utilizing open-ended questions to encourage patron augmentation of the initial request, using clarifying questions to refine the search strategy, avoiding jargon and unfamiliar terminology, and regarding the topic of inquiry objectively.

4. *Searching*: Here the guidelines include specific behaviors for conducting an information search as well as keeping the patron informed about the process. Recommended behaviors consist of a series of behaviors for constructing a competent search strategy, discussing the search strategy and sequence with the patron, explaining how to use sources, asking if additional information is needed after finding an initial result, and recognizing when to make a referral.

5. *Follow-up*: After a patron reviews the information provided, the librarian should engage in follow-up activities, such as asking if the question has been completely answered, returning to the patron after that patron has studied the initial sources, consulting with other librarians, referring to other agencies, and facilitating referral follow through.

These behaviors add up to standards that, when followed, increase the likelihood of both patron satisfaction with the transaction and patron success in obtaining needed information.

SETTING

In 1998 the Ohio Library Council (OLC), a nonprofit professional association serving primarily Ohio's public libraries, launched the grant-funded "Ohio Reference Excellence Initiative (OREI)." This project was designed to offer free basic reference training workshops to public, school, academic, and special library staff throughout the State of Ohio. The workshops consisted of two segments: one focusing on the reference interview and related interpersonal communication behaviors, and one dedicated to covering basic reference resources. The assumptions of the program are 1) in many small libraries reference questions are answered by library employees who lack professional training,

2) professional reference librarians require updates or refreshing on the reference process, and 3) new employees require basic training. The Ohio Reference Excellence Initiative workshops, combined with the previously developed *Ohio Reference Excellence: A Self-Study Reference Course* (a manual upon which the workshops are designed) and the introduction of a statewide back-up reference service provided by the State Library of Ohio and the Public Library of Cincinnati and Hamilton County, are intended to improve and ensure the quality of reference services in Ohio's libraries.

　　　　As part of the evaluation of the Ohio Reference Excellence Initiative, a number of methods, including surveys of participants and supervisors, were used for determining satisfaction with the workshops and progress in adopting appropriate reference interview techniques. One additional method was an unobtrusive study of interpersonal communication behaviors during reference interviews at libraries that sent a number of staff members to the workshops.

METHODOLOGY

The steps in conducting an unobtrusive study of the reference interview are:

1.　state goals and objectives,

2.　identify libraries to be studied,

3.　develop an evaluation form for observable behaviors,

4.　develop reference questions to be asked,

5.　identify and train proxies,

6.　engage in reference transactions, and

7.　analyze collected data.

Step 1: Goals and Objectives

　　　　The goals and objectives of this unobtrusive study were to determine if interpersonal communication behaviors taught in the Ohio Reference Excellence Initiative workshops were learned by participants and applied at their libraries, thus providing one indicator of the success and value of the workshops. Unlike many unobtrusive studies of reference services, the accuracy of the answer provided to an inquiry was not the focus. Instead, students acting as proxies asked reference questions and observed verbal and nonverbal behaviors of staff to determine whether or not desired reference behaviors were regularly exhibited.

Step 2: Libraries to Be Studied

　　　　Perhaps the most difficult aspect of this evaluation was that rather than performing a self-study of one's own library reference service, there was a need to examine the effects of workshop training in several libraries. Sites were selected for the unobtrusive study based on two criteria: libraries had to be located in the northern part of the state, and libraries had to have sent a large percentage of their staff to the workshop.

Location of the libraries was important because the students visiting them to observe reference transactions could not travel long distances. Using libraries with several workshop-trained staff members increased the odds of encountering a workshop attendee. However, observing staff members who were not workshop attendees was also valuable because one key assumption of the workshops was that attendees would return to their libraries and share the information on appropriate reference behaviors with others.

As a result, five public libraries were identified for the study. Each library had sent at least five people to the workshops for reference training.

Step 3: Develop Evaluation Form

The evaluation form was designed to be a checklist of desirable behaviors that could be easily and quickly completed by the proxies. Observed behaviors were to be coded as *Yes* (observed), *Partially* (somewhat observed), *No* (not observed), and, for some behaviors, *Not Applicable* (the reference interview never progressed to the point where the behavior could be observed). Selected behaviors from the *Ohio Reference Excellence: A Self-Study Reference Course* manual, mirroring those in "Guidelines for Behavioral Performance of Reference and Information Services Professional," were chosen to reflect the five major categories of approachability, interest, listening/inquiring, searching, and follow-up. Specific behaviors were selected that could be easily observed and remembered by observers. Also, a limited number of behaviors were selected so that the task of looking for these behaviors was manageable.

The final list of behaviors to be studied was

1. Approachability:
   - maintained eye contact
   - gave a friendly greeting

2. Interest:
   - spoke clearly
   - gave full attention

3. Listening/inquiring:
   - paraphrased comments
   - asked clarifying, open-ended questions
   - asked verifying questions

4. Searching:
   - went with patron to resources
   - found the answer in the first source
   - searched several sources
   - kept patron informed

5. Follow-up:
   - offered referrals
   - asked if question was answered

Additional items on the evaluation form included several open-ended questions designed to elicit comments from the proxies about the reference interview. These questions were

1. *Are you satisfied with the answer you received?*

2. *Do you think it was complete and accurate?*

3. *What were your general impressions of this transaction?*

4. *What else should we [the principal investigators] know about your experience?*

Other information on the evaluation form included the proxy's name, the name of the library that the proxy visited, the date of the visit, and how long the transaction took. A copy of the form appears in Figure 3.2.1.

NAME _____

LIBRARY VISITED _____

DATE OF VISIT _____

Name of the person who helped you: _____

This person . . .	YES	PARTIALLY	NO	
Maintained eye contact	1	2	3	
Gave a friendly greeting	1	2	3	
Spoke clearly	1	2	3	
Gave full attention	1	2	3	
Paraphrased my comments	1	2	3	
Asked clarifying, open-ended questions	1	2	3	
Asked verifying questions	1	2	3	
Went with me to resources	1	2	3	NA
Found the answer in the first source	1	2	3	
Searched several sources	1	2	3	NA
Kept me informed	1	2	3	
Offered referrals	1	2	3	NA
Asked if question was answered	1	2	3	

COMMENTS:

Are you satisfied with the answer you received? Do you think it was complete and accurate? Explain.

What were your general impressions of this transaction?

What else should we know about your experience?

Jeffrey N. Gatten and Carolyn J. Radcliff, May 1999

Figure 3.2.1. Evaluation Form for Unobtrusive Observation of Reference Behaviors

Step 4: Develop Reference Questions

Questions were devised that could naturally lead to a reference interview. For example, a proxy might ask, "Where are your books on cars?" when what the proxy really wanted was information on the number of automobiles produced in the U.S. annually. The idea was that if the staff member asked some probing questions, the specific information need would be discovered.

Through a review by practicing reference librarians, the questions were determined to be typical and relatively easy to answer with resources available in public libraries. Enough questions were developed so that each proxy would have two questions that were different from everyone else's.

Step 5: Identify and Train Proxies

For this project, students who were enrolled in the Kent State University School of Library and Information Science's (SLIS) Adult Services course in spring 1999 were required to be the proxies as one of their class assignments. The instructor's objectives for requiring participation were to provide students with first-hand experience with an evaluation of library services, to familiarize students with preferred reference behaviors, and to engage students in the research process.

One class session was dedicated to describing the project to the students, assigning reference questions to be asked at the libraries, training on the behaviors to be examined, practicing completion of the evaluation form, outlining the steps to be followed, facilitating practice sessions, and answering questions. Students were told about the project and informed of the role of proxies in going to designated libraries and engaging reference staff members in reference transactions.

The need for confidentiality was emphasized in that an unobtrusive study of this type can be effective only if the subjects are unaware of the artificial environment that is being created. It was also important that the proxies have no preconceived expectations of what they would experience or of the outcome of a transaction. Therefore, it was emphasized that proxies should not discuss the project with anyone, including their classmates. Proxies were told that all results of the study would be kept confidential and only reported in the aggregate. No individuals, including the proxies, were to be identified or associated with any library.

Proxies were instructed to become comfortable with their assigned questions by building their own stories about the specific query prior to visiting the libraries. They needed to be prepared to add nuggets of information in response to questions they might receive about their topic from the reference staff member. Proxies needed to be able to answer inquiries about why they wanted the information without divulging the true purpose of their visits.

The two principal investigators of this study engaged in role playing during the training session in order to give the students an opportunity to practice completing the evaluation form. Assuming the roles of a reference staff member and of a patron, the investigators performed various scenarios for the student proxies-in-training. The students then completed practice evaluation forms that were collected by the investigators. The results were tabulated and additional training was provided the following week to clarify inconsistencies in scoring the observable behaviors.

Students were also given a chance to study their simulated reference questions and to suggest changes or adaptations that would increase their comfort with the questions. These suggestions had to be reviewed and approved before they could be used.

Step 6: Engage in a Reference Transaction

In order to ensure that a sufficient number of reference inquiries were made at each library, the proxies were asked to make a total of four visits to at least two of the selected libraries. Each proxy was assigned two reference questions and each question was to be asked twice for a total of four inquiries. Proxies were not to ask the same question twice at any one library nor were they to ask both of their questions in one visit. Proxies were told to first re-familiarize themselves with the contents of the evaluation form immediately prior to entering a library. They were to approach the reference desk, ask their assigned questions, and respond directly to the specific questions asked of them by the reference staff member until the staff member determined that the process was concluded. After exiting the library, proxies were to complete the evaluation form as soon as possible.

Step 7: Analyze Data

Data from the evaluation forms were entered into a database and analyzed using the *SPSS for Windows*, version 8.0.1, statistical program. The evaluation form's alpha reliability was acceptable at 0.75, indicating that the proxies used the form consistently. (The item asking how long the transaction took was eliminated from the analysis because it proved to be unreliable.) The two main areas of interest were whether or not the desired behaviors were observed, and proxies' perceptions of the answers obtained and service provided.

FINDINGS

Ninety-six observations were recorded. All the interactions were successful in that the reference questions were asked without revealing the true nature of the project and all proxies received some amount of reference service. The transactions varied widely in terms of the desired reference behaviors and satisfaction with the assistance provided.

It was clear that not all desired behaviors were regularly exhibited by staff handling reference questions. In particular, those behaviors that center on listening and drawing out the patron occurred much less often than behaviors in the "approachable" category. Given that the proxies asked general questions that masked specific needs, the failure to identify the real need often led to dissatisfaction with the answer on the part of the proxy. See Table 3.2.1 for how often each behavior was observed.

In addition to looking for certain behaviors, proxies were asked to indicate whether or not they were satisfied with the answer received. These were narrative answers that were interpreted and coded as "yes," "partially," or "no." Table 3.2.2 shows that the proxies were fully satisfied slightly less than half the time.

Table 3.2.1. Observation of Reference Behaviors: Percentage of All Observations

Behavior	Observed	Partially Observed	Not Observed	Not Applicable
Spoke clearly	94%	6%	0%	
Gave full attention	80%	16%	4%	
Maintained eye contact	71%	26%	3%	
Friendly greeting	62%	28%	10%	
Went with me to resources	55%	4%	26%	14%
Kept me informed	43%	16%	42%	
Asked clarifying, open-ended questions	37%	18%	45%	
Found answer in first source	35%	4%	32%	27%
Asked verifying questions	34%	18%	48%	
Searched several sources	30%	1%	24%	40%
Paraphrased my comments	27%	24%	49%	
Asked if question was answered	17%	12%	72%	
Offered referrals	10%	1%	21%	67%

Percentages have been rounded and may not add up to 100%.

Ohio Reference Excellence: A Self-Study Reference Course.

Table 3.2.2. Satisfaction with Answer Received

Satisfied with Answer Received	Frequency	Percent	Cumulative Percent
Yes	46	48%	48%
Partially	12	13%	61%
No	37	39%	100%

Cross-tabulation of satisfaction with the various behaviors showed that nine behaviors were significantly associated with satisfaction with answer. The nine items were

1. spoke clearly,

2. paraphrased my comments,

3. asked clarifying, open-ended questions,

4. asked verifying questions,

5. went with me to resources,

6. found answer in first source,

7. kept me informed,

8. offered referrals, and

9. asked if question was answered.

The proxies were clearly looking for friendly and competent assistance, but regularly encountered only one or the other. For example,

> I received the answer I wanted, but I didn't care for the way she handled it. After finally getting to the real question, she handed me [a book] and said "It might be in there, I'm not sure," and she left to sit back down. I realized that I was unhappy (even though I received my answer) because the whole interview wasn't a pleasant one. She just seemed bothered by me.

> It took a little longer than we would have liked, and I had to prod with a couple search suggestions, but I got exactly what I was looking for.

> I didn't find her to be overwhelmingly helpful and friendly, but she was very knowledgeable and proficient and knew her sources well.

> She was friendly but did not answer my question.

Proxies were strongly dissatisfied when no attempt was made to discover their real needs. Comments from the proxies' evaluation forms bear this out:

> The librarian asked me one open-ended question to determine my "need" and then referred me by pointing to the [subject] reference area. She did not determine exactly what I was looking for and did not suggest any specific titles. (A patron could waste a lot of time looking through inappropriate books.)

> I was very dissatisfied. The librarian pointed to [subject] books in the far corner and left. She responded only to my preliminary request and asked me no questions at all, so she never discovered what was my true need for information.

I did not find an answer to my question. The librarian never learned my specific need and never asked me any questions at all.

INTERPRETATION

Results showed that not all desired behaviors were exhibited all of the time and that certain behaviors were associated with satisfaction. There are several possible interpretations of the observational findings. The most likely explanation is the obvious one: Staff providing reference service in these libraries are usually approachable and friendly, but they usually do not employ the various strategies available to identify a patron's hidden need and determine if the patron received what the patron wants.

It was hoped that the desired reference behaviors would be regularly demonstrated in libraries that sent several staff members to the OREI workshops. This did not happen with those behaviors that centered on listening/inquiring. The findings have significant implications for future workshops. First, adequate time and emphasis should be allocated in the workshops to covering the desired behaviors. Attendees should have a thorough understanding of the behaviors and why they are important. Through role-playing or other feedback methods, participants should learn to put the behaviors into practice. Second, workshop attendees should be encouraged and taught how to facilitate such behaviors among staff at their libraries.

Workshop planners may also need to identify any impediments to participants' learning and using the behaviors. For example, the failure to ask probing or follow-up questions in this study could signal a lack of self-confidence on the part of staff. If you know where the books on cars are located, but don't believe you can help with more difficult questions, then it's entirely natural to take a question like "Where are your books on cars?" at face value. And, if handling an inquiry taxed all of your reference knowledge and skills, would you want to ask the patron if "this completely answers your question"? What if the patron says "no" and you can think of no other sources? Such concerns could be identified and addressed in the workshop by providing reassurance and offering appropriate strategies.

Ideally, an initial evaluation of the effectiveness of workshop training would focus solely on the workshop participants, using a pre- and post-test to compare them before and after the training sessions. Such a comparison would reveal whether or not there were changes in the frequency of desired behaviors as a result of workshop training. That method was not available for this study but should be considered in future assessments.

In terms of satisfaction rates, the results must be interpreted cautiously. This study was designed to assess how well a particular style of workshop instruction leads to improvements in reference behaviors. It was not a study of how well reference service is performed in the observed libraries. The use of proxies and manufactured questions with hidden meanings do not necessarily reflect "real" patrons and their questions. Also, the proxies had certain expectations for reference behaviors of staff and they were primed to look for those behaviors as a required condition of being satisfied. For example,

She did not ask me any questions to find out my real question. She only asked me if I wanted books to take home or to use there. She then had me follow her to the reference section. She was very nice. If I wasn't studying to be a librarian, I would've been satisfied with the help she gave me. She was very friendly.

I was disappointed even though I found my answer.

CONCLUSION

The method developed here worked well in detecting the presence or absence of desired reference behaviors, which was one way to assess the value of the reference workshops. Having library science students available to act as proxies as part of a class assignment certainly contributed to the success of the unobtrusive observations. Students were highly motivated, not only because it was a class assignment, but also because they had a strong interest in how well librarians and other staff provide reference service. Some of the students were also doing reference work at other libraries and so could relate to the issue from the staff member perspective.

The evaluation of workshop learning was helpful because the results of this study will be used to focus and improve future workshops. The objective assessment of such an important aspect of reference work, as offered by the unobtrusive observation method, provides powerful guidance in the design and implementation of future workshops. The combination of this study with other methods of workshop evaluation (e.g., participant satisfaction) offers a comprehensive appraisal of the OREI workshops.

RESOURCES

Ohio Reference Excellence: A Self-Study Reference Course, 1997, Columbus: Ohio Library Council.

Reference and User Services Association (RUSA), 1996, "RUSA Guidelines for Behavioral Performance of Reference and Information Services Professionals," *RQ* 36 (Winter): 200–203.

Evaluating Collections

Connie Van Fleet

INTRODUCTION

Collection evaluation is concerned with determining the strengths and weaknesses of a collection of library materials in terms of the level of intrinsic quality, the extent to which that collection supports and furthers the library's mission and goals, and the value of that collection to the library's users and potential users. Collection evaluation is an integral part of the broader collection development process, which includes policy formulation, acquisition, selection, arrangement, processing, and deselection. Further, collection development includes applying those processes equally to print, audiovisual materials, digital materials, commercial online access services, and Internet sites.

Data gathering is the first step in the collection evaluation process. Collecting data, whether quantitative or qualitative, is a way to describe current conditions. Evaluation involves examining data in the context of appropriate organizational models and in terms of the library's mission. The resulting judgments about what the data mean form the basis of decisions for future action.

This discussion of collection evaluation is based on the following assumptions:

1. Providing access to multiple formats, including print, audiovisual materials, and electronic information, will continue as an important function of the library.

2. Different measures and evaluation contexts are appropriate for different purposes and settings.

3. Selection and interpretation of measures are grounded in the organizational model and philosophical context of the library (mission and goals).

4. Multiple measures or data points reveal a more complete and accurate picture of the collection, its use, and its value as well as the interaction of the variables studied.

5. Measurement supports evaluation. It does not substitute for it.

6. Evaluation leads to decision making.

TYPES OF COLLECTION EVALUATION TECHNIQUES

There are several basic typologies, or ways of classifying, collection evaluation techniques. Among these classifying criteria are the nature of the data, the focus of the technique, and the effect or area of judgment.

One classification system focuses on the nature of the data: quantitative and qualitative. Each has advantages. Quantitative data are numeric: they describe how many or how much. What is the library's circulation? What is the turnover rate? How frequently is a database accessed? Generally, quantitative data are considered to be absolute and objective, although the interpretation of the data may well be subjective. Measures that provide quantitative data have several advantages: they appear fair and accurate, external constituencies easily understand them, and they can be gathered and analyzed relatively easily. They are generally preferable for comparative techniques and often required by funding bodies.

Unfortunately, without careful attention to definition and application, assumptions about comparability and validity are often incorrect. For instance, while counting "searches" or "hits" may seem relatively straightforward, these measures may be defined and counted differently by each of the library's several database or software vendors. Quantitative measures that overlook local situational factors may not be appropriate or valid for all libraries. The value of numeric data that are easily aggregated is sometimes diminished because findings are available only in aggregate, giving a very superficial picture that overlooks individual differences.

Qualitative data typically are subjective. Does the library have a good collection? How much does the patron value the different aspects of the collection? Is that reflected by circulation statistics? Based in judgments, perceptions, or emotions, qualitative data are often difficult to accept as being directly comparable among respondents. Qualitative data are frequently anecdotal. It is much more difficult to standardize and compare findings, and the processes through which qualitative data are gathered are often time consuming and complex. Yet qualitative data are rich and can provide in-depth understanding of phenomena. Often stories have a profound emotional and political impact.

Another useful typology categorizes measures by focus: either collection-centered or user-centered. A variation on this classification has three categories: product (collection), process (provision), and outcome (use). This is a very traditional classification and is readily understood and applied.

Evans (1995) suggests a further useful typology that sorts collection evaluation procedures by the type of effect or judgment factor. This classification is a particularly useful organizing technique, as it more closely parallels organizational models and decision processes. These include measures of extent, efficiency, quality, performance, and effectiveness. Table 4.1 provides an overview of these measures, what they measure, and techniques most closely associate with the measures.

Table 4.1. Collection Evaluation Measures and Methods

Focus	What Is Measured?	Measures
Extent	Size	Counts, ratios, formulas, conspectus
Efficiency	Cost	Ratios, weighted systems
Quality	Intrinsic quality or goodness	List checking, citation analysis, impressionistic
Performance	Achievement of goals or purposes	Use, user satisfaction, availability
Effectiveness	Relationship between performance and efficiency	Cost-benefit analysis

DATA-GATHERING TECHNIQUES

Extent

This category includes measures of size. All measures of extent are quantitative and, by definition, collection-centered. These are most frequently gathered for use in describing a number of libraries and their collections and are included in such reports as the Federal-State Cooperative System statistics for public libraries and the Association of Research Libraries figures. They include counts, ratios, and formulas.

Counts or Tallies

These measures describe the size of the collection. They may include such data as

1. number of titles;

2. number of volumes;

3. growth rate (the same figure tracked over time to reveal trend data);

4. characteristics: format (audiovisual/electronic access/serials), age, language, or subject area; and

5. expenditures.

Ratios

Ratios are used to demonstrate the relationship between two counts and may include

1. size of collection in relation to population (volumes per capita),

2. collection budget in relation to total budget or other lines in budget (percentage of budget allocated to acquisitions), and

3. collection budget categories in relation to one another (percentage collection budget allocated to audiovisual materials or online database subscriptions).

Formulas

Formulas are often expressed in terms of the number of monographs or serial titles in relation to several factors, including number of students, level of study, and number of faculty. They are generally used to establish a recommended standard, usually in academic or school library collections.

Example: the Clapp-Jordan Formula for Academic Library
Collections

42,000 vol. base + 60 vol. (# full-time teaching faculty) + 10 vol.
(# students) + 2,400 vol. (subjects with masters) + 16,000 vol.
(subjects with doctorates)

Conspectus

The conspectus approach typically refers to a joint or cooperative collection development policy designed to analyze strengths and weaknesses of member libraries and to allocate primary collecting responsibilities. This approach is more common among research library consortia, such as the Research Library Group and the Association of Research Libraries. Such an arrangement will influence relative levels of collecting intensity and balance among an institution's subject-area collections.

Advantages and Disadvantages of Measures of Extent

Basic counts have all the advantages of quantitative data and can be gathered unobtrusively without disrupting the flow of service to patrons. Basic counts appear objective and ideal for comparative techniques, but they can be misleading. For instance, size of the service population may influence expectations for collection size or support. *Ratios*, which are frequently an expression of the relationship of the size of the collection or budget per capita, are an attempt to provide more nearly comparable data. Unfortunately, many elements in addition to size of population may affect the validity of comparing these figures. Socioeconomic status, education, age, and ethnicity of the community may all affect the comparability and interpretation of these figures, as can geographic region and environment (urban, rural, inner city, suburban). Additionally, simple counts of physical materials held at the local level are becoming increasingly misleading when not looked at in relation to online access services. Counts do not take into account local priorities or quality considerations. There is generally the implicit assumption that more is better.

Efficiency

This category describes the cost of providing materials. These measures are quantitative, typically collection-centered. They are nearly always expressed as ratios, although some systems use more complex weighted indices. Typical measures of efficiency include ratio and weighted systems.

Ratios

Efficiency ratios examine the relationship between a cost and count. For instance

1. Expenditure per capita, and

2. Average cost per item.

Weighted Systems

Weighted systems attempt to acknowledge that not all measures are of equal importance. Usually, a number of different indicators are evaluated and assigned relative weights to develop a composite score for an organization or phenomenon. A recent example of a weighted system is the HAPLR Index (Hennen 1999). In this system, the relationships among several public library data points are expressed by a system of weights. The data point is multiplied by its assigned weight, then all totals are added together for the library's composite score. Froehlich (Case Study 5.1) employs a weighting system in developing a rating scale for evaluating Web search engines. Libraries are divided according to population category and ranked by composite score.

Advantages and Disadvantages of Measures of Efficiency

Efficiency measures share the advantages of most quantitative measures in that they appear to be objective, and comparable, and are easy to analyze and understand. They can be gathered unobtrusively. As with counts, there are some basic assumptions. It is generally assumed, for instance, that higher expenditures per capita are good. In addition, lower expenditures per item delivered or acquired indicate greater efficiency and from this point of view are good. As anyone who has worked with governmental bidding processes or compared vendor contracts is aware, there are many factors that must be taken into account before efficiency measures can be considered comparable among libraries. A problem with the HAPLR system is representative of most efficiency measures. HAPLR applies a qualitative label—*best*—that is not the same as *more efficient* or *better funded*. In addition, it flies in the face of the Public Library Association's commitment to local planning, with its emphasis on locally developed priorities and evaluation strategies.

Quality

Quality measures focus on the intrinsic quality or *goodness* of the collection. They are based largely on the subjective judgment of experts, whether first- or secondhand. Selectors generally apply basic criteria (authority, scope, treatment, currency, arrangement, format, and special considerations) in selecting individual items. Kahn (Case Study 4.1) explains the use of qualitative criteria in evaluating reference materials and collections. These criteria apply if selecting print items for purchase or Web sites for menu links. Evaluation of a collection's quality takes place after items have been selected and more frequently relies on external lists and bibliographies. Although the results may be expressed in quantitative terms (we hold 26 of the 40 selected items), this is essentially a qualitative measure based on the subjective expert judgment of quality. Some weeding procedures use qualitative judgments in conjunction with use measures.

1. *List checking:* using standard lists or bibliographies to determine if the library holds identified materials or has provided links to identified sites. Halliday (Case Study 4.2) explains an innovative use of this method.

2. *Citation studies:* a variation on list checking. In essence, analyzing references of scholarly works, determining the most frequently cited materials, and creating a list of standard works. These may be used to ensure useful collections in scholarly disciplines or in developing professional collections in emerging areas of practice. Barkett (Case Study 4.3) uses a citation study to identify the disciplines and sources that contribute to the study of art history.

3. *Impressionistic*: a very subjective technique that relies on subject experts to develop individual approaches and impressions of the quality of a collection, often including opinions of selection policies and followed by subsequent use of list checking or other evaluative procedures.

Advantages and Disadvantages of Measures of Quality

Quality is essentially a subjective decision, depending on professional knowledge and judgment to apply standard criteria. There is some indication that funding bodies and constituents place a great value on perceived quality, whether or not their behavior indicates that quality is a prime consideration, and it is their expectation that librarians will develop "quality" collections. The advantage of *list checking* is that there is a great deal of apparent validity in relying on external expertise. The disadvantage is that external experts are not as familiar with the library's local constituencies and priorities for service, nor is there any attention to demand and use. Some list makers may well take need and demand into account, and some lists may create demand, but the focus is on the intrinsic quality of the item. *Citation analysis* is based on the assumption that the best works are those that are most frequently cited. Numerous studies suggest that there are many factors that influence citing practice. One of the most obvious is the ready availability of the work in question. That is, a work already in the library's collection is more likely to be cited that one that is not, regardless of quality. In addition, such a study may be time consuming and lack the validity of an externally compiled standard list. Although relying exclusively on qualitative and necessarily subjective analysis is problematic, the librarian's knowledge of the needs of the local community and professional judgment about the quality of the collection is an integral and essential part of many other evaluation methods.

Performance

Measures of performance focus on how well the collection fulfills its stated purpose from a variety of perspectives. Performance generally deals with three areas: use, user satisfaction, and accessibility.

Use Measures

Use measures are generally categorized as quantitative and patron centered. (Burton outlines the process of developing state-level use measures in Case Study 2.4.) The quality of materials may influence use, but it is the use itself that is viewed as the important aspect of collection performance. Although there are philosophical arguments about the meaning of *use*, most librarians consider that an item has been used if a patron borrows it or removes it from the shelf. Slote, aging studies, and CREW are actually weeding procedures that include an emphasis on use and so are included in this section.

1. *Circulation.* Circulation refers to the number of times patrons borrow library materials. This is a quantitative measure that is generally thought to be comparable and consistent. It has been translated to the electronic environment in terms of number of "hits." A number of factors, however, such as definition of a "circulation" or a "hit," the manner in which items are catalogued and processed or Web pages constructed, loan periods, renewal policies, and even the nature of the constituency must be considered before managers can be sanguine about relying solely on this measure.

2. *In-house use measures.* In-house use studies attempt to measure material use within the library. Various methods are used. Some involve staff observation of patrons and others involve interviewing patrons. Most are based on counts and may include counting materials marked in some way to indicate their removal from shelves, or tallies of survey or use cards inserted in items that are completed and returned by patrons. Staff counts of materials left on tables or in a gathering area are the most widely used, probably due to their inclusion in the Public Library Association's planning and measurement manuals. Generally, research indicates that table counts are time consuming and the resulting data are suspect (Rubin 1986).

3. *Slote.* The Slote (1997) method, although recognizing some intervening factors in determining the quality of library materials, relies on shelf-time (the time since the item's last circulation) as the key element in discarding an item. Interestingly, subsequent studies have indicated that Slote's method results in an overall increase in circulation (use) of the collection.

4. *Aging studies.* Aging studies are based on the concept of obsolescence of library materials, a bibliometric theory that contends that use declines with age of material in accordance with a very predictable pattern of diminishing returns. Aging can be understood in terms of the "80/20 Rule," which predicts that 80 percent of use will come from 20 percent of the collection. In the context of aging, it is usually the case that a large percentage of use is accounted for by a small percentage of the collection representing the most recent acquisitions (Wallace et al. 1990).

5. *CREW (Continuous Review, Evaluation, and Weeding)*. This method, codified by Segal (1980), relies on a combination of age of an item (varied by subject area), last use, and a variety of factors (MUSTY: misleading, ugly, superseded, trivial, and your collection has no use) for evaluation and weeding decisions.

6. *Web Server Logs*. In this method, a patron's interaction with the computer is recorded. At the most basic level, the log provides a list of sites visited. More detailed logs may be kept and analyzed to determine the nature and quality of the patron's interaction.

Advantages and Disadvantages of Measures of Use

A chief advantage of measures of use is that most of them can be gathered unobtrusively, that is, without disturbing patrons. Many, such as aging studies, Slote, and CREW, employ multiple approaches, using a basic quantitative measure as a method of selecting a sample of items for further subjective professional scrutiny. A key problem is that circulation and other use figures may become end goals rather than one data point indicating level of service or satisfaction. Although these figures appear objective and comparable, they may be subject to varying definitions. Figures may need to be interpreted differently for different constituent groups. For instance, many inner city public libraries have lower circulation figures but higher in-house use figures than suburban libraries. This may be perfectly appropriate to the different communities of users, but resource decisions based solely on level of use as defined by circulation are likely to have a negative and unjustified impact.

User Satisfaction Methods

User satisfaction measures focus directly on the perceptions of library users. They typically involve simply asking patrons for their reactions. The most common methods are surveys and interviews.

1. *Survey*. The survey method involves developing a list of questions relevant to the study and soliciting responses from individuals. Written surveys may involve distribution through mail or in the library or other public place. Some surveys are taken over the phone. Some are included on Web sites for online distribution and response. Each technique has a specific set of guidelines to ensure that the results are valid and reliable.

2. *Interview*. The interview method involves interacting with individuals, asking questions and receiving oral responses, then recording and analyzing responses.

3. *Focus groups*. Focus groups involve gathering selected individuals to provide qualitative data through a focused discussion led by an impartial facilitator. Focus groups allow for interaction among participants, more in-depth exploration of opinions and perceptions, and recognition of more spontaneous and unanticipated perceptions than other methods such as mail or telephone surveys.

Advantages and Disadvantages of Methods of User Satisfaction

The best, indeed the only way of finding out what people think or believe is to ask them. Surveys enable decision makers to gather opinions from a large number of people and to use the synthesized responses in determining broad levels of satisfaction. Survey construction and question asking are far more complex than they appear. Because the manner in which the question is asked may influence responses, it is important that survey instruments be carefully designed and tested.

A frequent problem with user satisfaction methods in evaluating library services is that only current users are included, presenting a distorted, or at least limited, perspective. Further, as many library users are familiar only with their local library, they may have limited knowledge of the range of library services available and as a result their expressed level of satisfaction may be a reflection of unrealistically high or low expectations.

D'Elia and Rodger (1996) point out several additional caveats about using satisfaction data in decision making. In addition to the subjectivity of responses, they note that such measures give no indication of the relationship between the patron's perceptions and the library's actual performance, nor do they suggest what changes would ensure satisfaction.

Availability Measures

Measures of availability determine whether materials are available to patrons on demand. Fill rates and response-time studies are typically categorized as accessibility (availability) measures. Arrangement, display factors, and amount and type of equipment available for displaying and copying nonprint formats (microfiche readers or computer workstations) may be important intervening variables in evaluating accessibility, but are not in themselves measures.

1. *Fill rates.* Surveys are the most frequently used data-gathering technique for fill rates, which are usually expressed as percentages (the ratio of number of items found divided by the number of items sought). Explicit procedures are provided in *Output Measures for Public Libraries*, which includes fill rates for items sought by title, author, or subject (Van House et al. 1987).

2. *Response time.* How long does it takes for a patron to receive an item once the item is identified? Although this appears to be a process–procedures question, it will influence collection decisions. Ultimately, the time it takes to deliver material to a patron will be a factor in whether additional copies should be purchased or if the wait entailed by interlibrary loan is acceptable. The balance of cost, responsiveness, availability, and priorities will determine whether the library emphasizes ownership (purchase) or access (subscription to an online document delivery service or full text database or reliance on interlibrary loan).

3. *Interlibrary Loan.* A study of interlibrary loan ratios (usually within a subject area) can be used to determine collection strength or weakness. The "collection balance indicator" is based on the following formula:

$$\frac{new\ acquisitions\ in\ class}{total\ acquisitions} - \frac{titles\ borrowed\ in\ class}{total\ titles\ borrowed}$$

The result is then multiplied by 100 to produce a whole number. A negative collection balance indicator suggests that the library might be relying too heavily on interlibrary loan materials to satisfy local patron need in a particular area.

Advantages and Disadvantages of Availability Measures

Availability measures have considerable appeal for library managers, as availability has an apparent and self-evident link to use and to patron satisfaction. Fill rates have significant face validity and represent a move toward matching expressed demand with actual material availability. They are widely used as measures, due largely to their inclusion (with specific procedures) in the output measures manuals. These measures are not without weaknesses, however. Weech (1988), in a report commissioned by the Public Library Association, expressed concern that the sampling procedures outlined in *Output Measures for Public Libraries* (Van House et al. 1987) would compromise internal validity. D'Elia's (1988) carefully constructed research presents continuing cause for concern. D'Elia found that there was no correlation between fill rates and resources available to patrons within the libraries studied and questioned basing standards or recommended performance levels for libraries on fill rates. Interlibrary loan analysis beyond delivery time must take into account cyclical special interests, as well as the local library's resources and roles.

Effectiveness

Effectiveness is typically approached through cost-benefit analysis. It is an attempt to demonstrate the relationship between performance and efficiency. It goes beyond the cost of providing a service in attempting to ascribe a value to the service. Smith (Case Study 2.3) has addressed cost-benefit analysis in terms of comparisons between the costs of library services and the cost of popular consumer services.

Cost-Benefit Analysis

Cost-benefit analysis is an accepted and clearly appropriate economic procedure to apply to library operations. It is rarely applied to collection evaluation in isolation, but rather as one service in an array of services. In a cost-benefit analysis, all actions are analyzed and identified, all costs and benefits are determined, monetary values are assigned to all costs and benefits, net benefits (benefits minus costs) are calculated, priorities are set and decisions made.

Advantages and Disadvantages of Measures of Effectiveness

Clearly, cost-benefit analysis is a process that has significant appeal for decision makers. For over two decades, researchers have attempted to apply this procedure to library operations. Kantor and Saracevic (1995) developed a substantial body of work in assigning value to academic library services. Currently Holt, Elliott, and Moore (1999) have popularized the technique in the public library milieu.

This is an exceedingly complex technique that requires substantial commitment of time and expertise on the part of individual libraries. There are significant problems in assigning monetary value to library services. Lancaster outlines several approaches, while warning that "it is exceptionally difficult, if not impossible, to express the benefits of library service in monetary units" (1993, 294). Kantor and Saracevic (1995) found that while research library users valued services very highly, especially relative to other university-supplied services, they had little experience purchasing information services and did not assign monetary values to the services that were commensurate with the cost of providing the services. Holt, Elliott, and Moore (1999) use the amount public library patrons would pay elsewhere in the community as a baseline for establishing value of services. Unfortunately, some of the resulting values are counterintuitive and serve to reinforce the need for multiple measures. For instance, the Holt, Elliott, and Moore analysis assigns zero value to storytelling programs, a service available without fee at bookstores in the community, because "the researchers could not find any way to set a reasonable price" (1999, 104). Nevertheless, the authors were able to report that "what we have proved is that on average for every dollar the public has invested in library services, the direct benefits just to library users is $4" (108). For now, it appears that cost-benefit analysis has more value to public libraries as a political strategy than as a technique for internal decision making.

CONCLUSION

Providing useful, quality collections of materials in all formats will continue to be an important function of libraries, particularly public libraries, into the foreseeable future. A wide variety of techniques are available to librarians that will assist in evaluating those collections. Carefully gathered data, analyzed in the context of the library's mission and the community's needs, form the basis for evaluation and effective decision making.

RESOURCES

D'Elia, George, 1988, "Materials Availability Fill Rates: Additional Data Addressing the Question of the Usefulness of the Measures," *Public Libraries* 27 (Spring): 15–23.

D'Elia, George, and Eleanor Jo Rodger, 1996, "Customer Satisfaction with Public Libraries," *Public Libraries* 35 (September/October): 292–97.

Evans, G. Edward, 1995, *Developing Library and Information Center Collections.* 3d ed. Englewood, CO: Libraries Unlimited.

Gorman, G. E., and B. R. Howes, 1989, *Collection Development for Libraries.* New York: Bowker-Saur.

Hennen, Thomas J., Jr., 1999, "Go Ahead, Name Them: America's Best Public Libraries," *American Libraries* 30 (January): 72–99.

Himmel, Ethel E., William James Wilson with the ReVision Committee of the Public Library Association, 1998, *Planning for Results: A Public Library Transformation Process.* Chicago: American Library Association.

Holt, Glen E., Donald Elliott, and Amonia Moore, 1999, "Placing a Value on Public Library Services at Saint Louis Public Library," *Public Libraries* 38 (March/April): 98–99+.

Kantor, Paul B., and Tefko Saracevic, 1995, *Studying the Cost and Value of Library Services: Final Technical Report.* Alexandria Project Laboratory, School of Communication Information and Library Studies, Rutgers, the State University of New Jersey. Technical Report APLAB/94-3/1 (Rev. Mar 95).

Lancaster, F. W., 1993, *If You Want to Evaluate Your Library. . . .,* 2d ed. Urbana, IL: University of Illinois, Graduate School of Library and Information Science.

Mandel, Carol A., 1988, "Trade-Offs: Quantifying Quality in Library Technical Services," *Journal of Academic Librarianship* 14 (September): 214–20.

McClure, Charles R. et al., 1987, *Planning and Role Setting for Public Libraries: A Manual of Options and Procedures.* Chicago: American Library Association.

Rubin, Richard, 1986, *In-House Use of Materials in Public Libraries.* Champaign, IL: University of Illinois at Urbana-Champaign, Graduate School of Library and Information Science.

Segal, Joseph, 1980, *Evaluating and Weeding Collections in Small and Medium-Sized Public Libraries: The CREW Method.* Chicago: American Library Association.

Slote, Stanley J., 1997, *Weeding Library Collections: Library Weeding Methods,* 4th ed. Englewood, CO: Libraries Unlimited.

Van House, Nancy A., Mary Jo Lynch, Charles R. McClure, Douglas L. Zweizig, and Eleanor Jo Rodger, 1987, *Output Measures for Public Libraries: A Manual of Standardized Procedures*, 2d ed. Chicago: American Library Association.

Wallace, Danny P. et al., 1990, *Age Analysis for Public Library Collections: Final Report.* Baton Rouge: Louisiana State University, School of Library and Information Science. ED 333889.

Weech, Terry L., 1988, "Validity and Comparability of Public Library Data: A Commentary on the Output Measures for Public Libraries," *Public Library Quarterly* 8, no. 3–4: 7–18.

Method @ A Glance: Qualitative Criteria

Purpose:

Assessing quality of materials, collections, services

Description:

The use of qualitative criteria is a method that allows librarians to focus professional expert judgment in a systematic and universally recognized manner.

Strengths:

In-depth of assessment, adaptable to local needs, reflective of multiple criteria

Use:

As part of a holistic approach to assessment

Data Needed:

Suggested criteria, expert knowledge

Sources of Data:

Firsthand examination

Organizational Models:

Decision-Process, Resource

Procedure:

1. Identify area to be evaluated.
2. Determine level of analysis.
3. Establish appropriate criteria.
4. Select expert evaluator(s).
5. Apply criteria.
6. Analyze results in context of other data.
7. Make resource and policy decisions.
8. Implement decisions.

Case @ A Glance: Using Qualitative Criteria to Evaluate Reference Resources

Purpose:	Determining the quality and appropriateness of a reference work and a reference collection
Description:	Val Greenwood's *The Researcher's Guide to American Genealogy* was evaluated using systematically derived qualitative criteria. These traditional selection and evaluation criteria were used as a framework for formulating criteria for evaluation of a reference collection.
Use:	To determine the potential usefulness of the selected resource as an addition to a reference collection or to engage in large-scale collection evaluation
Sources of Data:	Evidence gained from examination of the selected work; expert understanding of the criteria and processes for applying the criteria
Procedure:	1. Select potential work based on preliminary assessment of reference collection needs
	2. Apply qualitative criteria
	3. Combine results with quantitative indicators
	4. Make expert judgment regarding quality and usefulness
	5. Implement decision
	6. Extend to reference collection

CASE STUDY

$$\boxed{\textbf{4.1}}$$

Using Qualitative Criteria to Evaluate Reference Resources

Miriam J. Kahn

INTRODUCTION

Throughout their careers librarians are asked to evaluate collections, services, policies, expenditures, and other activities that effect the institution and its patrons, using a mixture of quantitative and qualitative criteria. With the increase in the types of formats available that contain information, it is essential to continue to apply the same evaluation and selection criteria to all media. The goal of this case study is to provide practical qualitative evaluation criteria for reference and research collections as a whole and print materials as items in and of themselves.

Librarianship has always been concerned with evaluating collections. The literature includes articles and books that describe evaluating collections under the subject headings *collection development*, *selection*, and *weeding*. The criteria outlined in the literature are almost always the same and hold true today.

Many of the traditional methods for evaluating collections suggest a quantitative analysis. That is, how many books total, or standard bibliographies, are owned by the library as compared to the number of librarians, size of budget, or type of library. The Association of Research Libraries (ARL) and American Library Association (ALA) rank libraries based upon these quantitative criteria, in addition to other factors.

Other methods are more concerned with qualitative analysis. Many of these are grounded in an understanding of the context for evaluation. *Does the collection reflect and support the mission of the library?* Public libraries have a very different overall mission than academic and special libraries. The former serves the local community's reading and reference needs and the reference and research collection will be as in-depth as the size of the library and the makeup of the community dictates. Academic libraries serve the needs of undergraduates, the more specialized needs of graduate students, and the in-depth, subject-specific needs of the research faculty, as well as carrying professional literature for the librarians and other professional groups on campus. Special libraries purchase in the specific area of the business or organization they serve, usually supporting a set of very focused and well-defined needs. School library media centers serve specific age ranges and levels, but a wide variety of subject needs, including the professional and pedagogical development of teachers.

Within libraries, different collections may serve different needs and so require different perspectives in assessing materials. Fiction collections and subgenres require a different evaluation knowledge base than nonfiction and evaluation of nonprint materials requires adapting basic evaluation criteria. For many years, nonprint library collections emphasized record albums, filmstrips, and 16mm film. Now nonprint formats include music on audiotape, videotape, and compact disc; movies on videotape, DVDs, and laser discs; audiobooks, available in complete or abridged versions, in fiction and nonfiction titles, and in a variety of formats designed for sighted or visually impaired listeners; and CD-ROMs, educational and recreational.

Although nonprint formats are not typically seen as suitable formats for reference and research collections, libraries have traditionally collected other nonprint materials, such as photographs and microfilm, to complement and supplement the reference and noncirculating collections. Audiovisual materials, microform collections, and other nonprint resources can be evaluated using the same basic criteria used for evaluating print materials. Evaluation criteria must be modified slightly, due to the nature of these collections. Particular attention must be given to organizational factors such as arrangement, access, and equipment support, as well as the durability and longevity of some media and the control mechanisms required by multipart materials. Many of these elements are addressed in Chapter 5, which provides an overview of evaluating the virtual library collection.

This case study will consider only the evaluation of reference materials and reference collections, including those used for ready reference and more extensive research, primarily in print on paper format. Basic evaluation procedures use several different approaches: expert judgment in assessing the intrinsic features of an item or collection (scope, authority, currency, and arrangement), list checking, and use studies.

EVALUATION OF REFERENCE SOURCES

No matter the type of library, good reference tools are essential for providing answers to patrons' questions. While assessing the reference collection for depth and breadth, individual books are often examined, with retention decisions determined by how well the item contributes to the mission of the institution and reflects collection development policy for that department.

To illustrate the evaluation of print materials, the evaluation criteria previously listed will be applied to a specific case, Val Greenwood's *The Researcher's Guide to American Genealogy* 2d ed., which is considered one of the best reference tools for genealogical research.

1. *Scope of text.* Does the book cover a broad subject generally or is the subject more narrowly defined and treated in greater depth? Does it fit within the reference department? Does it duplicate other resources in the same subject area?

    The Researcher's Guide to American Genealogy is broad in scope, covering the major topics and records examined while embarking on genealogical research. The author has attempted to cover the entire subject with a balanced approach to evaluating primary and secondary sources for their validity and verifiability. Coverage of each type of record is thorough, as is the background material discussing genealogical research as a whole. The second edition has updated the information in the first, added information on computers, family history, and understanding genealogical evidence. According to the "Preface,"

Greenwood removed the chapter on Canadian genealogy because there are now books on the topic that cover the subject matter more completely than a chapter would.

There may be another basic reference book on genealogical research, but the topic is a popular one, so overlapping coverage of this area is important. Taken as a whole, the work is suitable for retention in the reference or noncirculating section of the library.

2. *Authority of the author or organization.* Does the author or sponsoring organization appear knowledgeable? Are there previous publications by the author? Is the publisher reputable?

Val Greenwood has been teaching genealogy for more than 20 years and is cognizant of the various reference texts in the field, or the lack thereof. He is also familiar with the needs of beginning and experienced researchers. Genealogical Publishing Co., Inc. specializes in books on this subject.

3. *Currency.* Is the information contained up-to-date? Is currency an important criterion for the subject area?

Some of the prices for services and forms and some contact information are dated, a typical problem. Aside from the chapter titled "Computers in Genealogy," information is up-to-date and reliable. Information on researching public records, census materials, and the organization of research does not go out-of-date. The librarian reviewing this book should suggest supplementing the reference collection with a newer book on using computers and the Internet for genealogical research.

4. *Access points to the information/arrangement.* Is the book organized to allow the user to find specific information easily? Are there features that contribute to ease of use?

The author has included a 28-page index that contains *see also* references. The bibliography entries are included within chapters and as footnotes, not at the end of the book. Charts and illustrations are listed following the extensive table of contents and are reiterated in the index. The table of contents lists the type of record covered and then a list of those included within the chapter. The thoroughness of the table of contents, illustrations list, and index adds to the value of this reference tool.

5. *List checking.* Is the book listed in a standard bibliography or cited in other authoritative works?

The Researcher's Guide to American Genealogy is cited in all bibliographies in this subject area. It is cited in most standard books on genealogy and is widely held by public and academic libraries.

6. *Frequency of use.* Are there indications that either staff or patrons use this source frequently?

Based on the frequency with which others cite *The Researcher's Guide to American Genealogy*, it is used and consulted often. Purchasers of this book refer to it often. The first and second editions are often out in circulation, as is the reference copy in ready reference and the noncirculating sections of the library.

THE REFERENCE COLLECTION
AS A WHOLE

Librarians often find that utilizing a consistent conceptual framework for individual materials and for collections facilitates the evaluation process for both. The criteria that have been used previously to evaluate individual sources may be used with little adaptation to evaluate the reference collection as a whole. In evaluating a collection, it is important to remember that it is the impact of the collection as a whole, not of individual items, that is of most importance. A single text of a fairly narrow focus, or that supports one view of an issue, may well be balanced by other works within the collection.

1. *Scope.*

1.1 How does the scope and depth of the reference collection fit within the mission of the institution and its collection development policy? It is essential that librarians review these criteria before embarking upon weeding and collection development projects. Purchasing outside the mission of the institution means that critical funds are expended where they do not serve the needs of the community. When examining the scope of reference collections, look at the coverage of the subject areas as compared with the size of the library community and its reference needs.

1.2 Does the reference collection contain a little of everything? It is important to be able to answer questions of every nature at a main reference desk. The scope of a general reference collection is usually general in nature, containing encyclopedia, dictionaries, and basic reference tools for answering questions from all the subject disciplines.

1.3 What is the depth or breadth of the reference collection? The more academic or specialized the collection, the more in-depth the coverage of the reference collection in that area. There are encyclopedia and dictionaries for each subject as well as basic reference tools.
For example, a humanities reference collection would contain art dictionaries and encyclopedia as well as books about the works of major artists and art movements. The more in-depth the focus of this specialized reference department, the more works in that subject area are available in both reference and circulating collections. The opposite would be true of a small public library branch that serves the broader, but less in-depth reading needs of a community, especially where there is a main branch that serves as the "reference center of last resort." These small branches usually contain basic reference tools that deal on a more superficial level with a wide variety of topics and collect subject-specific tools.

2. *Authority.*

2.1 Is there a general sense of an authoritative collection? Examine the source of the major reference tools in the collection. Are they mainstream publications and reference tools?

2.2   For subject-specific reference collections: Do they originate from government agencies or prominent organizations? Are the authors renowned in their fields? Which of the publications are never used because there is no way to determine where the information came from?

3.   *Currency.*

3.1   On the average, how old are the major ready reference tools? Books of factual information should be as current as possible. Expensive items should be purchased on a rotating schedule, every two to three years, discarding the older editions.

3.2   Is the age of the collection appropriate to the purpose of institution and the subject matter? If the library serves historians and those in the literary disciplines, then older books should not be discarded, for older theories are important to understanding the primary texts. The same is true of collections that contain books on religion and philosophy. The core of this reference and research collection lies with the traditional texts supplemented by commentaries by contemporary scholars. Scientists require a heavier balance of journals to books.

3.3   Are a variety of approaches represented? Consider content and format in context of other materials. Research tools containing summaries of the knowledge of the field, such as subject-specific encyclopedia, dictionaries, or collected works of a person or discipline, are important to round out the reference collection. In this case, new editions do not always supersede old editions. They may be completely different in perspective and scope. Some may even index both editions in the newer version. Indeed just because there is a new edition does not necessarily mean that the old edition is out-of-date.

4.   *Access points/arrangement.* Can staff and patrons easily find materials in the reference and research sections of the library?

4.1   Does the catalog tell where the materials are located—circulating, reference, noncirculating? Is the area clearly identified?

4.2   Is the library large enough to have several reference desks divided by subject? If so, does each department have a core collection of reference materials close at hand that can answer factual questions?

4.3   Are the materials for answering quick factual questions housed with the rest of the collection or in a separate area? Is there overlap between the reference holdings and the circulating holdings so that patrons can take home books of a research nature that interest them?

4.4   Are there special reference collections that are not arranged in Dewey or Library of Congress Classification order or that are in a special area of the building? If so, how hard is it to find the special collection or to get access to the special collection?

4.5 Are there special finding aids for subject-specific collections? Are they up-to-date? Does staff distribute them to new staff and to patrons upon request?

5. *List checking.*

5.1 Does the collection have a representative selection of basic reference tools found on standard bibliographies? Compare the holdings of the reference and research (noncirculating) collection with standard bibliographies, keeping in mind the mission or purpose of the library. The more extensive the collection, the more items on the standard list. Small libraries should have the most basic core of reference and research materials, unless they provide no reference services at all. Even so, one should find dictionaries, encyclopedia, almanacs, and some other fact-finding reference tools at an information desk.

5.2 Are specialized lists available for subject-specific departments? Specialized bibliographies, finding aids, and reading requirements of the professors or schools in the area served by the library are good tools for evaluating focused collections.

5.3 How does the collection compare to those of comparable libraries? Review the recommended lists published by ARL or ALA committees to see how the library compares to others of its size, resource base, and mission. Try to focus on the research needs of your patrons as opposed to purchasing books and reference tools that are on the list, but not requested.

6. *Use.*

6.1 How often do reference items need to be reshelved? Does this vary by subject area?

6.2 Does the reference staff use some books more often than others? Why are some unused? Is a reference tool so new the staff hasn't discovered it yet? New reference tools should be available for examination by the staff or discussed in staff meetings and publications to alert librarians of their presence and uses.

6.3 Does use seem to follow patterns? Is there a yearly class assignment on that topic? Is the political section hot during the two months before an election?

Taken as a whole, the reference collection should be as full in scope as the patrons' needs require, as up-to-date as possible, and easy to locate and access for staff and patrons. In this way, the reference collection will be used and consulted, deficiencies identified and corrected, and out-of-date resources transferred to circulating stacks or discarded. This will keep the reference and research collections fresh and serving the needs of librarians and patrons.

CONCLUSION

Although the use of the Internet and other electronic formats in reference service continues to grow at a rapid pace, traditional print collections continue to form the basis for excellent reference collections. It is essential to remember that finding information on the Internet is not necessarily quicker than using a print source, nor is there any guarantee that the information will be accurate, authoritative, important, or even up-to-date. It is faster to look up some types of information, such as definitions, in a book. Other information, such as the current political representatives or the most popular movie this week, is easier to find and more current on the Internet. Different formats will serve different purposes; each will have strengths and weaknesses. Accuracy and currency are the trademarks of good reference service, regardless of the resource used to deliver the information.

Using a variety of established criteria to evaluate reference materials and collections on a regular basis continues to be an important responsibility of librarians in every type of library. Although the application of some evaluation criteria may need to be adapted to accommodate different formats, traditional evaluation procedures and criteria form a solid foundation for assessing individual items and entire collections. Stringent evaluation of resources in every format is important.

The evaluation process begins with recognizing the mission of the institution and its strategies for meeting the needs of users. Defining the project in terms of department, subject area, or collection is a crucial second step. Employing criteria that recognize and utilize a variety of methods results in a more effective and responsive collection. Procedures such as list checking and studying use patterns validate the librarian's judgment and assure that quality and utility are taken into account, but the librarian's expert judgment in qualitative areas and strong subject knowledge are at the heart of assessment.

RESOURCES

Greenwood, Val, 1990, *The Researcher's Guide to American Genealogy,* 2d ed. Baltimore: Genealogical Publishing.

Katz, William A., 1992, *Introduction to Reference Work*, 6th ed. New York: McGraw-Hill.

Method @ A Glance: List Checking

Purpose: Determining collection quality and congruence with library policy

Description: List checking is a methodology in which local holdings of library materials are compared to standard lists.

Strength: Quantitative, objective, efficient, externally valid, systematic, nonreactive (does not influence normal behavior)

Use: As part of collection evaluation and strategic planning

Data Needed: Appropriate lists, local holdings

Sources of Data: Local resource listings, standard lists

Organizational Model(s): Resource

Procedure:
1. Identify area of study, including place in organizational goals.
2. Identify, examine, compare, and select appropriate lists.
3. Define terms for local application.
4. Compare lists to holdings.
5. Analyze for trends.
6. Define decision areas.

Case @ A Glance: Identifying Library Policy Issues with List Checking

Purpose:	Evaluating a major urban public library's holdings of rock and roll audio recordings and developing policy recommendations
Description:	Library holdings were compared to three separate published standard discographies and a sampling of album sales charts from the *Billboard* weekly entertainment newspaper.
Use:	To guide collection management decision making and policy formulation
Sources of Data:	Holdings data from the library's online catalog; the *Rolling Stone* 200; *A Basic Music Library*; *Library Journal*'s Rock & Roll Hall of Fame; *Billboard*
Procedure:	1. Collection development policy examined to determine the role of popular music recordings in the library's mission
	2. Standard discographies identified as useful sources for comparison
	3. Album sales charts examined quarterly over a period of one year
	4. Library holdings determined by searching the online catalog
	5. Library holdings compared to the lists and the sales chart sample
	6. Findings analyzed to determine adequacy of holdings
	7. Decision areas identified based on analysis of holdings

CASE STUDY

4.2

Identifying Library Policy Issues with List Checking

Blane Halliday

INTRODUCTION:
THE LIST-CHECKING APPROACH

Collection evaluation and development is an essential library function. The study described in this case study is an evaluation of the popular music recordings collection of a major urban public library (MUPL). Evaluation was based on comparing the library's holdings to three separate published standard discographies and a sampling of album sales charts from the *Billboard* weekly entertainment newspaper. List checking is a standard, frequently used approach to collection evaluation (Curley and Broderick 1985).

This study followed six steps typical of list-checking evaluation procedures:

1. Identify area of study, including place in organizational goals;

2. Identify, examine, compare, and select appropriate lists;

3. Define terms for local application;

4. Compare lists to holdings;

5. Analyze for trends; and

6. Define decision areas.

AREA OF STUDY AND ORGANIZATIONAL GOALS

Popular music, and rock and roll music in particular, despite its growing stature in intellectual importance, has largely been ignored in the library literature (Cooper 1981). A brief search of *Library Literature* confirms this observation made nearly 20 years ago. Despite a strong 100-year existence, recorded music in general has not been accorded the respect given the printed word. Rock music plays a major role in today's society; it therefore behooves librarians, the keepers of society's history, to consider its place in their collections (Pymm 1993). Little, though, seems to have been written in reference to this aspect of popular culture and public libraries.

The debate over serious versus popular music is not new (Larkin 1992). Public libraries and librarians have struggled with the issue of collecting popular materials practically since the beginning of the profession. Few public libraries would argue the importance of collecting classics by the so-called masters (Twain or Bach), although acquisition of currently popular material continues to be a topic of debate. More than 15 years ago, LaBorie argued on behalf of popular music materials providing entertainment *and* intellectual benefits (1983). In terms of print materials, Rawlinson argues to "Give 'Em What They Want!" She defends the acquisition of popular materials if for no other reason than it is (should) be the public library's specialty. Further, because they are funded by the taxpayers' money, the public library should respond to the taxpayers' requests (Rawlinson 1990). An equitable balance *can* be found between the two disparate views of serious collections and popular demand.

Collection Development Policy

Four reasons are given for acquisitions of audio recordings in the "Materials Selection for Main Library" section of the MUPL's collection development manual:

1. To supplement and complement the print and other nonprint materials in all subject fields with a broad spectrum of sound materials.

2. To provide material that can be acquired and appreciated in audio form only.

3. To provide information that should be heard, rather than read, in order to be meaningful.

4. To provide entertainment, education, cultural enrichment, and an aesthetic experience through sound.

In addition to the library's general criteria for selection of all materials, special considerations for recordings include

1. Intrinsic value of the recording.

2. Quality of the performance of orchestra, soloist, conductor, or quality of the speaking voice.

3. Technical quality of the recording, fidelity of tone and voice.

4. The importance and significance of the recording artist, conductor, soloist, orchestra, or speaker in nonmusical recordings.

The Lists

Evaluation of the rock and roll music recordings holdings of the MUPL was based on comparison of local holdings, based on searches of the library's online catalog, three discographies, and a sample of sales chart data drawn from *Billboard*. The lists were chosen on the basis of authority and comprehensiveness, with the goal of providing a consolidated database indicative of the best rock and roll music recordings. The lists chosen were the *Rolling Stone* 200, *A Basic Music Library*, and *Library Journal*'s Rock & Roll Hall of Fame.

The *Rolling Stone* 200

Rolling Stone magazine's listing of "The *Rolling Stone* 200: The Essential Rock Collection," originally printed in the biweekly's May 15, 1997 edition, is an annotated discography that covers works released in all five decades of the rock era, from the 1950s through the 1990s. *Rolling Stone* is widely regarded as an excellent layman's guide to current trends in music and is indispensable as a librarian's selection tool for popular music. This listing is one of the few manageable (less than book length) discographies published on the subject. This list, as with any critical bibliography or discography, is subjective. However, as *Rolling Stone* editor, Jann S. Wenner, states in the article's introduction, "This is not a critics' or fans' poll, nor is it a document of the most popular albums of all time. It is an attempt to define a [home] CD library that offers a complete portrait of what rock & roll has been and what it has become" (1997, 46). The magazine assembled a panel of respected experts in the field of rock criticism to compile the list, including Rock & Roll Hall of Fame and Museum chief curator, James Henke. The definition of the genesis of the rock era was the emergence of Elvis Presley as an artist in the mid-1950s. The criteria for a work's inclusion were its inherent quality, impact, and significance. In the end, 200 titles were agreed upon, roughly arranged by decade, although dates were somewhat flexible based on a particular artist's or selection's primary year of impact. Again, the emphasis on this list is the *home* music library, consequently important features to librarians were not included, most notably catalog numbers for the items.

A Basic Music Library (BML3)

A Basic Music Library: Essential Scores and Sound Recordings, 3rd ed. (Davis 1997), is published by the Music Library Association division of the American Library Association and includes on its editorial board the Cleveland Public Library's William E. Anderson. This buying guide—designed by librarians for librarians—includes some 7,000 recordings and more than 3,000 scores. It is the first to include both of these related media together and in the area of popular music provides a tremendous leap forward in the legitimizing of the subject. The three genre areas to be looked at within the *BML3* for the purposes of this study were the Rhythm & Blues/Soul, Rap, and Rock classifications, which combined includes more than 800 titles. Each section contains a listing of essential recordings necessary to form a well-rounded, balanced collection in that genre. Further, recordings are marked to indicate collections levels. As MUPL fits the criteria for a large metropolitan system and thus the most comprehensive collection levels, all titles within each appropriate genre classification were examined for holdings.

Most of the titles listed in the *BML3* are in print and readily available on compact disc from the usual library-oriented distributors. Those titles not in print or not available in the CD format were not considered for this study. The arrangement of the selections in the *BML3* is alphabetical by artist within a genre, somewhat different from the *Rolling Stone*'s (roughly) chronological/alphabetical arrangement. Record labels and catalog numbers are included for each entry for ordering purposes. The breakdown of titles within the three genres examined is as follows: Rhythm & Blues/Soul—73 anthologies; 237 individual artist or group titles; Rap—8 anthologies; 36 individual artist or group titles; Rock—59 anthologies; 408 individual artist or group titles. A total of 821 individual titles from the *BML3* were examined. For this study, the Rap artists/titles were considered to lie within the Rhythm & Blues/Soul genre.

Library Journal's Rock & Roll Hall of Fame

This discography is based on a listing of the first 101 performing artists inducted into the Rock & Roll Hall of Fame and Museum. The list, originally published in the November 15, 1995 edition of *Library Journal (LJ)*, was meant to help "librarians choose among the gamut of options in music and pop culture collecting" (Annichiarico 1995, 32). The list offers one essential in-print (at the time) recording for each musician inducted into the Hall of Fame. For the most important artists, that choice is usually a boxed set. Considering the cost of these multidisc collections, a single CD alternative is listed for those libraries on a limited budget, a welcome difference from the *BML3* list. The alphabetical by artist discography listings include the title, label, label order number, number of discs (if a multidisc set), and the list price of the item (also if a multidisc set).

Billboard 200 Charts

Finally, the top 100 spots of the weekly *Billboard* 200 album charts were examined quarterly over the period of one year, beginning with the October 18, 1997 chart, followed by the January 17, 1998 chart, the April 18, 1998 chart, and the July 18, 1998 chart. These charts, compiled, collected, and reported by SoundScan, accurately demonstrate what the retail-buying public is currently interested in. They are nationally compiled from a statistically relevant sample of retail stores, as well as rack sales and therefore are not necessarily indicative of what is "artistically" or "intrinsically" valuable to a public library's collection over an extended period of time. However, as they are likely to reflect patron taste and requests and consequently are a valuable selection tool for librarians, they are considered for this study. Librarians often cite *Billboard* as a premiere source for information on current releases.

Comparison of Lists

The rationale for examining these four very different discographies or charts is to get as complete as possible picture of MUPL's holdings in the area of prerecorded popular music and to determine where the library is headed with its collection. All four are excellent selection tools for the library, yet each offers a unique perspective on the collection. The *Rolling Stone* discography is the basis for a medium-sized, well-conceived home collection of CDs that provides the layman with a financially affordable, well-rounded music library. At more than 800 titles, the *BML3* discography is obviously more in-depth; it gives a core collection of materials essential to a well-rounded music library within a public library setting. Some of the selected titles on this list are not necessarily as well known to the layman, but are essential for gaining a comprehensive portrait of the subject. The *LJ* listing tends more toward "greatest hits" collections and anthologies and offers (when possible) alternatives to the often pricey boxed sets. A little more than half of the *Rolling Stone* titles overlap with those on the *BML3* list, whereas 129 of its 145 represented artists overlap. Twelve of the *LJ* titles overlap with *Rolling Stone*, whereas 48 duplicate the *BML3*, less than half of all represented titles. Only five titles are shared by all three discographies.

The breadth of the *BML3* discography makes it unlikely that a majority of the titles would appeal to everyone. The artist–title selection is geared more toward a scholarly orientation. The *Rolling Stone* list's titles are designed to appeal to the average rock music buyer. The *LJ* selection is designed to provide the librarian with a simple introductory selection on the subject in a form that appeals to patrons as well. The *Billboard* charts examined are based entirely on current sales data; no critical assessment is involved in their creation. Due to the currency of these charts and this lack of critical relevance, the *Billboard* charts were analyzed separately from the other three sources. Looking at these provides the researcher with information on whether the library is developing the collection based on current trends or on retrospective artistic importance.

PROCEDURE: DEFINING LOCAL APPLICATION

What Counts

This study was limited to those recordings on compact disc (vs. vinyl LPs, audiocassettes, or other media sources), as the CD is the most popular format available and the one most likely to be available in the foreseeable future. Exceptions to this format criterion were those recordings not available in the compact disc format. These were indicated as necessary.

A title was considered a holding if it was readily available *anywhere* in MUPL's system. MUPL is part of an extensive regional system for sharing resources but audiovisual materials are not always part of this resource sharing for all member libraries. Because of this, titles owned by other regional system agencies, but *not* MUPL, were not considered holdings. As *LJ* offers alternative selections for some artists, an item was considered a holding if the library held any one of the suggested titles.

Findings

Data for this study were collected over a five-month time period, from June 1998 through October 1998, via MUPL's online catalog system. The catalog was examined for holdings on all of the titles, a total of more than 1,500 searches, not discounting title overlap. All searches were conducted as closely together as possible as titles are constantly being added to and removed from the collection. It should also be noted that during this time period (and beyond), MUPL was in the process of ordering many new titles and putting together an "opening day" collection in anticipation of the grand reopening of the library's remodeled wing in Spring 1999.

Rolling Stone 200

Titles from the *Rolling Stone* list were analyzed first. The results are illustrated in Table 4.2.1. Of the 200 titles from this "essential" listing, only 25 were available on compact disc in MUPL's collection, a mere 13 percent of the total. An additional 41 titles (20 percent) were classified as "missing" or "charged out/assumed lost," indicating they were at some point in the recent past available to the patron through the MUPL system. Combined, these titles represent a slightly improved 33 percent (66) of the 200 titles critiqued in the discography.

Table 4.2.1. Distribution of Holdings in Compact Disc Format of the *Rolling Stone* 200 by the Major Urban Public Library (N=200)

All Titles

Era	Total	Holdings		Missing		Combined	
	#	#	%	#	%	#	%
1950s	20	6	30	0	0	6	30
1960s	61	11	18	19	31	30	49
1970s	63	5	8	9	14	14	22
1980s	40	3	8	6	15	9	23
1990s	16	0	0	7	44	7	44
Totals	200	25	13	41	21	66	33

By Genre
Rock

Era	Total	Holdings		Missing		Combined	
1950s	14	4	28	0	0	4	28
1960s	52	9	17	15	29	24	46
1970s	48	4	8	7	15	11	23
1980s	27	3	11	4	15	7	26
1990s	15	0	0	6	40	6	40
Totals	156	20	13	32	21	52	33

R&B

Era	Total	Holdings		Missing		Combined	
1950s	6	2	33	0	0	2	33
1960s	9	2	22	4	44	6	66
1970s	15	1	7	2	13	3	21
1980s	13	0	0	2	15	2	15
1990s	1	0	0	1	100	1	100
Totals	44	5	11	9	20	14	32

Twenty of the *Rolling Stone* titles were classified as being from the era of the 1950s; 14 of those were from the category of "Rock" and 6 from "Rhythm & Blues (R&B)." MUPL held a total of 6 (30 percent) of these 1950s titles, 4 from rock and 2 from R&B. None were indicated in the catalog as "missing."

Sixty-one titles were relegated to the period of 1960s, 52 considered Rock, and 9 considered R&B. MUPL's catalog indicated holdings of 11 (18 percent) of these titles. By genre, MUPL held 9 of those 1960s titles classed as Rock, 2 classified as R&B. Those indicated as "missing" from the library's holdings were significant, 15 of the Rock titles and 4 of the R&B titles. Combining on-hand holdings with those missing (and at one time available through the system) suggests that 49 percent, or 30 of the titles of the 1960s were at one time available through MUPL.

The era of the 1970s represented the largest chunk of *Rolling Stone* titles, yet matched the 1980s for the smallest percentage of MUPL holdings. Five of 63 suggested 1970s titles (8 percent) were actually held by the library, 4 of 48 Rock and one of 15 R&B. Nine titles were missing, representing a combined percentage of 22 percent of 1970s titles presently owned or at one time owned by the system.

The percentages for the 1980s mirrored those of the 1970s. The library held 3 of the 40 suggested titles from this era, 8 percent, and all were from the Rock genre. Six, or 15 percent, of the titles were missing, a combined percentage of 23 percent of 1980s titles.

Of the 16 suggested titles from the 1990s, MUPL held none. However, 7 of them were indicated as missing, nearly one half; they were at one time available through the system. This could imply a bias toward more current releases, as well as the volatility of those releases; the current releases area being acquired due to patrons' demands and disappear due to excessive patron use without being purged from the OPAC.

Disregarding decades and just examining genres indicated little difference between Rock and R&B titles. The library held 13 percent of Rock and 9 percent of R&B, whereas 20 percent Rock and 23 percent R&B were missing or lost. The combined percentages were 33 and 32, respectively, of the *Rolling Stone* titles.

Basic Music Library (BML3)

The next set of titles analyzed was from *BML3's* "Rhythm and Blues, Soul, and Rap" and "Rock" sections. These numbers are represented in Table 4.2.2. Of 821 *BML3* recommended titles, the MUPL held 135, or 17 percent, a slightly better performance than on the *Rolling Stone* list. An additional 116 were classified as missing from the collection, creating a combined 31 percent of all suggested titles, implying that nearly one third of the titles are or were available at one time in the recent past. The overall performance on this "professionally oriented" discography was, then, roughly the same as with the "layman's" *Rolling Stone* list. The percentages within eras and genres varied considerably, though.

For the era of the 1950s, MUPL held 18 of a possible 121 essential titles (15 percent), with an additional 6 titles (5 percent) missing. Combined, MUPL had 24, or 20 percent of all *BML3* recommended titles from the 1950s. By genre, the library held 10 Rock titles (24 percent) of *BML3's* 42 and 8 R&B selections (10 percent) of *BML3's* 79 titles. Five (12 percent) of the Rock titles were missing, compared with one (one percent) of the R&B titles from the 1950s.

Table 4.2.2. Distribution of Holdings in Compact Disc Format of the BML3 by the Major Urban Public Library (N=821)

All Titles

Era	Total	Holdings		Missing		Combined	
	#	#	%	#	%	#	%
1950s	121	18	15	6	5	24	20
1960s	258	52	20	30	12	82	32
1970s	252	46	18	40	16	86	34
1980s	148	16	11	25	17	41	28
1990s	41	3	7	15	36	18	43
Totals	821	135	16	116	14	251	31

By Genre
Rock

Era	Total	Holdings		Missing		Combined	
1950s	42	10	24	5	12	15	36
1960s	145	40	28	21	14	61	42
1970s	155	29	19	19	12	48	31
1980s	105	15	14	19	18	34	32
1990s	20	1	5	9	45	10	50
Totals	468	95	20	73	16	168	36

R&B

Era	Total	Holdings		Missing		Combined	
1950s	79	8	10	1	1	9	11
1960s	113	12	11	9	8	21	19
1970s	97	17	18	21	22	38	40
1980s	43	1	2	6	14	7	16
1990s	21	2	10	6	28	8	38
Totals	353	40	11	43	12	83	24

The 1960s era was the largest within the *BML3* for number of titles, 258 of them. In all, MUPL held 52, or 20 percent of them. An additional 30 (12 percent) were missing from the collection, making for a combined percentage of 32 percent (82 titles). By genre, the library had 28 percent (40) of those titles within the parameters of Rock available from this era, with an additional 14 percent (21) missing. The combined percentage was 42 percent (61). R&B percentages were roughly half of those of Rock, at 11 percent (12) available and 8 percent (9) missing. Combining holdings with those titles missing yields 19 percent (21).

Of the 252 *BML3* suggested titles from the 1970s, the library held 46 (18 percent) and had nearly as many, 40 (16 percent), missing. The breakdown of owned titles by genre was 29 of those 46 belonging in Rock versus 17 that were R&B, representing fairly even (19 percent and 18 percent, respectively) percentages of the recommended titles. However, an additional 21 titles (22 percent) of the R&B titles were indicated in the catalog as missing, nearly twice the percent of Rock titles missing from the collection of *BML3* 1970s titles.

The *BML3* recommended 148 titles from the 1980s. MUPL held 16 (11 percent) of these with 25 more (17 percent) missing. Combined, 41 (28 percent) of all 1980s titles were accounted for. Only 1 (2 percent) of the holdings from this period was from the R&B category. Nineteen (18 percent) of the Rock titles were missing and 6 (14 percent) of the R&B releases were missing. Combined percentages included 34 (32 percent) of Rock titles accounted for and 7 (16 percent) of R&B titles accounted for.

As with the *Rolling Stone* 200 listing, the 1990s era again accounted for the smallest percentage of actual holdings and largest percentage of missing selections of recommended *BML3* titles. Three of 41 suggested titles (7 percent) were owned by the library; an additional 15 (36 percent) were missing. Combined, then, 18 titles (43 percent) were accounted for. By genre, only one Rock title (5 percent) was available, with 9 (45 percent) missing. In R&B, 2 (10 percent) of the suggested titles were actually available, with 6 titles (28 percent) missing. Disregarding time periods, 95 of 467 recommended Rock titles (20 percent) and 40 of 354 R&B titles (11 percent) were available. An additional 73 (16 percent) of Rock titles and 43 (12 percent) of R&B titles were missing from the collection. Combining both genres and again looking at time periods, percentages of missing titles indicate a clear pattern, rising from 6 (5 percent) of those from the 1950s to 15 (36 percent) of those from the 1990s.

Library Journal's Rock and Roll Hall of Fame

The final discography examined was the *LJ* list. The results are illustrated in Table 4.2.3. Twenty-nine of the 101 recommended selections (29 percent) were owned by the library, by far the best showing among the three lists. The percentage of missing titles (13 percent) was the smallest of the three. Because it included only Hall of Fame inductees, no titles were represented from the 1980s or 1990s. This could account for the list's relatively strong showing in terms of holdings for the library, as the works from these later periods represented on the *Rolling Stone* and *BML3* lists tended to be the ones most likely missing.

MUPL held 17 (34 percent) of titles from the 1950s with 4 (8 percent) missing. Nine rock titles (43 percent) were on hand, whereas 8 R&B selections (28 percent) were available, according to the OPAC. Three Rock titles (14 percent) and one R&B title (3 percent) were indicated to be missing. Combined, then, 21 (43 percent) of the titles from the 1950s were accounted for at MUPL. By genre, 12 (57 percent) Rock titles and 9 (31 percent) R&B titles were accounted for through the system.

The library held 8 (21 percent) of the recommended selections from the era of the 1960s. Seven (18 percent) were missing. By genre, the library had 5 of 19 suggested Rock titles (26 percent) with 3 (16 percent) missing. Combined, 8 (42 percent) recommended Rock titles from this era were accounted for. The numbers were somewhat reversed for R&B titles, with 3 (16 percent) on hand and 4 (21 percent) missing. Combined within this genre, 7 (37 percent) titles were accounted for. Combined across both genres, 15 (40 percent) titles were accounted for.

Table 4.2.3. Distribution of Holdings in Compact Disc Format of Library Journal's Recommended Rock and Roll Hall of Fame Inductees' Titles by the Major Urban Public Library (N=101)

All Titles

Era	Total	Holdings		Missing		Combined	
	#	#	%	#	%	#	%
1950s	50	17	34	4	8	21	42
1960s	38	8	21	7	18	15	40
1970s	13	4	31	2	15	6	46
Totals	101	29	29	13	13	42	42

By Genre
Rock

Era	Total	Holdings		Missing		Combined	
1950s	21	9	43	3	14	12	57
1960s	19	5	26	3	16	8	42
1970s	8	4	50	0	0	4	50
Totals	48	18	38	6	13	24	50

R&B

Era	Total	Holdings		Missing		Combined	
1950s	29	8	28	1	3	9	31
1960s	19	3	16	4	21	7	37
1970s	5	0	0	2	40	2	40
Totals	53	11	21	7	13	18	34

Four of 13 titles (31 percent) were available from the 1970s. Two (15 percent) were missing. Combined, 6 (46 percent) titles across both genres were accounted for at MUPL. All 4 titles held by MUPL were in the Rock genre, 50 percent of the suggested titles. No Rock titles were marked as missing, whereas 2 of the recommended R&B titles (40 percent) were indicated as missing.

Overall by genre, the library held 18 of 48 key Rock titles (38 percent) suggested by *LJ*, with 6 (13 percent) missing, implying that one half of those titles are or were available through the system. The R&B numbers were lower, 11 of 53 titles (21 percent) available with 7 (13 percent) missing, indicating 18 titles for a 34 percent combined percentage.

Billboard 200 Charts

The top 100 spots of weekly *Billboard* 200 Charts were examined quarterly over a period of one year beginning with October 18, 1997 and ending with July 18, 1998. These were studied working backwards from the examination of the previous original "classic" and "essential" discographies to determine how recent releases compared with established titles in terms of library holdings. There was, of course, no overlap with any of the previous discographies, due to *Billboard*'s currency. The results ran directly opposite to the recommended discography selections studied previously and are summarized in Table 4.2.4.

Table 4.2.4. Distribution of Holdings in Compact Disc Format of the First 100 Spots of Billboard Top 200 Album Charts by the Major Urban Public Library (N=400)

All Titles

Issue Date	Total	Holdings		Missing		Combined	
	#	#	%	#	%	#	%
10-18-97	100	87	87	0	0	87	87
1-17-98	100	89	89	0	0	89	89
4-18-98	100	87	87	0	0	87	87
7-18-98	100	83	83	1	1	84	84
Totals	400	346	87	1	<1	347	89

By Genre
Rock

Issue Date	Total	Holdings		Missing		Combined	
10-18-97	52	46	88	0	0	46	88
1-17-98	55	48	87	0	0	48	87
4-18-98	50	45	90	0	0	45	90
7-18-98	47	41	87	0	0	41	87
Totals	204	180	88	0	0	180	88

R&B

Issue Date	Total	Holdings		Missing		Combined	
10-18-97	30	24	80	0	0	24	80
1-17-98	30	27	90	0	0	27	90
4-18-98	37	31	84	0	0	31	84
7-18-98	35	29	83	1	3	30	86
Totals	132	111	84	1	<1	112	85

Other

Issue Date	Total	Holdings		Missing		Combined	
10-18-97	18	17	94	0	0	17	94
1-17-98	15	14	93	0	0	14	93
4-18-98	13	11	85	0	0	11	85
7-18-98	18	13	72	0	0	13	72
Totals	64	55	86	0	0	55	86

Holdings percentages for the four charts examined ranged from a low of 83 percent on the July 18, 1998 chart (the last and most recent date looked at) to a high of 89 percent on the January 17, 1998 chart. Only one title was classified as "missing" from any of the four charts (an R&B/Rap title, also from the July 18 chart). These percentages are contrasted with the range of holdings for the critical discographies of 12 percent of the *Rolling Stone* list, 17 percent of the *BML3* list, and 29 percent of the *LJ* list.

Breaking the numbers down by genres yielded similar results. Rock holdings percentages ranged from a low of 48 and 41, respectively (87 percent) on the January and July charts to a high of 45 (90 percent) on the April chart. Combining all four charts, the system held 180 of 204 Rock titles represented (88 percent). In the R&B/Rap category, the results were about the same, ranging from a low of 29 (83 percent) on the July chart to a high of 27 (90 percent) on the January chart. Combining the four charts and factoring in the single missing R&B/Rap title, MUPL had 112 of 132 (85 percent) accounting of this genre.

Because the *Billboard* 200 Charts track sales of *all* full-length albums, genres such as Country, Latin, and Classical were represented to varying degrees on the studied lists. They typically account for fewer than 20 percent of any given week's top sellers. As these genres were not the focus of this study, they were brought together in the category of "Other."

DECISION AREAS

Clearly, then, there is a bias toward obtaining current and recent titles, regardless of their long-term artistic merit or relevance to MUPL collection. This bias would also explain the low holdings percentage and high missing percentage of 1990s-era titles from the *Rolling Stone* and *BML3* listings (the *LJ* list stops with the 1970s). It is very likely these titles were obtained during their *Billboard* chart runs, as evidenced by the analysis of recent Top 200 charts, but ignored after that in terms of replacement. The charts are perhaps the easiest way for a library to obtain popular materials. The librarian need employ no critical assessment in making the decision to acquire a particular title. If it is near the top of the charts, immediate patron demand is assured. However, critical thinking about these popular materials can lead to *long-term* patron demand in that most "hits" of today are all but forgotten tomorrow, yet classics, regardless of format, will *always* be requested.

This study suggests the need to revisit the published collection development policy for sound recordings for MUPL. The term "compact disc" has not been added to the policy statement, nor is there any mention made of *what* sound recordings or genres to collect. Long-term goals of the collection are not included. Judging from the results of this study, the goal would appear to be short-term patron satisfaction.

CONCLUSION

It would appear that MUPL, a large research-oriented facility with a good reputation, concentrated on acquiring current "hits" as opposed to creating a sound recordings collection that could be used in serious scholarly research for the future. The fact that surprisingly little has been written recently reinforces this assumption. With budgets continuing to increase for nonprint materials and patron demand following suit, the time has come for public librarians to critically examine these (and other) popular culture materials as legitimate fixtures of their long-term collection development schemes.

RESOURCES

Annichiarico, Mark, 1995, "And the Beat Goes On," *Library Journal* 120 (November 15): 32–36.

"The *Billboard* 200. The Top-Selling Albums Compiled from a National Sample of Retail Store and Rack Sales Reports. Collected, Compiled, and Provided by SoundScan," *Billboard*. October 18, 1997; January 17, 1998; April 18, 1998; July 18, 1998.

Cooper, B. Lee, 1981, "An Opening Day Collection of Popular Music Resources: Searching for Discographic Standards," pp. 228–55 in *Twentieth Century Popular Culture in Museums and Libraries*, ed. Fred E. H. Schroeder. Bowling Green, OH: Bowling Green State University Popular Press.

Curley, Arthur, and Dorothy Broderick, 1985, *Building Library Collections*. Metuchen, NJ: Scarecrow Press.

Davis, Elizabeth A., 1997, *A Basic Music Library: Essential Scores and Sound Recordings*, 3rd ed. Chicago: American Library Associaton.

Halliday, Blane, 1999, "An Examination of Essential Popular Music Compact Disc Holdings at the Cleveland Public Library," Master's research paper, Kent State University, School of Library and Information Science.

LaBorie, Tim, 1983, "Introduction," *Drexel Library Quarterly* 19 (Winter): 1–3.

Larkin, Colin, 1992, "Introduction," pp. 9–15 in *Guinness Encyclopedia of Popular Music*, ed. Colin Larkin. Chester, CT: New England Publishing Associates.

Pymm, Bob, 1993, "It's Only Rock'N'Roll: Making A Case for Rock Music in the Research Library," *Australian Academic & Research Libraries* 24 (June): 78–82.

Rawlinson, Nora, 1990, "Give 'Em What They Want!" *Library Journal* 115 (June 15): 77–79.

Wenner, Jann S., ed., 1997, "The *Rolling Stone* 200: The Essential Rock Collection," *Rolling Stone* 760 (May 15): 46–100.

Method @ A Glance: Citation/Reference Analysis

Purpose:	Improving selection and weeding decision making
Description:	Citation/reference analysis is an approach in which patterns in the citations or references provided by publications are examined to identify prolific authors, seminal works, and core journals.
Strengths:	Quantitative, objective, nondisruptive, nonreactive (does not influence normal behavior)
Use:	As part of collection evaluation
Data Needed:	Citations to publications in a focused subject area
Sources of Data:	Selected publications; citation indexes
Organizational Model(s):	Resource, Decision-Process
Procedure:	1. Determine whether citation/reference analysis is an appropriate method.
	2. Identify an appropriate source of citations.
	3. Determine specific variables to be studied and how they will be defined and recorded.
	4. Gather data.
	5. Analyze data.
	6. Identify decision areas.
	7. Implement decisions.

Case @ A Glance: Conducting a Citation Analysis

Purpose: Identifying core authors and core journals in the field of art history

Description: A database of 1,140 citations from art history journal articles was compiled and analyzed.

Use: To guide collection management decision making; enhancing understanding of the literature of art history

Sources of Data: Citations from all articles published in *Art Bulletin* during a five-year period

Procedure:
1. Art history identified as an area appropriate for a citation study
2. *Art Bulletin* identified as a source of citation data
3. Citations recorded from issues of *Art Bulletin* published between March 1994 and June 1998. Citation data analyzed to identify trends
4. Decision areas identified

CASE STUDY

$$\boxed{4.3}$$

Conducting a Citation Analysis

Gina R. Barkett

INTRODUCTION: CITATION ANALYSIS

Citation analysis has been widely used in the scientific fields to identify prolific researchers and core journals. Libraries can use citation data in making decisions regarding selection and weeding of materials (Smith 1981). Gorman and Howes (1989) have discussed the advantages and limitations of citation analysis for collection evaluation. The data for this study, consisting of 1,140 citations, were collected from articles in issues of *Art Bulletin* over a five-year period (quarterly, March 1994–June 1998). This study followed the steps typical of citation studies:

1. Determine if the citation study is an appropriate method

2. Identify an appropriate source of citations

3. Determine specific variables to be studied and how they will be defined and recorded

4. Gather and analyze data

5. Identify decision areas.

ART HISTORY, SCHOLARSHIP, AND CITATION PRACTICE

The study of art history encompasses many disciplines. When conducting a study of a work of art, the art historian must keep in mind that many external factors have influenced the creation process. The artist's educational and religious backgrounds and exposure to the work of other artists, along with influences of the society in which the artist lived all have an effect. Renaissance artists were part of a culture that experienced new movements in religion and science, and this is illustrated in the art of this time. New understandings of proportion and perspective are demonstrated in the paintings of Leonardo da Vinci. Religious subject matter dominates the work of this period, with depictions of the Crucifixion of Christ, the Last Supper, and the Nativity. There was also a renewed interest during this period in the philosophical writings of Plato and Aristotle (Minor 1994). Pablo Picasso's art was heavily influenced by his experiences. The Spanish Civil War inspired one of his most famous works, *Guernica*, in 1937 (Janson 1986). This abstract mural expresses the state of fear felt by a society under attack. The more optimistic paintings of his rose period reflect his joy in the birth of his son at that time (Stein 1984). Such personal information about an artist, although not always published, gives the researcher further insight into why the work exists.

To place a work in its proper context, the researcher needs to possess knowledge about the period of history from which the work grew. Richard Brilliant suggests that the source of this knowledge may be the art library, providing its collection contains the necessary materials. He states

> Art historians may act like art critics in grasping the visual properties of objects, but they act like historians in surrounding the artifact with causes, effects, and circumstances—the ingredients of significance. The historical dimension of art history then requires the kind of information found in books, in periodicals, in old records, and in the varied forms of data collection and control which depend on texts and on writing. Learning about an art object diffuses the scholar's effort since context is a generalized abstraction; only gradually, as the connections become clear, can the historian close in on the subject of research. (1988, 125)

This illustrates the importance of a multidisciplinary collection for art libraries. Merely comparing one work of art to another can show stylistic similarities and influences, but it is not enough to substantiate its significance in history.

Citation analysis has been most commonly applied in scientific fields, which are typically heavily dependent on the journal literature. Citation analysis may have different applications in the humanities, in which journals are among many cited formats. Other cited formats include monographs, archives, personal manuscripts, and—in art history—catalogues from major museum exhibitions. Currency of cited materials, although vital to scientific publications, is not as important a factor in the humanities, in which works do not necessarily become obsolete (Koenig 1978). References to classic works of Greek and European philosophers, literary sources, and religious works are common. Art history is an interpretive discipline in which new studies offer alternative views on previous studies rather than discounting them. The sources cited by the researcher support the researcher's point of view on the subject. Brilliant (1988) lists three main objectives of art historians:

1. To interpret the object of study

2. To make clearly the argument that places the object in its historical context

3. To document this argument fully and to provide the reader with all of the information that is necessary to make a fair judgment of the study

The final two objectives on this list are fulfilled in large part by the citations to references made in the writing.

PROCEDURE

Source: Art Bulletin

The data for this study, consisting of 1,140 citations, were collected from articles in issues of *Art Bulletin* over a five-year period (quarterly, March 1994–June 1998). *Art Bulletin* is a scholarly publication of the College Art Association in New York City with a circulation of 9,500 (*Ulrich's* 1998). Its articles cover all periods of art history, are written by art historians from all over the world, and contain more comprehensive citations to other sources than do the other leading academic art journals consulted, including *Art Journal*, *Art History*, and *Art in America*.

Variables

In analyzing the data for this study, a coding sheet was used to illustrate the cross-disciplinary nature of art history research, the variety of formats cited, and the historical depth and international scope of the resources. Data were collected from the lists of sources most frequently cited that follow each article; the notes accompanying articles were not used.

1. The article *author's home country* was determined from the information on the author's present institutional affiliation that accompanies each article.

2. The *date of publication* refers to the specific edition of the work cited by the author.

3. *Subject disciplines* were defined by examining the title of each cited work and identifying the subject category of the Library of Congress classification system to which it is assigned.

4. The *format* of the work cited was identified by standard styles of citation used for monographs and articles from journals, and by specific labels in the citations themselves for exhibition catalogues, theses and dissertations, conference proceedings, and archival materials.

5. The *language* category refers to the language of the title of the cited work.

6. The *publishing country* refers to political entity (country) in which the city of publication was geographically located at the time of publication of the cited material.

FINDINGS AND ANALYSIS OF DATA

The following six categories were analyzed in the citation data collected for this study: the home country of the source author's academic institution; the date of publication of the cited work; the subject discipline of the cited work, determined from the title; the format of the cited material; the language of the cited work; and the country of publication for the cited work.

Home Countries of Authors

      Art Bulletin is an American publication; it is not surprising that 84.7 percent of the authors of articles that produced citations for this study were affiliated with American academic institutions (Table 4.3.1). English authors produced 4.5 percent (five) of the articles, and Canadian authors, 3.6 percent (four). European authors contributed six articles (5.4 percent) and there was one article each (0.9 percent each) from Israel and Mexico. These totals are probably influenced by the requirement of *Art Bulletin* that all articles be submitted in English.

Table 4.3.1. Home Country of the Journal Article's Author

Country	Frequency	Percent
United States	94	84.7
England	5	4.5
Canada	4	3.6
Germany	2	1.8
Scotland	1	0.9
Mexico	1	0.9
Italy	1	0.9
Israel	1	0.9
France	1	0.9
Czech Republic	1	0.9

Date of Publication

      Currency of materials is not as important in the humanities as it is in most other fields of study, as previously discussed. Works cited in art research can be from all periods of history. For this study, the date of publication refers to the date of the particular edition of the cited work. Many of the works cited are later editions and translations of classic works. For example, a citation for Dante Alighieri's *The Divine Comedy* was to a 1980 translation of the work by C. S. Singleton. Ovid's *Metamorphoses* was cited as a 1934 translation by F. J. Miller, and *Ars Poetica* by Horace was cited as a 1970 translation by H. R. Fairclough. Therefore, dates of publication can be deceptive; many of the cited works in this study date back to the Greek classical period in their original forms. Table 4.3.2 provides a breakdown of publication dates for works cited.

Table 4.3.2. Date of Publication

Date	Frequency	Percent
1980-89	297	26.1
1990-98	212	18.6
1970-79	158	13.9
1960-69	141	12.4
1800-99	83	7.3
1950-59	50	4.4
1700-99	36	3.2
1930-39	32	2.8
1600-99	31	2.7
1920-29	27	2.4
No date given	23	2.0
1900-09	22	1.9
1910-19	12	1.1
1940-49	12	1.1
Pre-1600s	4	0.4

Subject Discipline

One half of the citations in this study (583 or 51.1 percent) were to art materials (Table 4.3.3). This category refers to monographs on artists and periods of art styles, exhibition catalogues, works of art, and a few works dealing with music and dance. A significant number of citations were to historical materials (267 or 23.4 percent), sociology (82 or 7.2 percent), and religion (80 or 7.0 percent). Other fields of study drawn from in these art history studies include literature (62 or 5.4 percent), philosophy (28 or 2.5 percent), science (25 or 2.2 percent), and psychology (13 or 1.1 percent).

Table 4.3.3. Disciplines

Discipline	Frequency	Percent
Art	583	51.1
History	267	23.4
Sociology	82	7.2
Religion	80	7.0
Literature	62	5.4
Philosophy	28	2.5
Science	25	2.2
Psychology	13	1.1

Format

Researchers in the humanities, unlike those in the sciences, rely less on journal literature than on monographic works in their studies. This is due in large part to the importance of currency in science. Journals provide reports of the most current findings in a field, on a weekly, monthly, or quarterly basis. Obsolescence is not as significant a factor in art history; it is not surprising that the majority of citations (598 or 52.5 percent) were to monographs (Table 4.3.4). In comparison, references to journals, nearly all of them to art journals, totaled 163 (14.3 percent). Authors' citations to collections of works totaled 103 (9.0 percent) and citations to series, 83 (7.3 percent). Exhibition catalogues (50 or 4.3 percent) and archival materials (52 or 4.6 percent) were also cited relatively often.

Table 4.3.4. Format of Cited Material

Format	Frequency	Percent
Monograph	598	52.5
Journal	163	14.3
Collection	103	9.0
Series	83	7.3
Undefined archival material	52	4.6
Exhibition catalogue	50	4.4
Thesis/dissertation	26	2.3
Personal manuscript	25	2.2
Reference material	22	1.9
Conference proceedings	14	1.2
Microfilm	4	0.4

Language

Although citations to English-language works were by far the majority (663 or 58.2 percent), it is important to note that many of these were to editions that had been translated from other languages (Table 4.3.5). Knowledge of at least two foreign languages (including French, German, or Italian) is a requirement for advanced study in art history in most American institutions, as thousands of years of art were created in Europe and Asia before the Americas were settled. The most common languages of cited works other than English were Italian (156 or 13.7 percent), and French (147 or 12.9 percent) (Table 4.3.5). It is surprising that only 3.6 percent of citations (41) were to works in German, for much of the literature of northern European art is in German.

Table 4.3.5. Language of Cited Work

Language	Language Frequency	Frequency Percent
English	663	58.2
Italian	156	13.7
French	147	12.9
Chinese	42	3.7
German	41	3.6
Japanese	28	2.5
Spanish	28	2.5
Latin	19	1.7
Dutch	14	1.2
Greek	1	0.1
Other	1	0.1

Country of Publication

Places of publication were dispersed throughout the United States, Europe, and Asia, with a small number of publications from Australia, Canada, and Peru (Table 4.3.6). Although 41.7 percent of citations (475) were to works published in the United States, those works published in Europe as a whole (581) totaled 51 percent. As much of the world's art was created in Europe and Asia, and much of it remains there today, this is not unexpected.

Table 4.3.6. Publishing Country

Country	Frequency	Percent
United States	475	41.7
Italy	167	14.6
England	148	13.0
France	137	12.0
Germany	50	4.4
China	43	3.8
Japan	31	2.7
Netherlands	27	2.4
Spain	25	2.2
Austria	9	0.8
Belgium	7	0.6
Sweden	5	0.4
Switzerland	4	0.4
Peru	3	0.3
Canada	2	0.2
Australia	1	0.1
Greece	1	0.1
Ireland	1	0.1
Other	4	0.4

DISCUSSION, DECISION AREAS, AND CONCLUSIONS

This study has identified the main subject areas that influenced the research of art historians writing for *Art Bulletin* from March 1994 to June 1998: history; sociology; religion; and literature; and, to a lesser extent, philosophy; science; and psychology. In John Cullars's (1992) study of citations in fine arts monographs, he found the most citations to disciplines other than art to be to literature, history, biography, and religion. Citation studies can be useful in identifying these subject areas. However, it would be difficult to compile a specific list of titles in these subject areas for art libraries to add to their collections using this method. In this study, 1,140 citations were analyzed, and fewer than 10 titles were cited more than once. Unlike scientific research, studies in the arts are based on opinion rather than fact, and there are literally an infinite number of research topics to explore. A single work of art may yield a philosophical, religious, scientific, sociological, historical, or literary study, depending on the imagination and education of the researcher.

Perhaps the most effective way to compile a list of titles for collection development purposes would be to first isolate the main subject areas and analyze them individually to determine those titles most frequently cited. Another method would be to analyze studies from different periods of art separately. Studies in ancient Greek and Roman art may cite writers and philosophers from the same period, whereas research in French Impressionism may cite more sociological works, and Italian Renaissance studies may be influenced by religion. It may be more useful to collect citations from theses and dissertations if concentrating a study in this way. With either of these methods, it still may be most effective to use citation analysis in conjunction with other methods, as Smith (1981) suggested analyzing citation data in conjunction with circulation and interlibrary loan figures. Cullars (1992) supported the use of multiple methods when building a collection of fine arts materials, stating that it would be unwise to base such a collection solely on citation data in a field so based in interdisciplinary study. Interviewing local researchers or using questionnaires to determine on what resources they rely most frequently are other alternatives (Cobbledick 1994, Downey 1993, Larsen 1971, Stam 1984).

An art history study is never solely about art. This analysis identified some key disciplines that art researchers consult in their work and illustrated the international scope of the sources consulted. Further, there is a tendency to use older work and to rely on book materials, including monographs, series, collections, and exhibition catalogues.

Art history is a research-intensive discipline. Art historians gather information from many fields outside of the art world during the research process. By identifying the fields most often cited in their writings, information providers can become better prepared to serve their art researchers by developing more comprehensive collections.

RESOURCES

Barkett, Gina R., 1998, "A Study of the Multidisciplinary Influences on Art History Using Citation Analysis," Master's research paper, Kent State University, School of Library and Information Science.

Brilliant, Richard, 1988, "How An Art Historian Connects Objects And Information," *Library Trends* 37 (Fall): 120–29.

Cobbledick, Susie, 1994, "The Information-Seeking Behavior of Artists: Exploratory Interviews," Master's research paper, Kent State University, School of Library and Information Science.

Cullars, John, 1992, "Citation Characteristics of Monographs in the Fine Arts," *Library Quarterly* 62 (July): 325–42.

Downey, Maria, 1993, "A Survey of the Information-Seeking Practices of Artists in the Academic Community," Master's research paper, Kent State University, School of Library and Information Science.

Gorman, G. E., and B. R. Howes, 1989, *Collection Development for Libraries.* New York: Bowker-Saur.

Janson, H. W., 1986, *History of Art.* New York: Harry N. Abrams.

Koenig, Michael E. D., 1978, "Citation Analysis for the Arts and Humanities as a Collection Management Tool," *Collection Management* 2 (Fall): 247–61.

Larsen, John C., 1971, "The Use of Art Reference Sources in Museum Libraries," *Special Libraries* 62 (November): 481–86.

Minor, Vernon Hyde, 1994, *Art History's History*. Englewood Cliffs, NJ: Prentice-Hall.

Smith, Linda C., 1981, "Citation Analysis," *Library Trends* 30 (Summer): 83–106.

Stam, Deirdre Corcoran, 1984, "The Information-Seeking Practices of Art Historians in Museums and Colleges in the United States, 1982-83," doctorate dissertation, Columbia University.

Stein, Gertrude,1984, *Picasso*. New York: Dover.

 # Evaluating the Virtual Library Collection

Erica B. Lilly

INTRODUCTION

One of the most important responsibilities of a librarian is selecting, evaluating, and providing access to materials in a library collection. Traditionally, librarians have exercised these skills to judge the appropriateness of print, microform, and audiovisual materials for use by library patrons. Librarians have employed such long-standing tools as reviews, bibliographies, recommendations from colleagues, or publisher's predistribution copies to build collections responsive to the needs of their users.

The advent and increased availability of electronic resources, specifically those found on the Internet and World Wide Web, have added additional dimensions to this significant task. Wolfe (1996) observes that "Electronic resources offer nontraditional value to the collection . . . because [they] offer ease of use and additional information beyond what a print source provides" (115). However, the attributes of local control, ownership, and the innate sense of permanence that are an intrinsic part of the traditional collection development and management process cannot necessarily be applied in the chaotic environment of the Internet. As early as 1986, Sack noted that, "Despite patron confusion about widespread electronic information, use of the upcoming tools will be easy enough to allow each person to be his or her own librarian" (537). Time has proven this to be true. With the plethora of easily accessible Web resources and improving search tools, almost everyone has virtual carte blanche to networked information. The challenge for librarians is to evaluate and to select those electronic resources that best serve the information needs of their patrons and fit within the parameters of the library's collections. By doing so, we will provide access to quality electronic information of all types.

THAT WAS THEN . . .

Methods for judging and acquiring materials in nonbook formats (e.g., pamphlets, maps, clippings, visual or sound recordings, microforms, electronic journals, etc.) have been consistently developed and incorporated into existing selection plans (Bonk and Magrill 1979; Evans 1995; Fedunok 1996; Stanley 1995). Regardless of the exact nature of the material, its selection is "based ultimately on the same principles as for the selection of books: One seeks the best material available in terms of authority, accuracy, effectiveness of presentation, usefulness to the community, etc." (Bonk and Magrill 1979, 125). Maintaining access to these collections may be challenging, as they often require the purchase of expensive equipment and large amounts of staff time to ensure their continued viability and usefulness (Bonk and Magrill 1979).

Evans (1995) comments that, "Electronic formats will cause libraries and information centers to concentrate their attention on overall operations in a way never before required" (260). He goes on to state, "Electronic delivery of information requires delivery platforms, equipment, software, substantial user support, and time to assess the various services and products that producers offer" (1995, 260).

The addition of CD-ROMs into library settings represents an important, "early" example of librarians developing criteria upon which to judge the quality of and access to material in an electronic format. A selected overview of CD-ROM evaluation literature reveals these commonly suggested administrative, technical, and content guidelines (Herther 1988; Hoffman 1989; King 1991a, 1991b). Figure 5.1 summarizes these findings.

In each of the categories listed, the groundwork for evaluating future forms of electronic resources, such as those found on the Web, may be seen. Although each element is important, specific ones have greater impact. Administratively, although cost is always an issue in libraries, how a resource integrates with existing offerings and the level of training needed for staff and patrons to successfully use it is extremely important. Of particular consequence are all of the elements listed under *Content Considerations*, as the quality, timeliness, and reliability of any information source are critical. Technically, the availability of adequate hardware on which to run the product and characteristics of the search software that enhance its ease of use lend support to users of any electronic resource.

Access to CD-ROM material is generally at the discretion of the library that owns it. The library staff usually decides the venue in which patrons view this type of resource, whether it is installed on an individual workstation, served by a local area network for use in-house, or circulated as part of the collection. In most cases, the patron must be in the library at the time of use. The implied assumption is that simply by providing access to these resources, the library has determined that these resources are useful to patrons and that it retains some measure of control over them.

Administrative Considerations	Content Considerations	Technical Considerations
Funding Source(s) for Purchase (from a grant or standing budget line)	Accuracy and Documentation (how do search results compare with other similar materials? Are the directions comprehensible and usable?)	Hardware requirements (ease of installation, compatibility with existing equipment and other programs, timing of large-output searches)
Developing Procedures for Product Use (end user or staff mediated; sign-up or walk-up service)	Appropriateness (is the arrangement, content, and approach relevant to users?)	Database Quality (number of records, variety indexed fields, single or multiple access points)
Ongoing Costs of Supplies (computer workstation, printer, paper)	Ease of Use/Comprehension (is the product readable and instructions for use clear?)	Search Software (search modes B novice/expert; menu/command, display options, requirements for printing/downloading)
Integration with Existing Library Resources (location and enhancement to services)	Authority and Credibility (is the source of data and/or qualifications of contributors known; what is the reputation of the vendor?)	Number of Disks per Title (impact on the amount of CD-ROM drives needed)
Product Evaluation (user and staff perspectives)	Content Analysis (how valuable and comprehensive, is the information for its subject coverage?)	Vendor Service/Help (is product assistance by phone available?)
Training/Instructional Needs (of user and staff)	Information Quality (how does it compare to similar products?)	Demonstration Versions (is a demo available to evaluate before purchase; is there an obligation to buy after testing?)
Publicity to Library Patrons (adequate signage and means to inform users)	Revisions and Updates (are they timely?)	Product Contract, Service Agreement, and Warranty (are vendor and library expectations clearly understood?)
Adequate Space (is there room for the furniture and hardware needed to support the product?)	Overall Value/Interest/Worth (does it contribute to overall collection service and value?)	Product Maintenance (is the product difficult to support?)

Figure 5.1. Common Guidelines for Evaluating CD-ROMs

. . . THIS IS NOW

Tim Berners-Lee introduced the World Wide Web in 1991 ("Life on the Internet" 1998; Zakon 1999) and by doing so, made real Sack's vision of "widespread electronic information" and easy-to-use tools (Sack 1986). Berners-Lee envisioned the Web to be "an abstract (imaginary) space of information . . . [where] you find document[s], sounds, videos" (1999). The first graphical Web browser, Mosaic, became available in 1993, and Web service traffic on the Internet expanded to a 341,634 percent annual growth rate ("Life on the Internet" 1998; Zakon 1999). By 1995, Schwarzwalder notes that "The Web now provides real information in a form that reflects how people want to use it." He also states that "The Web allows anyone to become publisher and database provider" (1995). After 1995, the number of Web sites has increased considerably: *Hobbes Internet Timeline* shows that the 23,500 Web servers available in June 1995 had grown to more than 4.3 million in February 1999 (Zakon 1999). Based on a study of major Web search engines, Lawrence and Giles (1998) estimate that there are at least 320 million indexable Web pages available for access. Berners-Lee astutely observes that, "A familiar complaint of the newcomer to the Web, who has not learned to follow links only from *reliable sources* [author emphasis], is about the mass of junk out there. Search engines flounder in the mass of undifferentiated documents that range vastly *in terms of quality, timeliness and relevance* [author emphasis]" (1999).

"ON THE INTERNET, NOBODY KNOWS YOU'RE A DOG"

This quote, from the famous *New Yorker* cartoon (Steiner 1993), accurately depicts the current state of the Web. Brody notes, "Unlike the carefully catalogued stacks in a library, the Web often appears to be untouched by human judgement." (1998, 26) O'Neill observes that, "The web does not have a selection policy such as libraries where conscious decisions are made about what works will be acquired and maintained in the collections." (1998, 114) Historically, the Internet is a place of anonymity (Barr 1996). Anyone with access to the appropriate technology possesses the ability to make information available via the Web. (Janes and Rosenfeld 1996) There is no one entity in charge, and no one is acting in the role of quality assuror. Although this egalitarian and somewhat anarchical feature of the Web allows Web page authors untold freedom of expression, the lack of control creates serious problems for users. Lynch (1997) comments that, "Because of the greater volume of networked information, Net users want guidance about where to spend the limited amount of time they have to research a subject." (55) Tenopir (1996) unequivocally states "Bringing order out of information chaos is a natural role for librarians and is especially important in a world where each year . . . tens of thousands of new World Wide Web sites are created." (29)

LEVELS OF EVALUATION

The universe of networked information is a complex environment for library patrons to negotiate. The nature of this variable-information setting encourages its users, especially librarians, to assess its information from multiple perspectives. Unlike print, which exists in a more or less constant state from the time of publication, the quality and character of information on the Web may often be unpredictable. Sites and resources often appear and disappear with alarming regularity and with no notice or warning. Furthermore, successfully navigating the Web requires the necessary physical components (e.g., computer workstations and peripherals) as well as adequate technical support. Given this multifaceted situation, three levels of evaluating Web access may be exercised: intellectual, physical, and technological. *Intellectual access* may be defined as judging the quality of Web page content and design. *Physical access* involves more than just providing Internet access via a workstation; it also embraces two major ideas: adaptive computer equipment responsive to the needs of persons with disabilities and Web pages created using principles of universal design (Connell et. al. 1997; DO-IT 1998). *Technological access* may be measured by the quality of the available technical infrastructure. Aspects of this include network connection, computer workstation, available Web browser version, version of HTML used by Web page authors, Web site server log information, and use of Internet filters.

Intellectual Access

Kennedy (1998) perceptively observes that "Because the Web has been so 'overgrazed' by vanity publishers, quick-buck artists, and every individual or organization with an ax to grind, it requires more effort . . . to locate and identify high-quality information" (144). She also asserts that "Internet resources can and should be judged by the same stringent criteria by which you would evaluate any other information" (1998, 144). Pagell (1995) agrees, stating "We need to apply the same standards to Internet information that we apply to information from traditional providers" (9). Search engines do not provide reliable assistance in evaluating their results (Kirkwood 1998).

Many guidelines for assessing the content and design of a Web page find their origin in the literature of evaluating print materials (Brandt 1996; Rettig 1996; Smith 1997; Tillman and Howe 1999). These include accuracy, reliability, credibility and authority of author and sponsoring organization, comparability with related sources, stability of information, navigability, and others. A growing body of literature about evaluating Web pages suggests expanded criteria for assessing overall quality of this type of resource. Figure 5.2 summarizes several key elements common among them.

Authority

Web pages may be created by anyone with the appropriate skills, equipment, and server access. Determining the identity of a Web page or Web site author in terms of that person's expertise, reputation in the field, and overall credentials is a critical beginning to judging the quality and truthfulness of the information presented. Web pages often originate from an individual's personal account—indicated by a tilde (~) in the URL—and may require additional scrutiny.

Evaluative Aspect	Points of Consideration
Authority	Can the page author be easily identified (name, affiliation)? Is there contact information (e-mail, address, phone number)? Is information about the author available (credentials, expertise, noted in the field of study, publishing history)? Are sources of information used identified (pictures, graphs, etc.)? Is there evidence of peer review? Is the sponsoring organization reputable? Is the origin of the information obvious (based on URL and content) in the absence of any other identifying information? Does the site originate from someone's personal computer account (indicated by a ~ in the URL)?
Sponsoring Organization	Is it appropriate to be supporting the particular page or site? Is contact information present (webmaster, etc.)? Are its basic goals and values clearly stated? Is it known and/or respected in its field? Does the URL provide identifying information?
Accuracy	Are the facts well researched, well documented, and able to be verified? Is the information comparable to related resources in print or other media? Are the sources of information used clearly identified (i.e., bibliography)? Is the text free of grammar and typographical problems? Is the information up-to-date? Is the page content obvious separate from any advertising present? For research sites, are the methods of gathering information clearly stated? Has a recognized style manual for citing references and quoted material been used? Is there any indication of peer review or editorial oversight? Are there any obvious errors or omissions? Is the information complete? Can you tell if the page has been detrimentally altered in any way?
Objectivity	Is there more than one point of view presented? Is there bias subtly or obviously evident? Is the information provided as a public service? Is the intent of the page to influence user opinion? If the page topic is controversial, is the author's opinion clearly stated? Are the goals of the author/sponsoring organization clearly stated? Is there a hidden agenda in the content of the page or site? Is the tone of the page or site reasonable and balanced or intemperate or angry/critical? Is the language used ambiguous or manipulative? Are the presented ideas consistent or contradictory? Is there a conflict of interest with the sponsoring organization? Is the information easily identified as fact, opinion, or propaganda? Is the site inwardly focused or linked to external sites? Is the author's affiliation stated?

Currency	Is the page dated? Does the date represent time of creation, time of placement on the Web, or date of update? Is the material kept current or is it a static resource? If statistical or research data is presented, is the time of collection clearly stated? Is there an obvious commitment to ongoing maintenance? Is there a copyright statement and date? Is there a publication date for information presented at a conference or published in another format? Are the page links working and up-to-date? If there is no date present on the page, is there alternate means of determining it (e.g., viewing document's directory of page information)? Are different editions clearly noted?
Coverage	Is the treatment of the topic (selected or broad) clearly stated? Is a specific time period represented? Is the page complete or under construction? If there is a print equivalent of the Web page, is it obvious whether the entire work or only a portion is available electronically? Has any material used from sources out of copyright been updated? How comprehensive is the material? Is the material comparable with similar sites? Are the criteria for inclusion stated? Is included information mostly primary or secondary materials? Is the purpose of the page clear? Are the included page links relevant to the topic? Is the context in which the information is situated apparent? Is the intrinsic value of the material evident?
Scope	Is the purpose of the site clearly indicated? Is the intended audience identified? Is the chronological and geographical coverage stated? Are languages other than English included? Is the rationale for the site design given? Are the site goals listed? Is the level of resource complexity noted and appropriate (expert, layperson, student)? Are any limitations or disclaimers noted? Is there a statement of copyright? Is a schedule of updates listed? Are the criteria for link, resource selection, and exclusion stated? Is the purpose of advertisements on the site explained? Are reasons for the site breadth and depth stated?
Access	Is the page stable and easy to connect to? Does the URL change? Is the page viewable in text-only mode? Is access fee based? Is that clearly stated? Do the pages load quickly? Does the page support standard Web browsers and file formats? Does the page degrade gracefully when viewed by older browsers? Is a logon, password, subscription, or registration required? Do portal/directory services or search engines index the page? Is the page viewable by both high-end and low-end workstations? Is the page useable with software and hardware for people with disabilities? Is downtime announced in advance? Is the page written in standard HTML?

Figure 5.2 continues on page 172.

Design	Does the page appeal to its intended audience?
	Are the pages and site well organized?
	Are there consistent headers and footers of relevant information present?
	Can the users interact in interesting ways?
	Are secure transmissions available if needed?
	Are instructions available before interactive portions of the page or site?
	Is the text easy to read?
	Is the contrast between background and foreground sufficient?
	Are the visual metaphors used appropriate for its intended audience?
	Do the page features (searchable databases, animations, graphics, sound files, etc.) serve a purpose?
	Are the interactive features present explained and easy to use?
	  • Does the page fit the screen or require a large amount of scrolling to fully read?
	  • Does the page look good on the computer screen upon which it is being viewed?
	  • Have ergonomics been incorporated in the overall design?
	  • Is the design visually attractive, professionally understated, and appropriate?
	  • Is there a consistent look and feel to the pages on the site?
	  • Is the page and site user friendly and intuitive to use?
	  • Does the page work with older browsers?
	  • Are any icons present consistent and easy to interpret?
	  • Does the page accommodate persons with visual disabilities, low-end computers and text browsers?
	  • Are text alternatives to images available?
	  • Is a variety of media (visual, aural, numerical, and verbal) employed to support different learning styles?
	  • If frames are used, is there a no-frames option present?
	  • Are tables formatted properly to facilitate access by text browsers?
	  • Does the page "do more" than the equivalent printed page?

Ease of Use/ Navigability	Is a clearly organized scheme present that is appropriate for the material? Is each page titled? Are headings present for each section? Are the links descriptive and annotated? Is the page and site straightforward and user friendly? Are any required logons scripted in, so as to be invisible to the user? Is text broken up appropriately? Can the user access needed information within the minimal levels of nesting, three "clicks" or less? Do all links lead to somewhere "substantive?" Is the user expected to know how to use specialized software or have a high-end computer? Are there obvious elements to assist in moving around the site? Do any long pages contain internal links? Is a site index, search engine, or table of contents available on larger sites? Can the user get to any section from the table of contents? Can the information be accessed quickly, within three or less layers of screens? Is there a sense of context or place conveyed from within the page? Is getting back to the beginning of a section or to the home page easy? Is there a "Help" section and is it helpful? Do the interactive portions work properly? Is additional software needed use the page and is it noted and easy to obtain? Does the site "feel" friendly and easy to use?

General Content	Is the page or site title appropriate and descriptive? Is enough information present to make the visit worthwhile? Are the spelling and grammar correct? Is the information concise and nonrepetitive? Are links to more information on the topic relevant and carefully selected? Is the included information of high quality? Are reader expectations satisfied? Does the site contain unique information and/or special features? Is the emphasis on original material or a list of links to other sites? What is the context of the page; does it stand alone or is it part of a larger whole? Is there minimal use of jargon?
External Validation/ Evaluation	Does the site or page adhere to external design standards, such as Bobby (http://www.cast.org/bobby/ or HONCode (http://www.hon.ch/HONcode/Conduct.html)? Are the pages indexed by search engines or directory/portal sites? Do reviewing, rating or directory/portal services favorably cover the site or page? Is the site linked to by multiple Internet sites or cited frequently in other forms of literature.

Figure 5.2. Recommended Guidelines for Evaluating Web Page Content and Design

Sponsoring Organization

The identity of the organization that provides server space for the Web page or Web site provides important clues to the user concerning the context in which the information should be viewed. Every organization endorses specific goals and values. The Web pages that it supports reflect these beliefs.

Accuracy

The accuracy of a Web page or Web site directly determines its value to the user. Web pages with spelling, grammar, and factual errors call into question the overall reliability of the information presented. Evidence of editorial oversight, research methodology, and correct citations for quoted information further reinforces the credibility of the author and information presented. The presence of advertising should be examined for any influence that may be reflected in the Web page material.

Objectivity

People create Web pages and Web sites for many reasons, not all of them altruistic or noble. The Web is a flourishing environment in which to find information about controversial topics, with no obligation on the part of any Web author to present the truth or even a balanced viewpoint. Determining the level of bias, fact versus opinion, or hidden agenda present in the content of any Web page or site permits the reader to use the information safely and with confidence.

Currency

The Web has become a place where people often go first to search for information on a variety of topics once reserved for library research. For many areas, such as recent news events, business, health, or consumer topics, the most current information available is vital. Determining the time at which a page was created and placed on the Web permits the user to assess if it is maintained on an ongoing basis, updated, and generally valuable for the user's specific information need.

Coverage

Knowing the extent to which a topic is treated permits the reader to create reasonable expectations as to the usefulness of the Web page or site. Web pages may be extensions or supplements to printed publications. They may include only a specific time period. How comprehensive the material is will inform the reader as to whether visits to more Web sites on that topic will be necessary. When these characteristics are clearly stated or discernible, they permit the user to gain a more complete perspective on the information presented.

Scope

A Web page or site that clearly states its purpose, intended audience, goals, limitations, criteria for inclusion–exclusion, and design rationale furnishes the reader with important background and context in which to view the material presented. By observing how the information on a Web page conforms to these rules, the reader can more easily ascertain its reliability and believability.

Access

A many-faceted characteristic, access may be viewed from different standpoints. The stability of the page or site Uniform Resource Locator (URL) indicates that it may be reached on a stable and consistent basis. Pages that load quickly and that may be viewed properly on lower-end equipment, through text-only Web browsers, and are written in standard Hyper Text Markup Language (HTML) affirm that the needs of different segments of the Web-using population have been anticipated and addressed. Sites that require fee-based or other type of registration or that don't support common file formats may restrict usage by many who visit it.

Design

An appealing look, with uniform identifying information, sufficient contrast between background and foreground, and minimal scrolling, encourages the reader to explore and stay longer at a Web page or site. Consistent use of icons, an overall "look and feel," and contextual metaphors appropriate for the intended audience, lend credibility to the page or site. Accommodations of lower-end computer workstations, text-only browsers, and a variety of media in which to present information add to the reader's success in obtaining information.

Ease of Use/Navigability

A clearly organized scheme of movement around a Web page or site enhances the reader's ability to get to its information. The presence of a page title, section headings, and descriptive links indicate a certain attention to detail on the part of the Web page or site's creator that provide additional information to the user. Links that consistently move the reader to a substantive place or provide shortcuts to navigating very long Web pages give users a sense of confidence and skill in their use of the page or site.

General Content

The presence of an adequate amount of high quality information, whose context is clear and content unique, and that is free of spelling or grammatical errors, provides a satisfying experience for the reader. Concise, nonrepetitive, jargon-free text adds to the page or site's overall usefulness.

External Validation/Evaluation

By adhering to consistent, widely accepted design standards, Web pages or sites will be more easily used as well as located by readers.

LIBRARY USER INSTRUCTION

Librarians are uniquely suited to teach library patrons to evaluate Internet or Web-based information. This instruction may take place during a typical one-on-one reference desk interaction or in a classroom or group setting. One effective way of training users to think in terms of the evaluative categories is to use a worksheet. The benefit of using this approach is that it presents a written list of criteria against which to measure a specific Web page or site. This checklist imparts to the user those characteristics that convey the overall quality and reliability of the information on the Web page or site. A score may be assigned to each category (e.g., authority, currency, content, etc.), with a higher score indicating a "better" Web page or site. Figure 5.3. *Web Page Evaluation Worksheet* (Everhart, 1998) represents an excellent example of a Web evaluation checklist.

Web Page Evaluation Worksheet
1996 Dr. Nancy Everhart

Title of Web Site:

URL:

Directions: Use your judgment in allotting points for the various categories. Total the points for score.

Currency (0 to 15 Points)
The site has the date of last revision posted.
The site has been updated recently.
Frequency of planned updates and revisions is
  stated.

Content/Information (0 to 15 Points)
The information will be useful to our curriculum
  and/or student interest.
This information is not available in any other format
  elsewhere in my library.
The information on the topic is thorough.
The information is accurate.
The purpose of the page is obvious.
The information is in good taste.
The page uses correct spelling and grammar.

Authority (0 to 10 Points)
The authors are clearly identified.
The authors and/or maintainers of the site are
  authorities in their field.
There is a way to contact the author(s) via e-mail or
  traditional mail.
You can easily tell from the domain name where the
  page originates.

Navigation (0 to 10 Points)
You can tell from the first page how the site is organ-
  ized and what options are available.
The type styles and background make the page clear
  and readable.
The links are easy to identify.
The links are logically grouped.
The layout is consistent from page to page.
There is a link back to the home page on each
  supporting page.
The links are relevant to the subject.
The icons clearly represent what is intended.

Experience (0 to 10 Points)
The page fulfills its intended purpose.
The page is worth the time.
The page's presentation is eye-catching.
The site engages the visitor to spend time there.

Multimedia (0 to 10 Points)
Sounds, graphics or video enhance the site's
  message.

Treatment (0 to 10 Points)
Any biases towards the subject matter can be
  easily identified.
The page is free from stereotyping.
The page is age appropriate for content and
  vocabulary for its intended audience.

Access (0 to 5 Points)
You can connect quickly to the page.
The page is available through search engines.
The page loads quickly.
You can choose whether to download smaller
  images, text-only, or non-frame versions.

Miscellaneous (0 to 15 Points)
The page has received an award(s).
There are no per-use costs involved.
Interactions asking for private information are
  secured.
Information can be printed without the need to
  change your system configuration.
Information is presented in short enough segments
  so it can be printed out without backing up the
  system for other users.
The page has its own search engine for searching
  within the page.

TOTAL:

Scoring:

90 - 100 Excellent
80 - 89 Good
70 - 79 Average
60 - 69 Borderline Acceptable
Below 60 Unacceptable

Comments: _____

_____

Figure 5.3. Web Page Evaluation Worksheet

For permission to reprint contact: Dr. Nancy Everhart, St. John's University, Division of Library and Information Science, 8000 Utopia Parkway, Jamaica, NY 11439. (718) 990-1454. nancye@ptd.net.

PHYSICAL ACCESS

The issue of physical access to Web-based electronic information resources involves many components. Although every library differs in its environment, typical considerations include space for a sufficient number of high quality computer workstations (equipped with appropriate software) and peripherals (e.g., printers), and a reliable connection to the Internet. A comfortable working area coupled with quality equipment and minimal waiting time during high use periods contribute to a satisfying experience for most able-bodied library users.

Patrons with Disabilities

There are between 48 and 49 million people in the United States with a physical or learning disability (Cunningham and Coombs 1997; McNeil 1997). As our population grows older, the likelihood of developing a disability increases, and the number of persons with disabilities is expected to grow in the next several decades (McNeil 1997). People with disabilities have information needs just as any other persons, and the environment that a library provides for satisfying these needs is extremely important (Deines-Jones and Van Fleet 1995). The Americans with Disabilities Act (ADA) requires that programs and facilities be made accessible to people with disabilities (Crispen 1993). *The Library Bill of Rights* states that "Electronic information, services, and networks provided directly or indirectly by the library should be equally, readily and equitably accessible to all library users" (American Library Association 1996). Simply put, "All library information services, including access to electronic information, should be accessible to patrons regardless of disability" (American Library Association 1997). Library staff may potentially serve patrons with different types of disabilities. The nature of the specific disability will determine the level of accommodation the patron will need to successfully use a specific piece of computer equipment and view or interpret a computer screen or Web page.

TECHNOLOGICAL ACCESS

The availability of electronic information such as that found on the Web creates public demand for access. Meeting this need is a challenge faced by almost every library. Every library's technological environment is unique and develops through the influence of several factors. Initially, these begin with the budget line for technology needs, the number of systems personnel present to recommend, install, maintain, and support computer workstations and software, the number of trained library staff comfortable with using technology, and the size and overall information access philosophy of the library.

Once a library's technology infrastructure has been established, ongoing evaluation of its effectiveness will ensure that it remains a viable aspect of library service. There are several factors to consider when conducting an assessment. These may include (but are not limited to) such components as the network connection, the number of high-end computer workstations present, the version and type of Web browser installed, standard of HTML used by library Web page developers, analysis of library Web server logs, and use of Internet filters.

Network Connection

In order to access the Web, a library needs a connection to the Internet. The type of network connection will have a direct effect on how quickly a Web page, its images, applets, and other parts load and the speed at which a user may download or transfer files. Typical network connections include the following, in order of fastest to lowest speed, as defined by *PC Webopedia* ("Home Page" 1999):

1. T-1 Access—a dedicated phone connection that supports 1.544 Mbits per second.

2. Cable Modem—a modem designed to operate over cable television lines. The coaxial cable used by cable television companies offers extremely fast access to the Internet at speeds of up to 2Mbps.

3. ISDN—acronym for *integrated services digital network.* ISDN requires special metal wires and supports data transfer rates of 64 Kbps (64,000 bits per second).

4. Modem—acronym for *modulator–demodulator.* Modems work best with communications software and operate at speeds from as low as 300 bps to as high as 56,000 bps.

Computer Workstation

As the speed and capabilities of computers increase, so do those of the software they run. Web browsers are no exception. Newer, faster, high-end computers will provide a more satisfying and fuller Web experience for most users. Older, slower computers may lack the capabilities to fully exploit the multimedia aspects of the Web, for example, if they cannot run the most current version of Web browser software. Add-ons, such as speakers, sound cards or additional software may also be necessary. As discussed earlier, libraries must provide adaptive workstations so that persons with disabilities too may access Web and other electronic information.

Web Browser Software

There are many versions of Web browser software available to users. Libraries must decide which version to support and establish a cycle for implementing product upgrades. They must consider which plug-ins they will install to provide enhanced Web access. These can include software to hear sound files, experience virtual reality, or read files of various formats. Some browsers come with additional capabilities, such as the ability to send e-mail, compose Web pages, or access a newsreader. How a library supports these options in a public environment must be decided, especially if there are a limited number of computer workstations.

HTML Standards

Although libraries have no control over the quality and versions of HTML used in the Web pages accessed by their patrons, they can institute guidelines of good practice in-house. Libraries that use standard HTML and accessible design techniques will guarantee that anyone accessing their Web sites will do so successfully. Sullivan (1998) provides focused strategies on using a Web page's structure, content, and HTML tags to get noticed by search engine services. These include utilizing descriptive keywords, positioning them effectively within the document, providing substantive content, and using metatags. Checking pages through different HTML validation services such as *Bobby* (CAST 1998), SiteInspector (Link Exchange 1999), or the *W3C HTML Validation Service* (World Wide Web Consortium 1999) will allow library Web developers to present pages free of accessibility and HTML formatting errors.

Web Server Logs

Web server logs are a means of gathering useful evaluative information about a Web site. They provide "reverse access" in that they record the information concerning access to a Web page. Statistics gathered in Web logs may include data about the number of overall hits to a site, most requested pages, user demographics, most-used browsers and platforms used to reach the site, search engines and keywords used to locate the site, various page server errors, or both, and much more. Server log information may be used for Web site administrative purposes, for example, to determine the most and least used parts of a library's Web site, pages that cause access problems, and search engines indexing the site. Stout (1997) provides an excellent introduction to using and interpreting Web log statistics as well as identifying free and commercial software for analyzing them.

Internet Filters

The implementation of Internet filters in a library setting is an issue fraught with much controversy, involving Senate hearings, lawsuits, concerns for child safety, and First Amendment rights ("Filtering Legislation" 1999; Nichols 1998; Symons 1997). Some would contend that it puts librarians into the role of censor (Champelli 1997). Although the American Library Association affirms the right of access to information, regardless of its "alleged controversial content," (American Library Association 1997), the presence of Internet filtering technology in a library will influence access to electronic information for its patrons.

CONCLUSION

Evaluating access to the virtual library collection is in many ways an extension of the work that librarians have always done when considering materials to make available to library patrons. The ability to quickly access remote resources through the Internet and Web points to a growing "just-in-time" potential in the nature of library materials (Chen 1998). Universal access to the information content of Web pages and to the computing technology that makes that access possible opens up untold potential for all library users. When librarians impart the skills necessary to fully judge the quality of Internet and

Web-based information to library patrons, they truly become informed and discerning citizens, able to critically assess and utilize the information they find.

RESOURCES

American Library Association, 1996, "Access to Electronic Access to Information, Services, and Networks: An Interpretation of the *Library Bill of Rights*," http://www.ala.org/alaorg/oif/electacc.html. (Last accessed April 8, 1999.)

American Library Association, 1997, "Questions and Answers: Access to Electronic Information, Services, and Networks: An Interpretation of the *Library Bill of Rights*," http://www.ala.org/alaorg/oif/oif_q&a.html. (Last accessed April 8, 1999.)

Barr, Christopher, 1996, "Tattoos, Nose Rings, And Avatars," http://www.canada.cnet.com/Contents /Voices/Barr/091609/index.html. (Last accessed March 5, 1999.)

Berners-Lee, Tim, 1999, "Press FAQ," http://www.w3.org/People/Berners-Lee/FAQ.html. (Last accessed March 5, 1999.)

Bonk, Wallace John, and Rose Mary Magrill, 1979, *Building Library Collections*, 5th ed. Metuchen, NJ: Scarecrow Press.

Brandt, D. Scott, 1996, "Evaluating Information on the Internet," http://thorplus.lib.purdue.edu/~techman /evaluate.htm. (Last accessed March 28, 1999.)

Brody, Herb, 1998, "Untangling Web Searches," *Technology Review* 101 (July/August): 26.

Center for Applied Special Technology (CAST), 1999, "Welcome to Bobby 3.1.1," http://www.cast.org /bobby/. (Last accessed July 16, 1999.)

Champelli, L., 1997, "Understand Software that Blocks Internet Sites and Related Censorship and Safety Issues," http://www.monroe.lib.in.us/~lchampel/netady4.html. (Last accessed April 11, 1999.)

Chen, Ya-Ning, 1998, "The Internet's Effect on Libraries: Some Personal Observations," *LIBRES: Library and Information Science Research* 8, no. 1. Computer file. Available from the archives at listproc@info .curtin.edu.eu; file LIBRE8N1 CHEN. (Last accessed December 28, 1998.)

Connell, Bettye Rose et al., 1997, "The Principles of Universal Design," http://trace.wisc.edu/docs/ud_princ.htm. (Last accessed March 7, 1999.)

Crispen, Joanne L., ed., 1993, *The Americans with Disabilities Act: Its Impact on Libraries: The Library's Responses in "Doable" Steps*. Chicago: American Library Association.

Cunningham, Carmela, and Norman Coombs, 1997, *Information Access and Adaptive Technology*. Phoenix: Oryx Press.

Deines-Jones, Courtney, and Connie Van Fleet, 1995, *Preparing Staff to Serve Patrons with Disabilities*. New York: Neal-Schuman.

Disabilities, Opportunities, Networking and Technology (DO-IT), 1998, "World Wide Web Access: Accessible Web Design," http://weber.u.washington.edu/~doit/Brochures/Technology/universal.design.html. (Last accessed April 11, 1999.)

Evans, G. Edward, 1995, *Developing Library and Information Center Collections*, 3rd ed. Englewood, CO: Libraries Unlimited.

Everhart, Nancy, 1998, "Web Page Evaluation," *Emergency Librarian* 25 (May/June): 22.

Fedunok, Suzanne, 1996, "Hammurabi and the Electronic Age: Documenting Electronic Collection Decisions," *RQ* 36 (Fall): 86–90.

"Filtering Legislation Hearing, Round Two, More of the Same," 1999, *Library Hotline* 28 (March 15): 2.

Herther, Nancy K., 1988, "How to Evaluate Reference Materials on CDROM," *Online* 12 (March): 106–8.

Hoffman, Irene, 1989, "CD-ROM: A Planning Checklist," *OCLC Micro* 5 (October): 5.

"Home Page," 1999, *PC Webopedia*, http://webopedia.internet.com. (Last accessed April 11, 1999.)

Janes, Joseph W., and Louis B. Rosenfeld, 1996, "Networked Information Retrieval and Organization: Issues and Questions," *Journal of the American Society for Information Science* 47 (September): 711–15.

Kennedy, Shirley Duglin, 1998, *Best Bet Internet: Reference and Research when You Don't Have Time to Mess Around*. Chicago: American Library Association.

King, Alan, 1991a, "To CD-ROM or Not to CD-ROM, That is the Question!" *Online* 15 (March): 101–2.

———, 1991b, "Kicking the Tires: The Fine Art of CD-ROM Product Evaluation," *Online* 15 (May): 102–4.

Kirkwood, Hal P., 1998, "Beyond Evaluation: A Model for Cooperative Evaluation of Internet Resources," *Online* 22 (July/August): 66–72.

Lawrence, Steve, and C. Lee Giles, 1998, "Searching the World Wide Web," *Science* 280 (April 3): 98–100.

"Life on the Internet: Net Timeline," 1998, Public Broadcasting Service, http://www.pbs.org/internet/timeline. (Last accessed March 5, 1999.)

LinkExchange, 1999, "SiteInspector," http://siteinspector.com. (Last accessed April 11, 1999.)

Lynch, Clifford, 1997, "Searching the Internet," *Scientific American* 27 (March): 52–56.

McNeil, John, 1999, "Disabilities Affect One-Fifth of All Americans: Proportion Could Increase in Coming Decades, *Census Brief* 97–5. http://www.census.gov/population/www/pop-profile/disabil.html. (Last accessed April 8, 1999.)

Nichols, Jim, 1998, "ACLU to Sue Libraries Over Net Access," *Cleveland Plain Dealer*. December 10. http://www.cleveland.com/news/pdnews/metro/calibe.phtml. (Last accessed April 11, 1999.)

O'Neill, Edward T., 1998, "Characteristics of Web Accessible Information: Paper Presented at the 1997 IFLA Conference," *IFLA Journal* 24 (March): 114–16.

Pagell, Ruth A., 1995, "Quality and the Internet: An Open Letter," *Online* 19 (July/August): 7–9.

Rettig, James, 1996, "Beyond 'Cool': Analog Models for Reviewing Digital Resources," *Online* 20 (September/October): 52–54+.

Sack, John R., 1986, "Open Systems for Open Minds: Building the Library Without Walls," *College & Research Libraries* 47 (November): 535–44.

Schwarzwalder, Robert, 1995, "Annual Review of Technology Online—1995," *Database* 18 (December): 80–82.

Smith, Alastair G., 1997, "Testing the Surf: Criteria for Evaluating Internet Information Resources," *The Public-Access Computer Systems Review* 8, no. 3. Computer file. http://info.lib.uh.edu/pr/v8/n3/smit8n3.html. (Last accessed March 28, 1999.)

Stanley, Nancy Markle, 1995, "The Case for Acquiring and Accessing Electronic Journals in Libraries," pp. 29–34 in *Practical Issues in Collection Development and Collection Access: The 1993 Charleston Conference*, eds. Katina Strauch, Sally Somers, Susan Zappen, and Anne Jennings. New York: Haworth Press.

Steiner, P., 1993, Cartoon, *The New Yorker* 69 (July 5): 61.

Stout, Rick, 1997, *Web Site Stats: Tracking Hits and Analyzing Traffic*. New York: Osborne McGraw-Hill.

Sullivan, Danny, 1998, "Search Engine Design Tips," http://www.searchenginewatch.com/webmasters/tips.html. (Last accessed April 11, 1999.)

Symons, Ann K., 1997, "Sizing Up Sites: How to Judge What You Find on the Web," *School Library Journal* 43 (April): 22–25.

Tenopir, Carol, 1996, "Moving to the Information Village," *Library Journal* 121 (March 1): 29–30.

Tillman, Hope N., and Walt Howe, 1999, "Old Wine in New Bottles: Using the Internet to Access the Content You Need," http://www.tiac.net/users/hope/presentations/oldwine.html. (Last accessed March 28, 1999.)

Wolfe, Paula, 1996, "Evaluating Internet Resources: Criteria for Evaluation as a Collection Development Extension," pp. 213–17 in *Information Across the Waves: The World as a Multimedia Experience. Proceedings of the 21st Annual Conference of the International Association of Aquatic and Marine Science Libraries and Information Centers,* eds. James W. Markham and Andrea L. Duda. Fort Pierce, FL: International Association of Aquatic and Marine Science Libraries and Information Centers (IAMSLIC).

World Wide Web Consortium, 1999, "W3C HTML Validation Service," http://validator.w3.org/. (Last accessed April 11, 1999.)

Zakon, Robert Hobbes, 1998, "Hobbes' Internet Timeline Version 4.0," http://info.isoc.org/guest.zakon/Internet/History/HIT.html. (Last accessed March 5, 1999.)

Method @ A Glance: Rating Scale

Purpose:	Assessing services or materials against known evaluative criteria
Description:	Rating scales are a summarized form of expert judgment presented as quantitative scores that can be used in comparative analyses.
Strengths:	Efficient, systematic, externally valid, adaptable to local needs
Use:	As part of service and resource development and evaluation
Data Needed:	Numeric ratings of performance on specific criteria
Sources of Data:	Professional judgment
Organizational Model(s):	Goal, Resource, Open Systems, Decision-Process

Procedure:

1. Identify service or resource to be studied.
2. Identify or develop criteria.
3. Develop scoring mechanism.
4. Adapt to local context.
5. Apply rating scale.
6. Summarize findings.
7. Interpret findings.
8. Make recommendations.
9. Implement recommendations.

Case @ A Glance: Developing Search Engine Evaluation Criteria

Purpose: Identifying relevant criteria and developing a rating scale for evaluation of World Wide Web search engines

Description: Existing criteria for evaluating search engines were explored and a rating scale was developed.

Use: To evaluate search engines in a consistent and systematic manner

Sources of Data: Existing criteria and primary analysis

Procedure:

1. Literature on evaluation of search engines explored and synthesized

2. Criteria from the literature consolidated, categorized, and applied to individual search engines

3. Rating scale (checklist and weighting system) developed

CASE STUDY

5.1

Developing Search Engine Evaluation Criteria

Thomas J. Froehlich

INTRODUCTION

The proliferation of the World Wide Web has created an information environment of unprecedented scope. Access to millions of documents from the desktop, formerly no more than a dream, has become a startling reality. The transformation of the Web from an organizational tool to support a single researcher to an information utility available globally has not been without its downside. The World Wide Web was originally envisioned as a rather simple means of providing systematic, essentially intuitive access to what was at the time a rather limited number of Internet resources. It is basically an approach to manually classifying Internet information and as such is subject to the limitations of all traditional classification schemes. The Web was never intended as a retrieval tool and has little innate retrieval functionality. The result is a vast collection of information that can be made accessible only through ancillary retrieval tools known as search engines.

The good news is that there are many search engines on the Internet. Without them, how would it be possible to find anything? The bad news is that there are many search engines on the Internet and, given their diversity and competing claims for superiority, it is difficult to determine which is the best to use generally or the best to use for specific purpose. Despite mergers and acquisitions, search engines are propagating like rabbits, and there does not appear to be an end in sight. Most, if not all, search engines promise that they are the biggest and best in serving the information needs of their users. In general, the realities fall far short of the promises.

SEARCH ENGINE EVALUATION CRITERIA

This proliferation of search engines lends direct potential for inefficiency, error, and failure. As users fail to find the information they seek, they will inevitably turn to librarians as solvers of the dilemma of which search engine to use and how to use it. Unfortunately, without the guidance of a systematic approach to evaluating search engines, even otherwise effective information professionals may find themselves at a loss. It is clear that search engine evaluation criteria are necessary to cope with this matter.

There are many kinds of evaluation criteria. What makes the matter difficult is that although some of the evaluation criteria can be readily applied, most of them cannot. For example, in most cases, it is easy to determine the search capabilities of an search engine, such as if one can use Boolean operators. But other criteria are difficult to apply and these tend to be the more critical ones. For example, in order to know if one search engine is better than another, one should be able to know the size and coverage of each database the search engine interrogates and which its active agent, called variously a robot, webcrawler or spider, creates. Unfortunately, many, if not most, search engines do not disclose how they index sites, what sites they index (FTP sites, WWW sites, gopher sites, Usenet sites), how big their resulting database is, or what portion of the Web is indexed. Even if the user had a knowledge of one search engine's size, that user would have to know this value relative to the size of the databases of other search engines. Given this lack of information, it is difficult to make any kind of judgment.

The focus of this discussion is on the evaluation criteria that can be applied to search engines, not on criteria for evaluating the content of Web pages as information sources, subject directories, or metasearch engines. Each of these has its own set of evaluation criteria, although some criteria may cross some of these tools. One of the mistakes in developing evaluation instruments is to make one instrument function for a variety of different tools.

When developing an evaluation guide, there must be a defined objective for which evaluation criteria will be established. An evaluation checklist for search engines for use by schoolchildren would be different in character from one developed for medical librarians. The main interest here is to take a large framework—the value of search engines to facilitate the work of librarians and other information professionals, broadly conceived. It is recognized that the diversity of librarians and information professionals may contravene or modify the appropriateness or use of certain criteria for their specific contexts.

GENERAL CRITERIA FOR EVALUATING SEARCH ENGINES

Two key considerations must be kept in mind in developing criteria. First, different criteria or sets of criteria should have different weights. For example, the input interface (e.g., ease of use) is of less significance than the quality and quantity of output (i.e., database quality and relevance ranking). Second, criteria should be measured in different ways, resulting in different types of data. Some criteria require discrete answers:

1. yes

2. no

3. not available or not applicable, or

4. content related to the feature of concern, for example, the availability of Boolean operators might be "yes: AND, OR, NOT." That is, one would provide the list of available Boolean operators for that engine.

Other criteria should be scored with a range of values indicating a position on a continuum, for example, rating ease-of-use on a scale of five (*excellent*) to one (*poor*). An efficient and effective evaluation instrument should accommodate both types of measures.

Evaluation criteria can be divided into five categories:

1. nature and quality of the search engine database;

2. nature of the input interface;

3. nature of search capabilities;

4. nature of the display output, particularly of the relevance ranking, if one is employed; and

5. other considerations.

Database Criteria

The first set of criteria relates to the nature and quality of the database that a webcrawler, robot, or spider builds for a search engine. Although this information may not be readily available at the search engine site, Search Engine Watch at http://searchenginewatch.com/ keeps track of data on major search engines. Some of the data at this site are available free of charge, and some are available through an annual subscription. If one is concerned about such issues, it is well worth the cost of a subscription to this site.

The following are criteria for determining the quality of the database:

1. Size. In general, the larger the database, the more likely some retrieval of one's query term or terms will occur. Whether one gets more relevant hits is another matter, because the larger the database, the more likely is the possibility of noise and false drops.

2. Number of pages crawled per day. This refers to the number of pages that a search engine can index per day. In some cases, it is 3 million or 10 million Web pages.

3. Freshness. Because of the volatility of Web resources, they must be constantly checked for currency, if they are still there and if they have changed. Freshness indicates the age of the listings, from the best case (*one day*) to the worst case (*three weeks*).

4. Date added. Some search engines indicate when a Web page was added to the database, some indicate the date the file was created (when the original HTML code was created), and some indicate nothing. It is generally most desirable to know the date the file was created.

5. Submitted pages. Although a particular Web page may eventually be indexed, some search engines ensure indexing by permitting persons to submit their own pages. Search Engine Watch provides data on how soon a submitted page is likely to appear in its database. It can vary from a day to several weeks.

6. Nonsubmitted pages. These refer to the links that are derived from a submitted page. Although a submitted page may take only one to three weeks to appear in the database, this page itself is only crawled later and its links to other pages are then followed. It can vary from a day to months.

7. Depth. This refers to the number of pages beyond a submitted page a search engine will gather. According to Search Engine Watch, page gathering operates in two manners: no limit, in which case the spider will attempt to locate every page at a particular Web site and index it; and sampling, in which case the search engine takes a sample of the pages at a Web site and the sample size varies among engines. Obviously, the larger the sample, especially no limit, the better a particular Web site is represented. Search Engine Watch notes that there are hurdles that prevent the full indexing of the Web: some engines cannot cope with frames, images, password protected sites, and dynamically generated pages, and they are not indexed (Sullivan 1999).

8. Indexing. Does the spider or robot create selective text or full-text indexing? When the webcrawler seeks out Web pages, does it index just selected text (e.g., URLs, title, headings, and first 1000 words of the text) or does it index all the text? This issue is a matter of some consequence. For example, suppose that a search engine indexes the first 1,000 words of a particular site. If the site is a newspaper resource, in which there is typically a lead paragraph at the beginning of the article, such indexing is beneficial because major key words are contained in the lead paragraph and they will be included in the search engine's database index for that Web site. If the Web site contains a scientific article, major key words may be missed in the indexing. The important results of a scientific article often come at the end, in the conclusions, and if those conclusions occur after the first 1,000 words, then those words will not be included in the database index. It is not easy to determine whether a particular search engine indexes full-text or selected text.

9. Link popularity. Some search engines determine if a site is popular, that is, whether there are many links to it from other pages. Link popularity may be used by a search engine to determine whether a page is included in its database. Unfortunately, link popularity may or may not deal with quality: A Web page with conspiracy theories can be link popular, but really not of high quality.

10. Type of site. Another consideration for the set of criteria regarding the nature of the search engine's database is the kinds of sites that the robots seek for the database: gopher sites, FTP sites, Usenet sites, HTTP sites.

Input Interface

A second set of criteria has to do with the search engine interface. Considerations include

1. Interface modes. Does the interface support novice and a level or levels of expert (advanced) modes? What variations of expertise are demanded by each mode?

2. Ease of use. Is it easy to enter data? Are there a lot of advertisements that clutter the site?

3. Adequate help or instructions. Are the instructions or help clear and readily accessible for each of the modes? Is there a section on Frequently Asked Questions (FAQs)? Are they themselves easily searchable?

4. Universal accessibility. Does the interface support a variety of languages or make accommodations for individuals who are visually challenged or have other disabilities?

Search Capabilities

A third set of criteria applies to search capabilities. For many search engines, these criteria are generally the easiest to determine, because the answer to them is given in a tips button or help reference. Generally speaking, the greater the number of features listed next, the greater the ability to control the search and to obtain more precise results. Some of the search capabilities to consider include the following:

1. Truncation or the use of wildcards. When the user enters a search term, can that user truncate the term so that the user can get all variations of the world stem? Some engines may have automatic truncation, in which case the words as they are entered are reduced to stems and the stems are searched: *mathematics* would be reduced to *mathematic*, yielding *mathematics*, *mathematician*, *mathematical*, etc. In other search engines, partial query terms are used for the basis of retrieval, so that instead of truncation, *math* will retrieve variations of *mathematics* or *mathis* (e.g., Mathis der Mahler) for that matter, because *math* is a word fragment of the retrieved term.

2. Phrases. Phrases are queries with more than one word as a group. Many search engines require the use of quotation marks for exact phrase matching. *"Information Professional"* will retrieve these co-occurring terms in that order. Phrase searching, when available, serves the role of an adjacency operator.

3. Required words or prohibited words. This is an ability of the engine to require that a word or words ("required words") appear in a document, usually indicated with a plus (+) sign. Those words that must not appear in a document are represented by a minus (-) sign ("prohibited words"). The query *+librarian +payscale -men* would return Web pages that must each have *librarian* and *payscale* but with no occurrences of *men*. The use of the latter can be dangerous, for the text of the Web page may read "The issues studied here were those of women and not men." Because *men* is in the text the Web site or document would be excluded from the output.

4. Boolean operators or positional operators. Some search engines permit the use of the standard Boolean operators, AND, OR, and NOT or positional operators, such as NEAR. Is there a default operator? In some engines, if you enter *information retrieval* (no quotes, as for a phrase), the search retrieves documents containing either *information* OR *retrieval*, which may perplex the novice user who does not know that the default operator is OR. Can one change the default operator? Related to Boolean operators, does the search engine permit nested searches: for example, *data base OR database AND management*.

5. Stop words. Are nonsignificant words such as *a, and, of, the,* etc. entered in the database index when the database crawler or robot does the indexing? Some search engines publicize their stop word list (e.g., Deja News) and others may tell you what words are ignored in one's search request (e.g., Alta Vista).

6. Case sensitivity. Can one submit query terms that are case sensitive? This is particularly useful when looking for proper names, for example, *Black*.

7. Field search. Does the search engine permit the qualification of a search term to a field, such as title? If a search engine does permit a field search, these fields are generally different in character than that of a commercial database. In a commercial database, such as IAC PROMT, one can search for company name, descriptors, product name or code, event name or event code, geographic area, etc., fields that can provide extremely good precision for search results. Such precision is significantly less possible in general with search engines, because the fields that are searchable are fields built around the structure of a Web page: for example, title as words in the title field, or the URL, image, link, text, etc.

8. Date search. Does the search engine permit one to specify a date or a range of dates so that one can get the most current records, if that is a desirable element of search query?

Output and Display

A fourth set of criteria has to do with the output and its display. One of the more critical issues is that of relevance ranking, which will be treated rather extensively at first. Most, if not all, search engines produce an output in which they attempt to place the most relevant sites at the top of the output listing and then the other sites are ranked relative to the top site in declining order. In order to accomplish this ranking, search engines rely on two fundamental principles: term location and term frequency.

1. Term location. Each time a webcrawler or spider, that part of the search engine software that scans for Web sites on the Internet, creates an index of Web sites, it stores words from a Web site indicating what term or word it found and where the term or word occurred. If a word or term occurs in the title or in a header, the webcrawler may give it more weight in the database index than if it occurs in the text. Thus a term will be regarded as more valuable in certain locations rather than if it occurs elsewhere.

2. Term frequency. The more frequently a term occurs in a document, the more that term is given weight for that document/Web site and relative to other Web pages that have that term.

Both of these measures, term location and term frequency, although they are sometimes successful, are essentially flawed search and retrieval methods because they attempt to infer intellectual properties, such as the meaningful content of a Web site, from physical properties, the occurrence of a term and its location in that site. Nonetheless search engines use these to rank order the results. The initial results can vary from totally irrelevant sites to ones right on target. Why is this the case? First of all, what is often produced—the citations and their order—is what might be termed "raucous recall." Although the traditional measures of recall and precision are often implied, in traditional information recall is constrained to the database's subject-matter domain (that is, the result may not be relevant to a particular user's needs, but at least it reflects the same subject matter). With Internet search engines there are no such constraints.

Ranking

It seems even more facetious to call what the engines do in terms of ordering the output "relevance ranking" because many of the sites do not have any relevance and the ranking is at best obscure. Perhaps the most complex and perplexing dimension of search engines is how they produce their output. Most of them claim to use relevance ranking. Just how relevance ranking works is not simple. If one uses a single term in one's query, the issue of relevance ranking or ordering or prioritizing the Web sites for output appears to be relatively simple. Those Web sites that have the query term in the best locations (e.g., title) and with the highest term frequency will be the first ranked documents on output, and the ordering of the other documents or Web sites are ranked relative to the first, based on term location and frequency. The issue becomes much more complex when more than one term is used, and the complexity of the ranking algorithm escalates further with more than two terms. The user does not know—and in many ways is not supposed to know—how the algorithm works; that is part of the "trade secret" of the search engine. Each search engine has its own formula.

Methods for Adjusting Ranking. According to Search Engine Watch, the relevance ranking of a document can be boosted by such factors as link popularity or keywords in metatags, and deflated by a spam penalty. Also, for some search engines, less common words are given a higher relevance score, and so it behooves users to use less common terms in their queries. The user can perhaps further improve strategy, if the search engine allows it, by insisting on the occurrence of query terms in the document (required words or prohibited words, usually indicated by a + or -, as discussed earlier). But by and large the algorithm, which drives the search engine, is hidden from end users. And so most users are forced into a position of having to accept the algorithm of the search engine as the best available without knowing that to be case.

Informed Consent

Good engines should promote informed consent, that is, should indicate to users something of the nature of the engine and its coverage and expected result and the hazards of simple searches. But none of this appears at the query entry screen. No doubt search engine developers are economically motivated not to tell users how poor an engine is, for they are often paid by how many people click on their Web site.

Commercial Influences

There is one more issue regarding ranking, one that is ethical in nature. Does the search engine sell keywords (a company that buys a keyword will be guaranteed that a Web site will be found in the top 10 hits)? Can one tell? According to Search Engine Watch, only GoTo.com sells placement within its search results; none of the other major search engines do. However, they do sell advertisements that are linked to the user's keywords. In cases like these, the software designers modify the ranking algorithm so that sold keywords point users to the targeted sites of those who bought the keywords.

Other Considerations of Evaluation Criteria for Output

These may include whether there are one or more forms of display format; whether duplicates are eliminated; whether one can vary the number of results total or per screen; how a search engine generates a title for a Web page listing; whether the results are reusable (i.e., that one can refine a search within an already created search without reentering the original search with additional terms or qualifications). Search Engine Watch provides some detail about some of these criteria and how they are applied to specific popular search engines.

Other Evaluation Criteria

The last set of criteria is other considerations that do not quite fit the other categories:

1. Speed. How quickly does the engine respond, and how easily is it accessed?

2. Customization. Is the search engine personalizable?

3. Visual clarity. Are the parts of the query and output interfaces clear, readily comprehensible, and consistent?

4. Navigation. Is it easy to navigate from output page to sources and back again? Are navigational aids clear?

5. Links. Are links clearly distinguishable and do they conform to standard practices (except when there is genuine need to violate standard practices)? Are they reliable?

6. Subject directory. Is there a subject directory included to facilitate browsing?

DATA SOURCES

A basic evaluation problem is the lack of information available at the search engine site. Although there may be no onsite readily available answer, a number of Internet, monograph, and journal sources provide information that may be used in applying some of the earlier-mentioned criteria. (A list of these is included in the "Resources" section). Just because we cannot answer a question or apply a criterion does not mean that we should not query if an evaluative criteria be applied, for example, the nature of the ranking algorithm. Sometimes the only way in which an answer may be approximated is by carefully constructing a series of search queries, running them as similarly as possible across different engines, and comparing the results. Such a process is tedious and not entirely reliable, given that different engines have different coverage of the Internet, and the results can vary on the vagaries of the particular search query.

Most often, because of these difficulties, many comparative or evaluative schemes focus only on such factors as search capabilities and flexibility, variety of input interfaces, and nature of output, particularly the display aspects. But such schemes are rather shallow in nature as this case study has tried to establish. As a conclusion, a fairly robust example of a rating scale is provided as Appendix 5.1.1. In this instrument, each feature under consideration is given a yes/no/na/content answer. After checking all features in a particular section, the instrument asks for an overall impression for that section, using a range of values of five (*excellent*) to one (*poor*).

CONCLUSION

Developing useful and appropriate evaluation criteria and the processes for their application is a formidable but necessary task. This discussion provides a preliminary approach to identifying a ranked criteria tool for evaluating search engines. As the World Wide Web evolves and search tools become (hopefully) more capable and more sophisticated, new criteria will need to be added and existing criteria and their associated weights modified. With care and attention, it should be possible for librarians and other information professionals to gain the facility in evaluation necessary for making the World Wide Web a truly effective source of information to serve patron needs.

RESOURCES

Database: The Magazine of Database Reference and Review. Weston, CT: Online, Inc.

Ding, Wei, and Gary Marchionini, 1996, "A Comparative Study of Web Search Service Performance," pp. 136–42 in *ASIS '96: Proceedings of 49th ASIS Annual Meeting: Global Complexity–Information, Chaos and Control*. Medford, NJ: Information Today, Inc.

Free Pint. http:// www.freepint.com.co.uk.

Glossbrenner Alfred, and Emily Glossbrenner, 1999, *Search Engines for the World Wide Web*, 2d ed. Berkeley, CA: Peachpit Press.

Hock, Randolph, 1999, *The Extreme Searcher's Guide to Web Search Engines: A Handbook for the Serious Searcher*. Medford, NJ: CyberAge Books.

Maze, Susan, David Moxley, and Donna Smith, 1997, *Authoritative Guide to Web Search Engines*. New York: Neal-Schuman.

Searcher: The Magazine for Information Professionals. Medford, NJ: Learned Information.

Sullivan, Danny, 1999, "Search Engine Features Comparison Chart," *Search Engine Watch*. http://searchenginewatch.com/. (Last accessed April 22, 1999.)

Appendix 5.1.1

Evaluation Checklist

Database:

FEATURES		Search Engine: _____ URL: _____
	Coverage	
	Size	
	Pages Crawled per Day	
	Indexing	
	Depth (no limit/sampling)	
	Selected Text/Full Text	
	Accepts Submitted Pages	
	Update Frequency	
	Readily Available (Up time)	
	Other:	

Overall Impression of Database:

Quality and Size (5=excellent to 1=poor): _____

Coverage (5 to 1): _____

Quality of Indexing (5 to 1):Currency (Update Frequency) (5 to 1): _____

TOTAL: _____

Input Interface:

FEATURES	Search Engine: _____ URL: _____
Search Interfaces	
Querying versus Browsing	
Type or Select Operators or Fields	
Different Languages	
Accommodation of Disabilities	
Other:	

Overall Impression of Input Interface:

Visual Clarity (5=excellent to 1=poor): _____

General Ease of Input (5 to 1): _____

Ease of Moving among Modes (5 to 1): _____

TOTAL: _____

Search Capabilities and Flexibility:

FEATURES		Search Engine: _____ URL: _____
	Boolean Operators or Equivalent	
	Default Operator	
	Exact Matching	
	Case Sensitivity	
	Phrase Searching	
	Truncation/Wildcards	
	Proximity Searching	
	Natural Language Queries	
	Limit by Date	
	Limit by Language	
	Limit by Field	
	Stop Words	
	Required/Prohibited Words	
	Weighted Search	
	Use of Wildcards	
	Nested Search	
	Other:	

Overall Impression of Search Capabilities and Flexibility:

Search Flexibility and Control (5=excellent to 1=poor): _____

Ease of Use in Entering Queries (5 to 1): _____

TOTAL: _____

Output:

FEATURES		Search Engine: _____ URL: _____
	Relevance Ranking	
	Methods for Adjusting Ranking	
	Spamming Penalty	
	Link Popularity	
	Other:	
	Summary	
	Results per Page	
	Display Format/Options	
	Provide Date of Web Page Creation or Modification	
	Refine Results	
	Speed of Response	
	Other:	

Overall Impression of Ouput:

Quantity of Output (5=excellent to 1=poor): _____

Quality of Output (5 to 1): _____

Quality of Ranking Algorithm (5 to 1) : _____

Visual Clarity of Output (5 to 1): _____

Informativeness of Output (5 to 1) : _____

Ease of Navigation from Ranked List to Source (5 to 1): _____

TOTAL: _____

Help/Other:

FEATURES		Search Engine: _____ URL: _____
	Availability	
	Usability	
	Searchability	
	FAQs	
	Other:	

Overall Impression:

Accessibility of Help (5=excellent to 1=poor): _____

Ease of Use (5 to 1): _____

Adequacy of Help (5 to 1): _____

Clarity or Completeness of Explanations or Illustrations (5 to 1): _____

TOTAL: _____

OVERALL SCORE

Database—Total Points: _____ x 3: _____

Input Interface—Total Points: _____ x 1: _____

Search Capabilities and Flexibility—Total Points: _____ x 2: _____

Output—Total Points: _____ x 3: _____

Help—Total Points: _____ x 1: _____

Total: _____

Perfect SCORE: 205

Method @ A Glance: Guidelines

Purpose:	Ensuring that policies and procedures that reflect standard practice are consistently applied
Description:	Guidelines are a summarized, prescriptive form of expert judgment that codifies best practice.
Strengths:	Consistent, amenable to comparison, externally valid
Use:	As part of service and resource development and evaluation
Data Needed:	Professional or technical guidelines, data specified by the guidelines
Sources of Data:	Relevant and appropriate associations, other governing bodies, existing internal documents and procedures, procedures tailored to specific data-gathering needs
Organizational Model(s):	Goal, Critical Constituencies, Resource, Open Systems, Decision-Process, Customer Service
Procedure:	

1. Identify service or resource.
2. Obtain institutional commitment and support.
3. Identify or develop criteria (guidelines).
4. Adapt to local context.
5. Develop rules for implementation.
6. Offer awareness and training opportunities for affected individuals or administrative units.
7. Apply guidelines.

Case @ A Glance: Creating Accessibility Guidelines for Web Page Developers

Purpose:

Enhancing accessibility to the Kent State University World Wide Web site for individuals with disabilities

Description:

A set of guidelines for accessible Web pages was developed as a means of creating an institutional focus for improving the accessibility of Kent State University Web pages.

Use:

To improve access to information for students, faculty, staff, and other individuals with disabilities

Sources of Data:

National standards, published literature, local input

Procedure:

1. National standards and published literature sources examined to determine legal requirements and best practices

2. Input gathered from university committees and interested individuals

3. Draft guidelines developed

4. Draft guidelines referred to the university's Americans with Disabilities advisory committee for official approval and development of implementation policies

CASE STUDY

5.2

Creating Accessibility Guidelines for Web Page Developers

Erica B. Lilly and Pamela R. Mitchell

THE SETTING

Kent State University (KSU) is an eight-campus system, of which the Kent Campus is the largest residential campus in Northeast Ohio. Nearly 21,000 students are enrolled. About 78 percent of these students are undergraduates, and 74 percent of all students have full-time status. There are more than 10,000 students enrolled across the seven regional campuses, the majority of whom are part-time students (Kent State University 1998).

The KSU World Wide Web site (http://www.kent.edu/) is a multipurpose information resource that provides an initial point of contact to potential students and connects current students, faculty, and staff to information about campus services, academic departments, links to the regional campuses, and more.

Students on all eight campuses have access to a variety of computer lab facilities. The Kent campus alone provides close to 40 computing labs, many of which are open, public labs. Several labs are also located in dormitory complexes, and others are restricted in use to majors of specific departments. There are multiple labs located across the regional campuses.

IMPETUS

According to recent KSU statistics, there are approximately 530 students on the Kent campus and 120 students throughout the regional campuses who identify themselves as having a disability (Jannarone 1999). Among the 4,036 faculty employed on the Kent and regional campuses, 55 individuals identify themselves as persons with disabilities (Rule 1999).

The Americans with Disabilities Act (ADA) requires that programs and facilities be made accessible to people with disabilities (Crispen 1998). To further support this effort, the U.S. Access Board (also known as the Architectural and Transportation Barriers Compliance Board), whose responsibility it is to implement the ADA since its passage in

1990, has developed a set of electronic and information technology accessibility standards for government agencies. These recommendations, which include specifications for Web sites, are found in the final report of the Electronic and Information Technology Access Advisory Committee (1999). In addition, the U.S. Department of Justice has issued "Compliance Instructions" to assist federal agencies in making their computer and Internet systems more accessible to persons (United States Department of Justice 1999a). Specific instructions for Web page accessibility are based on guidelines recommended by the World Wide Web Consortium's (W3C) *Web Accessibility Initiative* (WAI) (World Wide Web Consortium 1999a, 1999b).

Library staff may potentially serve patrons with different types of disabilities. The nature of the specific disability will determine the level of accommodation the patron will need to successfully use a specific piece of computer equipment and view or interpret a computer screen or Web page. Cunningham and Coombs (1997) group four major disabilities into the following categories:

1. Vision Impairments: Persons with low vision, functional vision, color blindness, and blindness are included in this category. They may have difficulty in seeing computer screens, keyboards, or reading printed materials. These individuals may also have problems using a standard mouse to interact with electronic information (Paciello 1996; Trace Research and Development Center 1998b).

2. Mobility Impairments: People who use wheelchairs as well as those with limited hand usage are placed in this category. Persons with paralysis, missing limbs, and limited body control or movement may fit in either group. Wheelchair accessibility and limited use of standard computer input and output devices are major problems for people with mobility disabilities. Alternatives to the typical keyboard and mouse are mouth stick, headpointer, eyegaze-operated keyboard, or infrared device (Paciello 1996; Trace Research and Development Center 1998b).

3. Hearing Impairments: People who are hard-of-hearing or who are deaf may not have difficulty in using standard computers. However, they will require other accommodations (e.g., text equivalents) to make information that includes sound more accessible to them.

4. Learning Disabilities: These individuals may experience visual perception difficulty as well as aural processing problems. Use of computers to convey and retrieve information may compensate for the presence of some learning disabilities.

ADAPTIVE WORKSTATIONS

Appropriately adapted computer workstations provide gateways to the Internet for many people with disabilities (Cunningham and Coombs 1997). Cunningham and Coombs suggest beginning with easy, low-cost approaches to providing computer access and moving on to high-tech solutions when the simpler ones won't work. Unfortunately, there is no one universal configuration that will work in every library situation, as there are many technologies for differing disabilities and multiple hardware and software packages for each (Coombs 1990).

The hardware and software of any adaptive computer workstation must be selected with the needs of the library's patrons firmly in mind. Each disability has specific barriers and compensatory strategies (Cunningham and Coombs 1997). There are numerous vendors and products available to implement an adaptive workstation for patrons with disabilities. Cunningham and Coombs (1997), the University of Washington (1999), Trace Research and Development Center (1998a), Disability Mall (1999), the Alliance for Technology Access (1997), and Oregon State University's Technology Access Program are excellent starting places to begin research.

STANDARDS DEVELOPMENT AT KENT STATE UNIVERSITY

The development of the *Kent State University ADA Web Accessibility Initiative and Guidelines (Accessed Considered (AC) Guidelines)* was undertaken as a means of developing an institutional focus for improving the accessibility of KSU Web pages (Figure 5.2.1). There has been an increasing awareness on campus related to the need for such an effort, but no coordinated mechanism or set of guidelines existed. The University ADA Compliance Committee, the University Council on Technology, the Office of Academic Computing and Technology, Libraries and Media Services, Learning Technology Services, the Department of University Relations and Marketing, and the Office of Affirmative Action are key KSU entities that have all made efforts to address the issue of Web accessibility in the past two years.

The growth of Web pages at KSU has been exponential, and it was clear that immediate, readily implemented guidelines and support were needed to impact changes in the accessibility of those pages. The "Access Considered" initiative was proposed through the Technology Subcommittee of the KSU ADA Compliance Committee and reviewed by that body. The initial focus will be to promote greater accessibility of academic and administrative Web pages. A secondary focus will be encouraging Web site authors to "retrofit" existing pages to meet the *AC Guidelines*.

Kent State University ADA Web Accessibility Initiative and Guidelines

DRAFT 2

Purpose

This purpose of this page is to enhance and coordinate efforts at Kent State University (KSU) in Web accessibility for persons with disabilities. It provides an initial set of supporting guidelines and resources to assist all Web developers at KSU to create Web documents that show considerations for individuals with disabilities.

"Access Considered" Guidelines

The KSU/ADA Committee affirms the importance of Web page design that supports access by persons with disabilities. The W3 Page Authoring Guidelines (also linked below) provide a critical set of carefully considered guidelines for Web page authors. In order to assist with the transition to more accessible Web pages by University personnel, a set of "starter" guidelines has been developed. These guidelines provide a set of Web authoring considerations that are relatively easy to implement and should result in Web pages that offer improved access for persons with a variety of disabilities. The "Access Considered" Guidelines (Mitchell and Lilly,1999) are a voluntary set of considerations for Web page authors at KSU. Pages that meet "access considered" criteria are eligible for a custom icon representing this level of compliance. Inclusion of the "A.C." icon will be based on an honor system and guidelines for inclusion of the icon.

The following are the criteria for the 1999 version A.C. status:

- Provides a clear and consistent navigation scheme within and across all authored pages.
- Provides a high contrast between background and text.
- Provides text size of 12-14 point font equivalent minimum.
- Provides "No Frames" and "No Tables" optional pages OR does not use frames or tables.
- Provides ALT descriptions for all: graphics, audio and/or video files.
- Provides e-mail alternative to form-based input.
- Provides general navigation instructions for persons with disabilities.

Selected Sites for Creating Accessible Web Pages

It's important to make Web pages accessible (in some cases, its the law!):

- Disability Rights Activist
- EASI Web Law

A painless starting place:

- Sixty Second Tutorial on Web Access

Resource Sites:

- W3 Page Author Guidelines (current version)
- Bobby Validator
- Jim Lubin's Web Access Links

Examples of Accessible Web Sites:

- National Center to Improve Practice
- WGBH
- Trace Center

Document History:
1st draft: 2/21/99 by Pam R. Mitchell
Revised draft: 3/2/99 by Pam R. Mitchell
2nd draft: 4/2/99 by Erica Lilly

Figure 5.2.1. Kent State University ADA Web Accessibility Initiative and Guidelines

Kent State University ADA Web Accessibility Initiative and Guidelines. Kent State University.

METHOD

KSU recognizes the importance of a universal set of standards and guidelines for Web page accessibility, as reflected in the W3C's "Web Content Guidelines 1.0" (1999b). The KSU *AC Guidelines* were developed as an intermediate step toward full compliance with the W3C *Guidelines*. The following considerations were applied in selecting our "critical subset" of page authoring guidelines:

1. ease of implementation by Web authors,

2. general benefits to the Web site (e.g., clear site navigation), and

3. impact on users with disabilities.

The *AC Guidelines* also provide links to selected Web sites about creating accessible Web pages.

Our process will reward Web authors for this intermediate level of compliance through an honor system of recognition similar to "Bobby" (Center for Applied Special Technology 1999). Once KSU Web page authors have met the *AC Guidelines*, they will be eligible to place the KSU *AC* icon on their page(s) to indicate this accomplishment.

We plan to publicize the *AC Guidelines* through the KSU Web site and a variety of internal University print publications and listservs. In addition, we will collaborate with the University's Faculty Professional Development Center to assist with the dissemination of information about these guidelines to facilitate the creation of accessible, Web-based instructional materials.

Procedures for occasional monitoring of sites' appropriate use of the logo will be developed through the Technology Subcommittee of the ADA Compliance Committee.

FINDINGS

It is too early to see the impact of the *AC Guidelines* on KSU Web sites at this time. However, anecdotal communication with various University Web site designers has revealed some concern about the effect on the design and maintenance of their Web sites. We believe that incorporating these guidelines, based on those of the W3C, should eliminate the need to develop and maintain two Web sites containing the same information, but rather contribute to the overall accessibility of their current Web site to everyone.

Interpretation

It is our sense that implementation of the *AC Guidelines* will be a gradual process, most likely adopted for use first on newly created pages and by the more conscientious campus Web designers. As the W3C *Guidelines* become more widely adopted internationally and accessibility features continue to be incorporated into the multitude of Web authoring tools, greater numbers of accessible Web pages and sites will be developed everywhere, not only at KSU.

Action

The current draft of the *AC Guidelines* was reviewed by the KSU ADA Compliance Committee. When its assessment is complete, suggested changes will be incorporated. The larger campus community will then be given the chance to view and comment upon them. We hope that this opportunity will encourage KSU Web authors to think about accessibility issues as they create Web sites. Once the final draft is finished, we look forward to full endorsement and encouragement of use by the KSU administration.

Evaluation

Because this project is in the early stages of development, procedures to evaluate its effectiveness have yet to be fully developed. Initial steps to measure the use of the *AC Guidelines* on the KSU Web site will probably include the following:

1. examining the site for Web pages displaying the *AC* logo,

2. spot checking the pages for accessibility in text-based Web browsers or using the Bobby tool, and

3. testing the pages for accessibility using adaptive computer equipment.

Future evaluative techniques may include these steps:

1. surveying Web page authors concerning their implementation of the *AC Guidelines*, and

2. conducting Web page usability studies with KSU faculty, staff, and students with disabilities.

We expect to revise the *AC Guidelines* as needed based on W3C updates to its *Guidelines* and in response to the Web's constantly changing technology.

RESOURCES

Alliance for Technology Access, 1997, "Products Which Enhance Access to the WWW," http://www.ataccess.org/access.html. (Last accessed April 11, 1999.)

Center for Applied Special Technology, 1999, "Welcome to Bobby 3.1.1," http://www.cast.org/bobby/. (Last accessed July 16, 1999.)

Coombs, Norman, 1990, "Electronic Access to Library Systems for Users with Physical Disabilities," *Public-Access Computer Systems Review* 1, no. 1: 43–47.

Crispen, Joanne L. ed., 1993, *The Americans with Disabilities Act: Its Impact on Libraries: The Library's Response in "Doable" Steps.* Chicago: American Library Association.

Cunningham, Carmela, and Norman Coombs, 1997, *Information Access and Adaptive Technology.* Phoenix, AZ: Oryx Press.

Disability Mall, 1999, "Computers: Hardware and Software," http://www.disabilitymall.com/ecomput .html. (Last accessed April 11, 1999.)

Electronic and Information Technology Access Advisory Committee, 1999, "Final Report. May 12, 1999," http://www.access-board.gov/pubs/eitaacrpt.htm. (Last accessed July 16, 1999.)

Jannarone, Anne. (ajannaro@kent.edu). 1999, April 20. Re: A quick clarification of student ADA stats . . . E-mail to Erica Lilly (elilly@kent.edu).

Kent State University, 1998, "The Kent Student Community," http://www.kent.edu/ra/stupro/page1.htm. (Last accessed April 18, 1999.)

Mitchell, Pamela R., and Erica B. Lilly, 1999, "Kent State University ADA Web Accessibility Initiative and Guidelines—Draft 2," http://www.library.kent.edu/~elilly/ada/access_considered.html. (Last accessed July 16, 1999.)

Oregon State University Technology Access Program, 199?, "Adaptive and Augmentative Equipment," http://osu.orst.edu/dept/tap/adaptive.htm. (Last accessed April 10, 1999.)

Paciello, Mike, 1996, "Making the World Wide Web Accessible for the Blind and Visually Impaired," *Florida Libraries* 39 (January/February): 5+.

Rule, Judith, 1999, April 12, conversation with E. Lilly, Kent, OH.

Trace Research and Development Center, 1998a, "Accessibility Products for Microsoft Windows, Windows NT, and Windows 95," http://www.trace.wisc.edu/docs/win_access_prod/winacces .htm#enlarger. (Last accessed April 10, 1999.)

———, 1998b, "A Brief Introduction to Disabilities," http://trace.wisc.edu/text/univdesn/populat/populat.html. (Last accessed April 8, 1999.)

United States Department of Justice, 1999a, "Section 508 Instructions and Documents," http://www.usdoj .gov/crt/508/508docs.html. (Last accessed July 16, 1999.)

———, 1999b, "Web Accessibility Checklist," http://www.usdoj.gov/crt/508/webpage.pdf. (Last accessed July 16, 1999.)

University of Washington Computing and Communications Adaptive Technology Lab, 1999, "Resources in the Adaptive Technology Lab," http://www.washington.edu/computing/atl/DOCS/atl.use.html. (Last accessed April 9, 1999.)

World Wide Web Consortium, 1999a, "W3C HTML Validation Service." Available http://validator.w3.org/.

World Wide Web Consortium, 1999b, "Web Content Guidelines 1.0," http://www.w3.org/TR/WAI -WEBCONTENT/. (Last accessed July 16, 1999.)

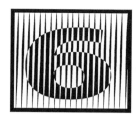

The Nature of Evaluation

Danny P. Wallace

INTRODUCTION

The preceding chapters have concentrated on broad areas that are common focuses of library evaluation and have provided detailed cases that describe the application of methods of evaluation to specific library needs. This concluding chapter addresses the nature of evaluation as a means of providing guidance on the development of programs and methods of evaluation. Building and nurturing the culture of evaluation described in Chapter 1 requires understanding more about the nature and origins of evaluation and the ways in which evaluation influences library activities.

THE CONTEXT FOR EVALUATION

Working within the context of the systems approach to evaluation requires understanding the context within which evaluation takes place. The need for library evaluation derives from several important contexts, which may apply simultaneously. Effective understanding of these contexts and their origins may serve to foster understanding and effective employment of evaluation processes and techniques. Failure to understand the context for evaluation may lead to evaluation activities that are inappropriate, ineffective, or even harmful.

The Societal Context

A library is a manifestation of the society it supports and the society that supports it. Any society is an exceedingly complex organism that cannot easily be understood. Some appreciation for the societal context, though, is essential to effective evaluation. Societies are defined by a myriad of characteristics, including place, time, economics, politics, and other factors. The modern library is a product of a host of societal influences, local and universal, historical and contemporary, pragmatic and philosophical, immediate and long term. Evaluation is and must be a response to the societal context of the library. Changes in the societal context should be reflected in changes in library operations; effective evaluation is essential to determining how the library should respond to societal change.

As society undergoes change, it may be necessary to engage in evaluation processes that reposition libraries to better suit societal evolution. Although the public perception of libraries, particularly public libraries, is generally positive, there is reason to believe that the public's *understanding* of libraries is limited. There is an ongoing need to seek new ways of presenting the public with understandable assessments of the value of libraries and library services. The promotional tool "Libraries—A Capital Investment," described in Case Study 2.3, provides concise data that compare the costs and values of library services to those of other popular services. This is a form of comparative evaluation that positions libraries in the societal context in an understandable and accessible manner.

The Professional Context

Librarians are members of a highly specialized professional group with an established set of professional concerns, ethics, policies, and practices. No library can operate in isolation from the profession of librarianship. The American Library Association and its subsidiary divisions, such as the Association of College and Research Libraries, the Public Library Association, and the American Association of School Libraries, define the professional context for libraries to a considerable extent. Established professional standards can readily serve as a model on which to base local evaluation activities; national guidelines for reference behaviors, for instance, served as the model on which the evaluation project described in Case Study 3.2. Library managers must also look to ancillary professional associations and to governmental agencies for professional guidance in areas not directly related to the delivery of library services, such as accessibility for individuals with disabilities (Case Study 5.2).

Although the philosophies and policies of national professional associations do not necessarily bind local evaluation, those philosophies and policies are always available for local application and provide a set of guideposts for evaluation. Conflicts between library administration and community pressure can be resolved by relating professional association policies and recommended procedures to local evaluation activities.

The Institutional Context

Every library exists within the structure of some institutional setting. Although the concept of *library* is not necessarily tied to an institution called a *library*, most libraries are defined at least in part by their institutional identity. Evaluation carried out in the library is by extension carried out on behalf of the institution that governs the library. Each of the cases presented in this book describes an approach to evaluation carried out in a specific library for a carefully designated purpose. To a substantial extent, institutional needs drove each of the evaluation processes described in the case studies. Although every library is governed by a unique combination of institutional needs and requirements, there are fundamental similarities that make it possible to extend methods and techniques developed in one institutional setting to other environments. Although the approach to evaluating reference behaviors described in Case Study 3.2 was developed for application in a public library network, there is every reason to believe that it can be directly adapted for use in a university library or other setting.

The Administrative Context

Evaluation is basically an administrative function. Regardless of who carries out the actual evaluation, the library's administration is responsible for the evaluation and its results. This means that evaluation at any level must have explicit or implied administrative consent. More importantly, it suggests administrative commitment to act on the outcomes of the evaluation. In the absence of such commitment, evaluation of any kind is an empty and futile exercise. Evaluation can be used as an approach to consciously altering the administrative structure of a library. Total Quality Management, described in Case Study 2.1, is essentially an approach to evaluating the operating structure of an enterprise with the goal of improving the processes and services provided by that enterprise.

The Functional Context

To be meaningful, useful, and beneficial, evaluation must lead to some pragmatic result. Ultimately, that result is either the replacement of some existing function with a new function or a decision to perpetuate the existing function. In this context more than any other, objectivity is essential. If replacement of the existing function is not a possibility, there is no need for evaluation. If retention of the existing function is not a possibility, particularly if the replacement has already been selected, there is no need for evaluation. Evaluation in the functional context assumes a commitment to acting on the outcomes of the evaluation process. The Ohio Measuring Library Services project described in Case Study 2.4 was predicated on the assumption that public libraries could and would change their approaches to measuring basic library operations. The desire to implement new measures was necessarily accompanied by a series of activities and events designed to build a shared commitment to functional change.

The Technological Context

Although it is certainly possible to overstate the impact of the technological context on evaluation and decision making, it is impossible to deny that changing technology inherently has a significant impact on what libraries and librarians do and how those things are done. Evaluation must take into account the technological context. At the same time, evaluation of technology and its use is essential to understanding the technological context. It is frequently the case that the introduction of new technology has a polarizing effect on those individuals who are affected by the change, with some people embracing the new technology—because it represents change—and others rejecting the new technology—because it represents change. It is much too often the case that neither camp has engaged in any meaningful evaluation of the new technology.

The introduction of new technologies has had a profound impact throughout the history of libraries and library services. The emergence of new ways of achieving library goals must be accompanied by evaluation of the technology itself and of the impact of the new technology on existing processes, products, and services. Continuity in the provision of services is frequently maintained by adapting established evaluation techniques to new technologies, as has been done with the development of criteria for evaluating World Wide Web search engines (Case Study 5.1).

The Patron Context

The ultimate context for evaluation is benefit to the patron. If there is no potential for patron benefit, any outcome of evaluation becomes suspect. Even when the process or product to be evaluated is buried deeply in the bowels of obscure library processes and procedures, the patron must be the central focus for evaluation. It is imminently difficult to imagine any library activity for which the patron is not the ultimate beneficiary of competent evaluation.

A currently popular expression in the library profession emphasizes the need for libraries to be *client centered*. This term derives from the business world and carries with it the implication that the central purpose is not to be profitable but to provide profit. In the corporate context, the message to be sent is that the company does not exist to make money, but to provide useful products or services to its customers. The principle of being client centered extends to the library context in a desire to be focused not on information resources, but on information needs.

Appreciation for the patron or client context leads to the need to involve and engage the library's clientele in evaluation of library services, processes, and products. Bringing the client into the evaluation process has a bonding effect that sends the message that patron input is important. The desire for useful and usable client input is the principle that underlies methods such as focus groups, which are described in Case Study 2.2. Client input also drives the ongoing search for standards for professional performance such as those imbedded in the Wisconsin–Ohio Reference Evaluation Program (Case Study 3.1).

ASSIGNING VALUE

Within the framework of an appropriate context or contexts, evaluation is literally and fundamentally the process of assigning value. The assignment of value can have many motives and many meanings. Likewise, evaluation takes place for many reasons and in many contexts, and in most cases is done for multiple simultaneous purposes that can be understood from a variety of points of view. The concept of evaluation is tied to a number of related concepts; a clear vision of the origins and linkages of any particular evaluation activity is a requirement for successful evaluation.

Value and Values

Value can be assigned only within the structure of some recognized system of values. Values are a human phenomenon that mixes elements of personal, group, and societal influence. The organizational models discussed in Chapter 2 are examples of value systems and their impact on evaluation. Individuals develop idiosyncratic value systems that shape their understandings of the universe. Free public library service is treated as a basic value by many residents of the United States and is a core value of the country's library profession. Societies develop, foster, and in some cases enforce value systems that vary according to geography, economics, and history.

Within an overall societal context, value systems vary across subgroups or cultures. Free public library service may be highly prized in general, but there are undoubtedly segments of the population to whom, for various reasons, free public library service is irrelevant or is viewed negatively.

Evaluation, then, must recognize the various value systems that affect the entity being evaluated. Evaluation is not value neutral. Working from the assumption that free public library service is a core value inherently shapes the goals, methods, and outcomes of evaluation of public library services. If the goal of evaluation is to determine whether a thing is good, then the question of who determines what is good or bad must be addressed. A first essential of evaluation is to understand and work within the value systems that apply.

Value and Benefit

It is easy to assume that those things that are valuable are necessarily beneficial or, conversely, that value derives from benefit. Because benefit is itself a function of prevailing value systems, determining benefit is an uncertain process. Benefits, like values, are closely tied to individual and group perceptions of importance. One person's benefit may be another's detriment. Many of the most fundamental sources of disagreement with regard to intellectual freedom, for instance, have to do with value-driven differences in perception of the benefit of open access to information.

Historically, it has been relatively simple to assign a relationship between value and benefit in economic analysis, but much more difficult in attempts to evaluate social processes. How well does a professional school meet the expectations of its various constituent groups? Do existing measures of library performance accurately reflect library activities? Does explicit instruction in basic reference service provision result in improved reference behavior? Each of these questions identifies a specific benefit and the value that might be associated with it, but turning such statements of benefits and values into operational evaluation processes is a difficult and frequently elusive proposition.

Benefit may be expressed in economic terms by comparing the costs of different products or services and allowing relative cost to serve as an indicator of relative benefit. Knowing that the annual cost for public library service to a family of four is less than one half the cost of admission for the same family to a typical amusement park, as described in Case Study 2.3, can help build understanding of the relative investment in the two services and emphasize the efficiency with which public libraries expend the public funds in their trust.

Value and Goals

Because evaluation is so tied to diverse value systems and varying perceptions of benefit, it is paramount to develop specific goals for any evaluation process, project, or product. Although evaluation cannot take place outside the value system context, the establishment of explicit goals for evaluation serves as a constant anchor in a sea of varying values and conflicting perceptions of benefit. A goal speaks to some set of tasks to be accomplished and the need to determine if they are accomplished in an appropriate manner. When carefully stated, evaluation goals serve to override the negative potential inherent in conflicting value systems.

Although it may be difficult to determine the impact a formal course of study in effective reference service has on the usefulness patrons derive from library reference services, it is quite feasible to set a specific goal of a desirable set of reference behaviors and determine to what extent those behaviors are exhibited by reference staff, as is described in Case Study 3.2. Turning a generic statement of value or benefit into a specific, tangible goal with observable or even measurable outcomes provides for precision and consistency in evaluation. At the same time, the value or benefit desired is retained in a form that can be easily and uniformly understood.

Value and Quality

At its heart, the purpose of evaluation is to ascertain quality—how good something is, how well something is done, how effectively a goal is achieved, how appropriate a service is, how efficiently a service is delivered. Quality is a tenuous and amorphous concept. There is no universal measure of *goodness*, no obvious definition of *correctness*, no yardstick marked in units of *quality*. As a result, it is usually necessary to develop specialized tools that are assumed to somehow aid in determining quality even though the tools themselves do not directly address quality. It is perilous to lose track of the distance between what the tool actually measures and the phenomenon being evaluated. The old expression "a pint's a pound the world around" and the more modern "one size fits all" are excellent examples of the danger of divorcing the measure from the thing being measured.

There is a strong link between the concept of quality and the process of setting goals. In the absence of carefully determined quality goals, there is a tendency to assume that the only acceptable indicator of quality is perfection. Although it is intuitively true that meeting all the needs of every patron is desirable, it is equally obvious that meeting all the needs of every patron is impossible. Quality must be assessed in terms of what is possible as well as what is desirable. Bourne (1965) has written of the "90 Percent Library," a conceptual basis for understanding that, because perfection is generally unattainable, perfection as a goal is usually unattainable. The 90 Percent Library model is predicated on the notion that it is possible to identify an optimal, attainable level of performance and to shape library services, operations, and processes in terms of achieving a targeted success rate rather than failing to perform perfectly.

A frequently cited and oft-lamented principle in library evaluation is the so-called 55 Percent Rule, in which it is posited that reference questions are answered completely and correctly about 55 percent of the time (Hernon and McClure 1986). Although studies of reference accuracy have actually reported a wide range of success rates, a fundamental limitation of most such studies is failure to identify a target rate that defines acceptable quality. If 55 percent is not good enough, what is? If 100 percent is not attainable, what is a desirable rate of success? Are there strategies and techniques that can be effectively employed to influence reference accuracy and allow a library to achieve a predetermined success rate? Does reference accuracy legitimately vary among types of libraries, across geographic locations, or according to time of day, difficulty of question, or some other factor? Using a standardized evaluation instrument, such as the Wisconsin–Ohio Reference Evaluation Program (discussed in Case Study 3.1), provides a basis for making such comparative quality assessments.

Ultimately, effective evaluation must be tied to some set of operational definitions of the specific factors associated with the determination of quality. Evaluation must then be carried out in the context of some target level of quality that is rational, reasonable, and verifiable. Without a clear understanding of what constitutes quality, evaluation will tend either to overlook flaws or to exaggerate them. The role of expert professional opinion in establishing targets for quality assessment is paramount and is reflected in the approaches to verifying the quality of individual sources as well as collections as a whole found in Case Study 4.1.

Value and Quantity

Quantification is the most obvious and most frequently employed approach to indirectly assessing quality. Although it is possible to set nonquantitative quality targets, adding the element of quantification lends precision, consistency, and replicability. A desire to know if the library is being used, which in the context of some value systems is taken as being a positive indicator of quality, translates into counts of conspicuous acts of use such as circulation transactions, numbers of questions asked, door counts, and related measures. Quality can be quantified through methodologies such as citation analysis, which provides a basis for identifying core resources that transcends the scope of expert judgment (Case Study 4.3). These quantitative indicators are especially attractive in that they are easily amenable to comparison. They can be compared over time for a single location, among locations for a single library system, and across locations for a broader geographic area. They can be applied consistently and with an impressive degree of validity.

Unfortunately, no quantitative measure is more than what it is. In the current context, circulation is counted primarily in terms of numbers of bar codes scanned. Circulation must be, in some sense, an indicator of use, but transaction counts reveal nothing regarding the nature of that use. Circulation counts may mean one thing in a suburban middle class community and something completely different in an inner city neighborhood. Counts of questions asked or even of staff perceptions of questions answered are a very indirect reflection of if patron needs are met. A study carried out at the University of Illinois in the mid-1980s found little relationship between public library patron perceptions of the quality of reference service and factual assessment of whether questions were correctly answered (Wallace 1983, 1984). A possibly apocryphal study from several years ago revealed that turnstile counts consistently show more patrons entering libraries than leaving.

Ultimately, the drive to quantify leads to the lament that "if you can't count it, it doesn't count." Counting is useful only when the distance between the quantifiable measure and the quality of the phenomenon being evaluated is thoroughly and thoughtfully understood. Bigger and more are not necessarily better; smaller and less are not necessarily worse.

A fundamental aspect of the relationship between value and quantity is assurance that measures are meaningful. This requires revisiting measures at appropriate intervals to reassess their usefulness. Circulation transactions as an indicator of the volume of library use must be re-examined in an age of digital transactions that do not generate circulation counts. The Ohio Measuring Library Services project, outlined in Case Study 2.4, is a rare example of a comprehensive and systematic reassessment of standardized approaches to quantifying library operations.

APPROACHES TO EVALUATION

Ad Hoc/As Needed/As Required

Much, perhaps most, evaluation is carried out on the fly as a more-or-less emergency procedure. A problem arises, there is a perceived need for an immediate solution, and some sort of attempt is made at evaluating the problem as a means of deriving a solution. Sometimes the problem is imposed from outside via political, social, or economic influences. The library community has no need to look far for examples of societal pressures to examine problems defined by pressure groups. An impressive number of very immediate evaluation needs center around the opportunity to take advantage of a funding opportunity with a fixed deadline. Governance or governmental bodies are well known for their tendency to demand quick responses to esoteric needs to evaluate specific functions.

The major problem with on-demand evaluation is that there is no meaningful integration of evaluation and planning. If a member of the library board suddenly demands to know "why the library is not meeting the needs of small businesses," an on-demand evaluation of whether the library is in fact doing so is unlikely to be something that can be carried out in a time frame that will soothe the board member. Turning an on-demand evaluation into an integral element of the library's planning will take even more time and will likely constitute a de facto admission that the board member's concern was justified. The best response to such a demand for short turnaround evaluation is a pre-existing evaluation process, which requires an element of forethought that cannot be guaranteed. Having in place the results of an evaluation activity for which no external request had been made, however, has fulfilled many a real need. Relying on ad hoc evaluation is an invitation to missed opportunities and frantic compliance with unreasonable deadlines.

Externally Centered

External forces drive many of the evaluation processes carried out in libraries. Most state libraries and many other library agencies request standardized statistical reporting, with the implication that there is a compelling reason to comply. These statistical reporting practices are developed in response to demands from a range of levels from local to federal. The development of new state standards and new measures of public library services—a process that must take place as new technologies and societal evolution reshape the nature of library services—is a force to which libraries must respond.

Reporting data on an annual basis to a state agency is not in and of itself an act of evaluation. Every public librarian with responsibility for delivering statistical or other data in response to an external demand should be thinking and planning in terms of the local application and benefit of such data. The externally centered need to report should not be viewed as self-justifying. The essential challenge is to look for the local benefit to be derived from reporting to external sources.

Internally Centered

The most interesting and most immediate evaluation needs are those that arise from perceptions of local problems. External demands help establish comparative baselines; internal demands produce solutions to tangible problems. Deriving approaches to internal problems is, however, a problem in itself. External demands for statistical reporting have the advantage of being structured, repetitive, and predicable. Internal demands require creativity, critical thinking, development of new tools for evaluation, and allocation of local resources. They also demand a commitment to evaluation. It is in many cases easier to let the problem go or pretend that it is addressed in external reporting than to make the administrative commitment to seek a solution. Only when a real commitment is made can internally centered evaluation be meaningful and beneficial.

Creating an internally centered approach to evaluation requires developing a program of meaningful environmental scanning in which the internal operations of the library, the external demands of agencies to which the library is responsible, the constituents the library serves, and the political entities that subject the library to scrutiny are systematically polled to provide data for evaluation. Ultimately, responding to internal evaluation needs can be expected to lead to a new understanding of the library and may result in a major paradigm shift, such as introduction of Total Quality Management as an approach to structuring the library's operations.

Research Centered

Research is a very special focus for evaluation. Herbert Goldhor, former director of the Library Research Center at the University of Illinois, frequently lamented that every evaluation project was *almost* a research study. What research adds to evaluation is the potential for extension to other environments. When applied appropriately, evaluation techniques reveal useful information not only about the library for which the evaluation project was conducted, but also for other libraries with similar evaluation needs.

Carrying out an evaluation project in a research mode is not an easy process. The needs and problems of the Anytown Public Library are not obviously or inherently of interest to any other library. The essence of research is documenting and reporting those aspects of the local evaluation process that are potentially applicable to other environments. This is a tricky process. The trickiest part of all is understanding, believing, and acting on the principle that if one library has a problem, other libraries probably have the same problem. The greatest impediment to sharing useful results of local evaluation activities is the mistaken belief that the local situation is so unique that no one else has the same problems. Every library problem is indeed a potential research project, and every librarian should strive to be aware of the needs of other librarians with similar problems.

EVALUATION AND DECISION MAKING

Evaluation and decision making are inextricably linked. Evaluation is sterile when it fails to lead to effective decision making. No responsible library practitioner has the resources to devote to evaluation for the sake of evaluation. At the same time, decisions not based on evaluation are legitimately subject to charges of capriciousness and arbitrariness. The challenge is to find the most efficient approach to evaluation that will lead to the most effective basis for making decisions that are in some sense correct.

The Need for Decisions

Management can be accurately described as a system of decisions. The effectiveness of management is a direct function of the correctness and appropriateness of decision making. The need for decision making arises from the mission, goals, objectives, strategies, tactics, and environment of the library. Some decisions are unique and emergent; others are recurring and routine. Ultimately, though, the need to make frequent, high quality decisions is absent only in a nonfunctional or dysfunctional setting. Because effective decision making is dependent on evaluation, an effective library requires appropriate evaluation.

Authority for Decision Making

The ability to make decisions derives from the authority granted to various individuals and groups to make decisions. In a typical public library, decisions are made variously by individual staff members, the director, the board, the governing body of the political entity with which the library is affiliated, the voting public, and governmental agencies at the local and state levels. Generally speaking, useful evaluation can take place only when endorsed by the entity or agency empowered to make decisions based on the outcomes of evaluation.

Any evaluation activity should be undertaken only with due regard to the policies, procedures, and traditions that determine authority for decision making.

Types of Decisions

Ihrig (1989) defined the following categories of important library decisions:

1. Planning and Decision Making—those decisions having to do with setting future directions and goals for the library.

2. Staff Leadership—those decisions having to do with determining staff roles in carrying out planning initiatives and achieving goals.

3. Financial—those decisions that affect the allocation of resources for the achievement of goals.

4. Intellectual Freedom—those decisions that derive from the philosophical and ethical principles espoused by the profession.

Planning and Decision Making

The need for effective decision making in planning can be found in the initiatives that produced the Public Library Association's series of planning tools, including *A Planning Process for Public Libraries*, *Planning and Role-Setting*, *Planning for Results*, and two editions of *Output Measures for Public Libraries*. Effective planning is dependent on evaluation and required as part of the evaluation process. Planning is expected to be action oriented—to lead to implementation of that which is planned.

A major focus for planning decisions is collection evaluation and management. As the needs of the library and its public change, it is essential to have in place systems and tools for assessing the nature and quality of the collection. Established collection assessment techniques, such as list checking, may need to be modified and adapted to reflect the evolution of the collection. The approach to evaluating a rock and roll compact disc collection described in Case Study 4.2 is an example of such creative adaptation of an established approach.

Staff Leadership Decisions

The need for staff development in libraries has increased dramatically in recent decades. Changes in the technological, organizational, and societal contexts of libraries have made staff responsibilities at all levels more complex and more varied. The reliance on ad hoc, on-the-job training that characterized what passed for staff development during most of the history of libraries has been frequently found lacking as a solution to current education and training needs. Effective evaluation of staff needs, staff abilities, and staff development opportunities is essential to making appropriate decisions regarding staff goals and staff roles in planning and implementation. The approaches to reference service evaluation and staff development included in Case Studies 3.1 and 3.2 are concrete examples of the need for staff leadership decision making.

Financial Decision Making

Evaluation plays an obvious role in financial decision making. Resource allocation for library support is rarely magnanimous, and demands from institutions and the public for accountability, particularly in publicly funded settings, are increasingly tangible and immediate. Handling a library's resources is a critical task that necessitates careful and continuous evaluation and rapid feedback. Financial decision making is more than budgeting expenditures. The model for relating library expenditures to public expenditures for other consumable services provided in Case Study 2.3 helps place the financial decision making necessary in libraries in a broader context as a means of furthering public understanding of how far their financial investment in libraries extends.

Intellectual Freedom Decision Making

Intellectual freedom is a fundamental tenet for most librarians. Responsiveness to intellectual-freedom challenges and proactive planning to support the principles of intellectual freedom require effective environmental scanning and assessment. Intellectual freedom is a complex concept that includes the elements of intellectual access, physical access, and technological access discussed in Chapter 5 and exemplified in Case Study 5.2.

Evaluating Decisions

The most difficult evaluation question of all is "Was that the correct decision?" Decisions are expected to lead to results, and results are expected to serve as validators of decisions. If the goal of evaluation is to drive decision making, then the process of "evaluating the evaluation" described in Chapter 1 cannot be considered complete until the decisions based on the evaluation have themselves been evaluated. Decisions are evaluated by further evaluation of the operations, processes, services, or products affected by the decisions.

The need to engage in evaluation to guide decision making combined with the need to evaluate decisions to create an environment in which evaluation must be ongoing to be effective. Episodic or one-time evaluation is of limited potential for having a meaningful impact on the library. Evaluation when done properly is an approach to continuous quality improvement, to ensuring that things are indeed getting better all the time. Ultimately, the key to evaluating decisions is determining if improvement has indeed taken place and if new targets for improvement can be identified from the results of the evaluation process. When examination of the results of the evaluation leads to new approaches to evaluation, the circle of evaluation has been regenerated and the culture of evaluation is at its most effective.

RESOURCES

Bourne, Charles P., 1965, "Some User Requirements Stated Quantitatively in Terms of the 90 Percent Library," pp. 93–110 in *Electronic Information Handling*, eds. Allen Kent and Orrin E. Taulbee. Washington, DC: Spartan.

Hernon, Peter, and Charles R. McClure, 1986, "Unobtrusive Reference Testing: The 55 Percent Rule," *Library Journal* 111 (April 15): 37–41.

Himmel, Ethel E. et al., 1998, *Planning for Results: A Public Library Transformation Process*. Chicago: American Library Association.

Ihrig, Alice B., 1989, *Decision Making for Public Libraries*. Hamden, CT: Library Professional Publications.

McClure, Charles R. et al., 1987, *Planning and Role Setting for Public Libraries: A Manual of Options and Procedures*. Chicago: American Library Association.

Palmour, Vernon E., 1980, *A Planning Process for Public Libraries*. Chicago: American Library Association.

Van House, Nancy et al., 1987, *Output Measures for Public Libraries: A Manual of Standardized Procedures*, 2d ed. Chicago: American Library Association.

Wallace, Danny P., 1983, "An Index of Quality of Illinois Public Library Service," pp. 1–46 in *Illinois Library Statistical Report 10*. Springfield, IL: Illinois State Library.

———, 1984,"An Index of Quality of Illinois Public Library Service, 1983," pp. 61–84 in *Illinois Library Statistical Report 14*. Springfield, IL: Illinois State Library.

Zweizig, Douglas, and Eleanor Jo Rodger, 1982, *Output Measures for Public Libraries: A Manual of Standardized Procedures*. Chicago: American Library Association.

BIBLIOGRAPHY

Aggarwal, Sumer. 1993. "A Quick Guide to Total Quality Management." *Business Horizons* 36 (May/June): 66–68.

Alliance for Technology Access. 1997. "Products Which Enhance Access to the WWW." http://www.ataccess .org/access.html. (Last accessed April 11, 1999.)

Aluri, Rao, and Mary Reichel. 1994. "Performance Evaluation: A Deadly Disease?" *Journal of Academic Librarianship* 20 (July): 145–54.

Amabile, Teresa M. 1998. "How To Kill Creativity." *Harvard Business Review* 76 (September/October): 77–87.

American Library Association. 1995. *ALA Handbook of Organization, 1995/96.* Chicago: American Library Association.

———. 1996. "Access to Electronic Access to Information, Services, and Networks: An Interpretation of the *Library Bill of Rights.*" http://www.ala.org/alaorg/oif/electacc.html. (Last accessed April 8, 1999.)

———. 1997. "Questions and Answers: Access to Electronic Information, Services, and Networks: An Interpretation of the *Library Bill of Rights.*" http://www.ala.org/alaorg/oif/oif_q&a.html. (Last accessed April 8, 1999.)

American National Standards Institute, Inc. 1983. *American National Standard for Library and Information Sciences and Related Publishing Practices–Library Statistics. ANSI Z39.7–1983.* New York: American National Standards Institute, Inc.

Annichiarico, Mark. 1995. "And the Beat Goes On." *Library Journal* 120 (November 15): 32–36.

Ashar, Hanna, and Sharon Geiger. 1998. "Using the Baldrige Criteria to Assess Quality in Libraries." *Library Administration & Management* 12 (Summer): 147–55.

Atkinson, Philip E. 1990. *Creating Culture Change: The Key to Successful Total Quality Management.* Bedford, UK: IFS Ltd.

Baker, Sharon, and F. W. Lancaster. 1991. *The Measurement and Evaluation of Library Services.* 2d ed. Arlington, VA: Information Resources Press.

Barker, Joel A. 1990. *Discovering the Future: The Business of Paradigms.* Barnsville, MN: ChartHouse International Learning Corporation. Videocassette.

Barkett, Gina R. 1998. "A Study of the Multidisciplinary Influences on Art History Using Citation Analysis." Master's research paper. Kent State University, School of Library and Information Science.

Barr, Christopher. 1996. "Tattoos, Nose Rings, And Avatars." http://www.canada.cnet.com/Contents/Voices /Barr/091609/index.html. (Last accessed March 5, 1999.)

Beals, Ralph. 1942. "Implications of Communications Research for the Public Library." pp. 159–81 in *Print, Radio, and Film in a Democracy*, ed. Douglas Waples. Chicago: University of Chicago.

Berners-Lee, Tim. 1999. "Press FAQ." http://www.w3.org/People/Berners–Lee/FAQ.html. (Last accessed March 5, 1999.)

"The *Billboard* 200. The Top-Selling Albums Compiled from a National Sample of Retail Store and Rack Sales Reports. Collected, Compiled, and Provided by SoundScan." *Billboard* October 18, 1997; January 17, 1998; April 18, 1998; July 18, 1998.

Binkely, Dave, and Tom Eadie. 1989. *Wisconsin–Ohio Reference Evaluation at the University of Waterloo.* CALCUL Occasional Paper Series No. 3. Canadian Association of College and University Libraries.

Blandy, Susan, Lynne Martin, and Mary Strife, eds. 1992. "Assessment and Accountability in Reference Work." *The Reference Librarian* no. 38.

Bonk, Wallace John, and Rose Mary Magrill. 1979. *Building Library Collections*. 5th ed. Metuchen, NJ: Scarecrow Press.

Bourne, Charles P. 1965 "Some User Requirements Stated Quantitatively in Terms of the 90 Percent Library." Pp. 93–110 in *Electronic Information Handling*, eds. Allen Kent and Orrin E. Taulbee. Washington, DC: Spartan.

Brache, Alan, and Geary Rummler. 1997. "Managing an Organization as a System." *Training* 34 (February): 68–74.

Brandt, D. Scott. 1996. "Evaluating Information on the Internet." http://thorplus.lib.purdue.edu/~techman /evaluate.htm. (Last accessed March 28, 1999.)

Brilliant, Richard. 1988. "How An Art Historian Connects Objects and Information." *Library Trends* 37 (Fall): 120–29.

Brody, Herb. 1998. "Untangling Web Searches." *Technology Review* 101 (July/August): 26.

Brown, Barbara J. 1992. *Programming for Librarians: A How-To-Do-It Manual*. New York: Neal-Schuman.

Brown, Janet. 1994. "Using Quality Concepts to Improve Reference Services." *College & Research Libraries* 55 (May): 211–19.

Bunge, Charles A. 1984. "Planning, Goals, and Objectives for the Reference Department." *RQ* 23 (Spring): 306–15.

———. 1990. "Factors Related to Output Measures for Reference Services in Public Libraries: Data from Thirty–Six Libraries." *Public Libraries* 29 (January/February): 42–47.

———. 1994. "Evaluating Reference Services and Reference Personnel: Questions and Answers from the Literature." *The Reference Librarian* 43: 195–207.

Cameron, Kim S., and David A. Whetten. 1983a. "Organizational Effectiveness: One Model or Several?" pp. 1–24 in *Organizational Effectiveness: A Comparison of Multiple Models*, ed. Kim S. Cameron and David A. Whetten. New York: Academic Press.

———, 1983b. "Some Conclusions About Organizational Effectiveness." pp. 261–77 *in Organizational Effectiveness: A Comparison of Multiple Models*, eds. Kim S. Cameron and David A. Whetten. New York: Academic Press.

Carson, Kerry David, Paula Phillips Carson, and Joyce Schouest Phillips. 1997. *The ABCs of Collaborative Change: The Manager's Guide to Library Renewal*. Chicago: American Library Association.

Center for Applied Special Technology. 1999. "Welcome to Bobby 3.1.1." http://www.cast.org/bobby/. (Last accessed July 16, 1999.)

Champelli, L. 1997. "Understand Software that Blocks Internet Sites and Related Censorship and Safety Issues." http://www.monroe.lib.in.us/~lchampel/netady4.html. (Last accessed April 11, 1999.)

Chatterjee, Sangit, and Mustafa Yilmaz. 1993. "Quality Confusion: Too Many Gurus, Not Enough Disciples." *Business Horizons* 36 (May/June): 15–18.

Chen, Ya-Ning. 1998. "The Internet's Effect on Libraries: Some Personal Observations." *LIBRES: Library and Information Science Research* 8, no. 1. Computer file. Available from the archives at listproc @info.curtin.edu.eu;_file LIBRE8N1 CHEN. (Last accessed December 28, 1998.)

Churchman, C. West. 1968. *The Systems Approach*. New York: Delacorte Press.

Cobbledick, Susie. 1994. "The Information-Seeking Behavior of Artists: Exploratory Interviews." Master's research paper. Kent State University, School of Library and Information Science.

Connell, Bettye Rose et al. 1997. "The Principles of Universal Design." http://trace.wisc.edu/docs/ud _princ.htm. (Last accessed March 7, 1999.)

Coombs, Norman. 1990. "Electronic Access to Library Systems for Users with Physical Disabilities." *Public-Access Computer Systems Review* 1, no. 1: 43–47.

Cooper, B. Lee. 1981. "An Opening Day Collection of Popular Music Resources: Searching for Discographic Standards." Pp. 228–55 in *Twentieth Century Popular Culture in Museums and Libraries*, ed. Fred E. H. Schroeder. Bowling Green, OH: Bowling Green State University Popular Press.

Crawford, Gregory. 1994. "A Conjoint Analysis of Reference Services." *College & Research Libraries* 55 (May): 257–67.

Crispen, Joanne L. ed. 1993. *The Americans with Disabilities Act: Its Impact on Libraries: The Library's Response in "Doable" Steps*. Chicago: American Library Association.

Cullars, John. 1992. "Citation Characteristics of Monographs in the Fine Arts." *Library Quarterly* 62 (July): 325–42.

Cullen, Rowena. 1992. "Evaluation and Performance Measurement in Reference Services." *New Zealand Libraries* 47 (March): 11–15.

Cunningham, Carmela, and Norman Coombs. 1997. *Information Access and Adaptive Technology*. Phoenix, AZ: Oryx Press.

Curley, Arthur, and Dorothy Broderick. 1985. *Building Library Collections*. Metuchen, NJ: Scarecrow Press.

Curran, Charles, and Philip M. Clark. 1989. "Implications of Tying State Aid to Performance Measures." *Public Libraries* 28 (November/December): 348–54.

Davis, Elizabeth, ed. 1997. *A Basic Music Library: Essential Scores and Sound Recordings*. 3d ed. Chicago: American Library Association.

De Geus, Arie. 1997. "The Living Company." *Harvard Business Review* 75 (March/April): 51–59.

Deines-Jones, Courtney, and Connie Van Fleet. 1995. *Preparing Staff to Serve Patrons with Disabilities*. New York: Neal-Schuman.

D'Elia, George. 1988. "Materials Availability Fill Rates: Additional Data Addressing the Question of the Usefulness of the Measures." *Public Libraries* 27 (Spring): 15–23.

D'Elia, George, and Eleanor Jo Rodger. 1996. "Customer Satisfaction with Public Libraries." *Public Libraries* 35 (September/October): 292–97.

———. 1994. "Public Opinion about the Roles of the Public Library in the Community: The Results of a Recent Gallup Poll." *Public Libraries* 33 (January/February): 23–28.

D'Elia, George D., and Sandra Walsh. 1985. "Patrons' Uses and Evaluations of Library Services: A Comparison Across Five Public Libraries." *Library and Information Science Research* 7 (January): 3–30.

Deming, W. Edwards. 1985. "Transformation of Western Style of Management." *Interface* 15 (May/June): 6–11.

Ding, Wei, and Gary Marchionini. 1996. "A Comparative Study of Web Search Service Performance." pp. 136–42 in *ASIS '96: Proceedings of 49th ASIS Annual Meeting: Global Complexity—Information, Chaos and Control*. Medford, NJ: Information Today.

Disability Mall. 1999. "Computers: Hardware and Software." http://www.disabilitymall.com/ecomput.html. (Last accessed April 11, 1999.)

DO-IT (Disabilities, Opportunities, Networking and Technology). 1998. "World Wide Web Access: Accessible Web Design." http://weber.u.washington.edu/~doit/Brochures/Technology/universal.design.html. (Last accessed April 11, 1999.)

Downey, Maria. 1993. "A Survey of the Information-Seeking Practices of Artists in the Academic Community." Master's research paper. Kent State University, School of Library and Information Science.

Electronic and Information Technology Access Advisory Committee. 1999. "Final Report, May 12, 1999." http://www.access–board.gov/pubs/eitaacrpt.htm. (Last accessed July 16, 1999.)

Emerson, Katherine. 1984. "Definitions for Planning and Evaluating Reference Services." pp. 63–79 in *Evaluation of Reference Services*, eds. Bill Katz and Ruth A. Fraley. New York: Haworth Press.

"The Enlightened Manager's Guidebook." 1998. *Inc.* 19 (October): 45–51.

Evans, G. Edward. 1995. *Developing Library and Information Center Collections*. 3d ed. Englewood, CO: Libraries Unlimited.

Everhart, Nancy. 1998. "Web Page Evaluation." *Emergency Librarian* 25 (May/June): 22.

Fedunok, Suzanne. 1996. "Hammurabi and the Electronic Age: Documenting Electronic Collection Decisions." *RQ* 36 (Fall): 86–90.

"Filtering Legislation Hearing, Round Two, More of the Same." 1999. *Library Hotline* 28 (March 15): 2.

Free Pint. http:// www.freepint.com.co.uk.

Glossbrenner Alfred, and Emily Glossbrenner. 1999. *Search Engines for the World Wide Web*. 2d ed. Berkeley, CA: Peachpit Press.

Goldhor, Herbert. 1987. "An Analysis of Available Data on the Number of Public Library Reference Questions." *RQ* 27 (Winter): 195–201.

Gorman, G. E., and B. R. Howes. 1989. *Collection Development for Libraries*. New York: Bowker-Saur.

Gorman, Kathleen. 1987. "Performance Evaluation in Reference Services in ARL Libraries." SPEC Kit 139. Washington, DC: Office of Management Studies, Association of Research Libraries.

Green, Louise Koller. 1988. "Assessing the Effectiveness of Reference Services: A Difficult But Necessary Process." *Catholic Library World* 59 (January/February): 168–71.

Greenbaum, Thomas L. 1988. *The Practical Handbook and Guide to Focus Group Research*. Lexington, MA: Lexington Books.

Greenwood, Val. 1990. *The Researcher's Guide to American Genealogy*. 2d ed. Baltimore: Genealogical Publishing.

"Guidelines for Behavioral Performance of Reference and Information Services Professionals." 1996. *RQ* 36 (Winter): 200–203. Also available at http://www.ala.org/RUSA/.

Haley, Frances, and Connie Van Fleet. 1996. *Measuring Library Services: A Joint Project of the Ohio Library Council and The State Of Ohio. Final Report*. Columbus: Ohio Library Council.

Halliday, Blane. 1999. "An Examination of Essential Popular Music Compact Disc Holdings at the Cleveland Public Library." Master's research paper. Kent State University, School of Library and Information Science.

Hallman, Clark N. 1981. "Designing Optical Mark Forms for Reference Statistics." *RQ* 20 (Spring): 257–64.

Harari, Oren, and Linda Mukai. 1990. "A New Decade Demands a New Breed of Manager." *Management Review* 79 (August): 20–25.

Heim, Kathleen M. 1982. "Stimulation." pp. 120–53 in *The Service Imperative for Libraries*, ed. Gail A. Schlachter. Littleton, CO: Libraries Unlimited.

Hennen, Thomas J., Jr. 1999. "Go Ahead, Name Them: America's Best Public Libraries." *American Libraries* 30 (January): 72–76.

Hernon, Peter. 1987. "Utility Measures, Not Performance Measures, for Library Reference Service?" *RQ* 26 (Summer): 449–59.

Hernon, Peter, and Charles R. McClure. 1986. "Unobtrusive Reference Testing: The 55 Percent Rule." *Library Journal* 111 (April 15): 37–41.

————. 1987. *Unobtrusive Testing and Library Reference Services*. Norwood, NJ: Ablex.

————. 1990. *Evaluation & Library Decision Making*. Norwood, NJ: Ablex.

Herther, Nancy K. 1988. "How to Evaluate Reference Materials on CD-ROM." *Online* 12 (March): 106–8.

Himmel, Ethel E., William James Wilson with the ReVision Committee of the Public Library Association. 1998. *Planning for Results: A Public Library Transformation Process*. Chicago: American Library Association.

Hock, Randolph. 1999. *The Extreme Searcher's Guide to Web Search Engines: A Handbook for the Serious Searcher*. Medford, NJ: CyberAge Books.

Hoffman, Irene. 1989. "CD-ROM: A Planning Checklist." *OCLC Micro* 5 (October): 5.

Holland, Thomas P. n.d. *Organizational Effectiveness in the Human Services*. Cleveland, OH: Case Western Reserve University, Mandel Center.

Holt, Glen E., Donald Elliott, and Amonia Moore. 1999. "Placing a Value on Public Library Services at Saint Louis Public Library." *Public Libraries* 38 (March/April): 98–99+.

"Home Page." 1999. *PC Webopedia*. http://webopedia.internet.com. (Last accessed April 11, 1999.)

Houghton, James R. 1993. "It's Time for a New Management System." *USA Today* 121 (March): 62–63.

Ihrig, Alice B. 1989. *Decision Making for Public Libraries*. Hamden, CT: Library Professional Publications.

"Information Services for Information Consumers: Guidelines for Providers." 1990. *RQ* 30 (Winter): 262–65.

Janes, Joseph W., and Louis B. Rosenfeld. 1996. "Networked Information Retrieval and Organization: Issues and Questions." *Journal of the American Society for Information Science* 47 (September): 711–15.

Janson, H. W. 1986. *History of Art*. New York: Harry N. Abrams.

Kantor, Paul B., and Tefko Saracevic. 1995. *Studying the Cost and Value of Library Services: Final Technical Report*. Alexandria Project Laboratory, School of Communication Information and Library Studies, Rutgers, the State University of New Jersey. Technical Report APLAB/94-3/1 (Rev. Mar. 95).

Katz, Bill, and Ruth A. Fraley, eds. 1984. "Evaluation of Reference Services," *The Reference Librarian* no. 11.

Katz, William A. 1992. *Introduction To Reference Work*. 6th ed. New York : McGraw-Hill.

————. 1997. "Reference Service Policies and Evaluation." *Introduction to Reference Work*, Vol. II. 7th ed. New York: McGraw-Hill.

Kennedy, Shirley Duglin. 1998. *Best Bet Internet: Reference and Research When You Don't Have Time to Mess Around*. Chicago: American Library Association.

Kent State University. 1998. "The Kent Student Community." http://www.kent.edu/ra/stupro/page1.htm. (Last accessed April 18, 1999.)

Kesselman, Martin, and Sarah Barbara Watstein. 1987. "The Measurement of Reference and Information Services." *The Journal of Academic Librarianship* 13 (March): 24–30.

King, Alan. 1991a. "To CD-ROM or Not to CD-ROM, That is the Question!" *Online* 15 (March): 101–2.

————. 1991b. "Kicking the Tires: The Fine Art of CD-ROM Product Evaluation." *Online* 15 (May): 102–4.

Kirkwood, Hal P. 1998. "Beyond Evaluation: A Model for Cooperative Evaluation of Internet Resources." *Online* 22 (July/August): 66–72.

Koenig, Michael E. D. 1978. "Citation Analysis for the Arts and Humanities as a Collection Management Tool." *Collection Management* 2 (Fall): 247–61.

Krueger, Richard A. 1994. *Focus Groups: A Practical Guide for Applied Research*. 2d ed. Thousand Oaks, CA: Sage Publications.

——. 1997. *Involving Community Members in Focus Groups*. Focus Group Kit, vol. 5. Thousand Oaks, CA: Sage Publications.

——. 1997. *Moderating Focus Groups*. Focus Group Kit, vol. 4. Thousand Oaks, CA: Sage Publications.

——. 1998. *Analyzing and Reporting Focus Groups*. Focus Group Kit, vol. 6. Thousand Oaks, CA: Sage Publications.

——. 1998. *Developing Questions for Focus Groups*. Focus Group Kit, vol. 3. Thousand Oaks, CA: Sage Publications.

——. 1998. *Focus Group Kit*. Thousand Oaks, CA: Sage Publications.

LaBorie, Tim. 1983. "Introduction." *Drexel Library Quarterly* 19 (Winter): 1–3.

Lancaster, F. W. 1993. *If You Want to Evaluate Your Library. . . .* 2d ed. Urbana, IL: University of Illinois, Graduate School of Library and Information Science.

Larkin, Colin. 1992. "Introduction." Pp. 9–15 in *Guinness Encyclopedia of Popular Music*, ed. Colin Larkin. Chester, CT: New England Publishing Associates.

Larsen, John C. 1971. "The Use of Art Reference Sources in Museum Libraries." *Special Libraries* 62 (November): 481–86.

Larson, Carole. 1994. "Developing Behavioral Reference Desk Performance Standards." *RQ* 33 (Spring): 347–49.

The Last Whole Earth Catalog. 1974. Menlo Park, CA [?]: Portola Institute.

Lawrence, Steve, and C. Lee Giles. 1998. "Searching the World Wide Web." *Science* 280 (April 3): 98–100.

"Life on the Internet: Net Timeline." 1998. Public Broadcasting Service. http://www.pbs.org/internet/timeline. (Last accessed March 5, 1999.)

Line, Maurice B. 1979. "Review of *Use of Library Materials: The University of Pittsburgh Study*." *College & Research Libraries* 40 (November): 557–58.

LinkExchange. 1999. "SiteInspector." http://siteinspector.com. (Last accessed April 11, 1999.)

Lynch, Clifford. 1997. "Searching the Internet." *Scientific American* 27 (March): 52–56.

Lynch, Mary Jo. 1983. "Measurement of Public Library Activity: The Search for Practical Methods." *Wilson Library Bulletin* 57 (January): 388–93.

Mackey, Terry, and Kitty Mackey. 1992. "Think Quality! The Deming Approach *Does* Work in Libraries." *Library Journal* 117 (May 15): 57–61.

Mandel, Carol A. 1988. "Trade-Offs: Quantifying Quality in Library Technical Services." *Journal of Academic Librarianship* 14 (September): 214–20.

Maslow, Abraham H., with Deborah Stephens and Gary Heil. 1998. *Maslow on Management*. New York: John Wiley.

Maze, Susan, David Moxley, and Donna Smith. 1997. *Authoritative Guide to Web Search Engines*. New York: Neal-Schuman.

McClure, Charles R. et al. 1987. *Planning and Role Setting for Public Libraries: A Manual of Options and Procedures*. Chicago: American Library Association.

McNeil, John. 1999. "Disabilities Affect One-Fifth of All Americans: Proportion Could Increase in Coming Decades." *Census Brief* 97–5. http://www.census.gov/population/www/pop–profile/disabil.html. (Last accessed April 8, 1999.)

Mears, Peter. 1993. "How to Stop Talking About, and Begin Progress Toward, Total Quality Management." *Business Horizons* 36 (May/June): 11–14.

Minor, Vernon Hyde. 1994. *Art History's History*. Englewood Cliffs, NJ: Prentice-Hall.

Mitchell, Pamela R., and Erica B. Lilly. 1999. "Kent State University ADA Web Accessibility Initiative and Guidelines—Draft 2." http://www.library.kent.edu/~elilly/ada/access_considered.html. (Last accessed July 16, 1999.)

Morgan, David L. 1997. *Planning Focus Groups*. Focus Group Kit, vol. 2. Thousand Oaks, CA: Sage Publications.

———. 1998. *The Focus Group Guidebook*. Focus Group Kit, vol. 1. Thousand Oaks, CA: Sage Publications.

Muir, Holly J. 1995. "Benchmarking: What Can It Do for Libraries?" *Library Administration & Management* 9 (Spring): 103–6.

Murfin, Marjorie E. 1995. "Assessing Library Services: The Reference Component." pp. 1–15 in *The Reference Assessment Manual*, comp. and ed. Evaluation of Reference and Adult Services Committee, Reference and Adult Services Division, American Library Association. Ann Arbor, MI: Pierian Press.

Murfin, Marjorie E., and Charles A. Bunge. 1988. "Responsible Standards for Reference Service in Ohio Public Libraries." *Ohio Libraries* 1 (April/May): 11–13.

Murfin, Marjorie E., and Gary M. Gugelchuk. 1987. "Development and Testing of a Reference Transaction Assessment Instrument." *College & Research Libraries* 48 (July): 314–36.

Murfin, Marjorie E., and Jo Bell Whitlatch, eds. 1993. *Research in Reference Effectiveness: Proceedings of a Preconference Sponsored by the Research and Statistics Committee, Management and Operation of Public Services Division, American Library Association, San Francisco, California, June 26, 1992*. Chicago: Reference and Adult Services Division, American Library Association.

National Center for Higher Education Management Systems. Dennis Jones, Project Director. 1977. *Library Statistical Data Base: Formats and Definitions*. Boulder, CO: National Center for Higher Education Management Systems.

Nichols, Jim. 1998. "ACLU to Sue Libraries Over Net Access." *Cleveland Plain Dealer*. December 10. http://www.cleveland.com/news/pdnews/metro/calibe.phtml. (Last accessed April 11, 1999.)

Nord, Walter R. 1983. "A Political-Economic Perspective on Organizational Effectiveness." pp. 95–133 in *Organizational Effectiveness: A Comparison of Multiple Models*, eds. Kim S. Cameron and David A. Whetten. New York: Academic Press.

Ohio Reference Excellence: A Self-Study Reference Course. 1997. Columbus: Ohio Library Council.

O'Neil, Rosanna M. 1994. *Total Quality Management in Libraries: A Sourcebook*. Englewood, CO: Libraries Unlimited.

O'Neill, Edward T. 1998. "Characteristics of Web Accessible Information: Paper Presented at the 1997 IFLA Conference." *IFLA Journal* 24 (March): 114–16.

Oregon State University Technology Access Program. 199? "Adaptive and Augmentative Equipment." http://osu.orst.edu/dept/tap/adaptive.htm. (Last accessed April 10, 1999.)

Orenstein, David. 1999. "Developing Quality Managers and Quality Management: The Challenge to Leadership in Library Organizations." *Library Administration & Management* 13 (Winter): 44–51.

Paciello, Mike. 1996. "Making the World Wide Web Accessible for the Blind and Visually Impaired." *Florida Libraries* 39 (January/February): 5+.

Pagell, Ruth A. 1995. "Quality and the Internet: An Open Letter." *Online* 19 (July/August): 7–9.

Palmour, Vernon E., Marcia C. Bellassai, and Nancy V. DeWath. 1980. *A Planning Process for Public Libraries*. Chicago: American Library Association.

Parasuraman, A., Leonard L. Berry, and Valerie A. Zeithaml. 1991. "Perceived Service Quality as a Customer-Based Performance Measure: An Empirical Examination of Organizational Barriers Using an Extended Service Quality Model." *Human Resource Management* 30 (Fall): 335–64.

Peischl, Thomas M. 1995. "Benchmarking: A Process for Improvement" *Library Administration & Management* 9 (Spring): 99–105.

Peitz, G. S., and E. F. Moherek. 1993. "Front-line Leaders: A Balance Between People and Systems." *HR Focus* 70 (May): 17.

Phillips, Steven. 1993. *Evaluation*. London: Library Association.

Pierce, Sydney. 1984. "In Pursuit of the Possible: Evaluating Reference Services." *The Reference Librarian* 11 (Fall/Winter): 9–21.

Powell, Ronald R. 1997. *Basic Research Methods for Librarians*. 3d ed. Greenwich, CT: Ablex.

Public Library Management Forum Standards Review Committee, Illinois Library Association. 1996. *Serving Our Public: Standards for Illinois Public Libraries*. Springfield: Illinois Library Association.

Pymm, Bob. 1993. "It's Only Rock'N'Roll: Making A Case for Rock Music in the Research Library." *Australian Academic & Research Libraries* 24 (June): 78–82.

Ranganathan, S. R. 1964. *The Five Laws of Library Science*. Bombay: Asia House.

Rawlinson, Nora. 1990. "Give 'Em What They Want!" *Library Journal* 115 (June 15): 77–79.

The Reference Assessment Manual. 1995. Comp. and ed. Evaluation of Reference and Adult Services Committee, Reference and Adult Services Division, American Library Association. Ann Arbor, MI: Pierian Press.

Reference and User Services Association. 1996. "RUSA Guidelines for Behavioral Performance of Reference and Information Services Professionals." *RQ* 36 (Winter): 200–203.

"Report on the Library and Information Services Policy Forum on Impact of Information Technology and Special Programming on Library Services to Special Populations." 1996. Funded by the National Center for Education Statistics and Co-sponsored by the U.S. National Commission on Libraries and Information Science with the Cooperation of the Office of Library Programs and the National Institute on Postsecondary Education, Libraries, and Lifelong Learning. Alexandria, Virginia. May 20-21, 1996.

Rettig, James. 1996. "Beyond 'Cool'—Analog Models for Reviewing Digital Resources." *Online* 20 (September/October): 52–54+.

Riggs, Donald E. 1993. "Managing Quality: TQM in Libraries." *Library Administration & Management* 7 (Spring): 73–78.

Robbins, Jane, Holly Willett, Mary Jane Wiseman, and Douglas L. Zweizig. 1990. *Evaluation Strategies and Techniques for Public Library Children's Services: A Sourcebook*. Madison, WI: University of Wisconsin-Madison, School of Library and Information Studies.

Rothstein, Samuel. 1961. "Reference Service: The New Dimension in Librarianship." *College & Research Libraries* 22 (January): 12.

Rubin, Richard. 1986. *In-House Use of Materials in Public Libraries*. Champaign, IL: University of Illinois at Urbana-Champaign, Graduate School of Library and Information Science.

Sack, John R. 1986. "Open Systems for Open Minds: Building the Library Without Walls." *College & Research Libraries* 47 (November): 535–44.

Schneider, Benjamin. 1983. "An Interactionist Perspective on Organizational Effectiveness." pp. 27–54 in *Organizational Effectiveness: A Comparison of Multiple Models*, eds. Kim S. Cameron and David A. Whetten. New York: Academic Press.

Schwarzwalder, Robert. 1995. "Annual Review of Technology Online — 1995." *Database* 18 (December): 80–82.

Seashore, Stanley E. 1983. "A Framework for an Integrated Model of Organizational Effectiveness." pp. 55–70 in *Organizational Effectiveness: A Comparison of Multiple Models*, eds. Kim S. Cameron and David A. Whetten. New York: Academic Press.

Segal, Joseph. 1980. *Evaluating and Weeding Collections in Small and Medium-Sized Public Libraries: The CREW Method*. Chicago: American Library Association.

Senge, Peter M. 1994. *The Fifth Discipline Fieldbook: Strategies and Tools for Building a Learning Organization.* New York: Doubleday.

Shearer, Kenneth. 1993. "Confusing What Is Most Wanted with What Is Most Used: A Crisis in Public Library Priorities Today." *Public Libraries* 32 (July/August): 193–97.

Slote, Stanley J. 1997. *Weeding Library Collections: Library Weeding Methods.* 4th ed. Englewood, CO: Libraries Unlimited.

Smith, Alastair G. 1997. "Testing the Surf: Criteria for Evaluating Internet Information Resources." *The Public-Access Computer Systems Review* 8, no. 3. Computer file. http://info.lib.uh.edu/pr/v8/n3 /smit8n3.html. (Last accessed March 28, 1999.)

Smith, Linda C. 1981. "Citation Analysis." *Library Trends* 30 (Summer): 83–106.

Smith, Mark L. 1996a. *Collecting and Using Public Library Statistics: A How-To-Do-It Manual for Librarians.* New York: Neal-Schuman.

———. 1996b. "Using Statistics To Increase Public Library Budgets." *The Bottom Line: Managing Library Finances* 9, no. 3: 4–13.

Stalker, John C., and Marjorie E. Murfin. 1996. "Quality Reference Service: A Preliminary Study." *Journal of Academic Librarianship* 22 (November): 423–29.

Stam, Deirdre Corcoran. 1984. "The Information-Seeking Practices of Art Historians in Museums and Colleges in the United States, 1982-83." D.L.S. diss., Columbia University.

Standards Task Force, Ohio Library Development Committee, Ohio Library Council. Mary Pat Essman, Chair. 1996. "Standards for Public Library Service in Ohio. Draft Document for Discussion. 12 August 1996."

Stanley, Nancy Markle. 1995. "The Case for Acquiring and Accessing Electronic Journals in Libraries." pp. 29–34 in *Practical Issues in Collection Development and Collection Access: The 1993 Charleston Conference*, eds. Katina Strauch, Sally Somers, Susan Zappen, and Anne Jennings. New York: Haworth Press.

Starbuck, William H., and Paul C. Nystrom. 1983. "Pursuing Organizational Effectiveness That Is Ambiguously Specified." pp. 135–61 in *Organizational Effectiveness: A Comparison of Multiple Models*, eds. Kim S. Cameron and David A. Whetten. New York: Academic Press.

Stein, Gertrude. 1984. *Picasso.* New York: Dover.

Steiner, P. 1993. Cartoon. *The New Yorker* 69 (July 5): 61.

Stewart, David W., and Prem N. Shamdasani. 1990. *Focus Groups: Theory and Practice.* Thousand Oaks, CA: Sage Publications.

Stout, Rick. 1997. *Web Site Stats: Tracking Hits and Analyzing Traffic.* New York: Osborne McGraw-Hill.

Sullivan, Danny. 1998. "Search Engine Design Tips." http://www.searchenginewatch.com/webmasters/tips.html. (Last accessed April 11, 1999.)

———. 1999. "Search Engine Features Comparison Chart." *Search Engine Watch.* http://searchenginewatch.com/ (Last accessed April 11, 1999.)

Sweeney, Richard. 1997. "Leadership Skills in the Reengineered Library: Empowerment and Value Added Trend Implications for Library Leaders." *Library Administration & Management* 11 (Winter): 30–41.

Symons, Ann K. 1997. "Sizing Up Sites: How to Judge What You Find on the Web." *School Library Journal* 43 (April): 22–25.

Tenopir, Carol. 1996. "Moving to the Information Village." *Library Journal* 121 (March 1): 29–30.

Thompson, Kenneth R. 1998. "Confronting the Paradoxes in a Total Quality Environment." *Organizational Dynamics* 26 (Winter): 62–74.

Tillman, Hope N., and Walt Howe. 1999. "Old Wine in New Bottles: Using the Internet to Access the Content You Need." http://www.tiac.net/users/hope/presentations/oldwine.html. (Last accessed March 28, 1999.)

Trace Research and Development Center. 1998a. "Accessibility Products for Microsoft Windows, Windows NT, and Windows 95." http://www.trace.wisc.edu/docs/win_access_prod/winacces.htm#enlarger. (Last accessed April 10, 1999.)

———. 1998b. "A Brief Introduction to Disabilities." http://trace.wisc.edu/text/univdesn/populat/populat.html. (Last accessed April 8, 1999.)

Trotta, Marcia. 1993. *Managing Library Outreach Programs: A How-To-Do-It Manual for Librarians*. New York: Neal-Schuman.

Tyckoson, David. 1992. "Wrong Questions, Wrong Answers: Behavioral vs. Factual Evaluation of Reference Service." *The Reference Librarian* 38: 151–74.

United States Department of Justice. 1999a. "Section 508 Instructions and Documents." http://www.usdoj.gov/crt/508/508docs.html. (Last accessed July 16, 1999.)

———. 1999b. "Web Accessibility Checklist." http://www.usdoj.gov/crt/508/webpage.pdf. (Last accessed July 16, 1999.)

University of Washington Computing and Communications Adaptive Technology Lab. 1999. "Resources in the Adaptive Technology Lab." http://www.washington.edu/computing/atl/DOCS/atl.use.html. (Last accessed April 9, 1999.)

Van De Ven, Andrew H., and Diane L. Ferry. 1980. *Measuring and Assessing Organizations*. New York: John Wiley.

Van Fleet, Connie. 1998. *Measuring Library Services 1998: A Joint Project of the State Library of Ohio and the Ohio Library Council. Manual and Training Guide*. Columbus: Ohio Library Council.

Van Fleet, Connie, and Joan C. Durrance. 1993. "Public Library Leaders and Research: Mechanisms, Perceptions, and Strategies." *Journal of Education for Library and Information Science* 34 (Spring): 137–53.

———. 1994. "Public Library Research: Use and Utility." pp. 1–16 in *Research Issues in Public Librarianship: Trends for the Future*, ed. Joy M. Greiner. Westport, CT: Greenwood.

Van Fleet, Connie, and Frances Haley. 1997. "Clarity, Consistency, and Currency: A Report on the Ohio 'Measuring Library Services' Project." *Advances in Library Administration and Organization* 15: 35–62.

Van House, Nancy A., Mary Jo Lynch, Charles R. McClure, Douglas L. Zweizig, and Eleanor Jo Rodger. 1987. *Output Measures for Public Libraries: A Manual of Standardized Procedures*. 2d ed. Chicago: American Library Association.

Van House, Nancy A., Beth T. Weil, and Charles R. McClure. 1990. *Measuring Academic Library Performance: A Practical Approach*. Chicago: American Library Association.

Von Seggern, Marilyn. 1987. "Assessment of Reference Services." *RQ* 26 (Summer): 487–96.

Wallace, Danny P. 1983. "An Index of Quality of Illinois Public Library Service." pp. 1–46 in *Illinois Library Statistical Report 10*. Springfield, IL: Illinois State Library.

———. 1984. "An Index of Quality of Illinois Public Library Service, 1983." pp. 61–84 in *Illinois Library Statistical Report 14*. Springfield, IL: Illinois State Library.

Wallace, Danny P. et al. 1990. *Age Analysis for Public Library Collections: Final Report*. Baton Rouge: Louisiana State University, School of Library and Information Science. ED333889.

Weech, Terry L. 1988. "Validity and Comparability of Public Library Data: A Commentary on the Output Measures for Public Libraries." *Public Library Quarterly* 8, no. 3-4: 7–18.

Wenner, Jann S., ed. 1997. "The *Rolling Stone* 200: The Essential Rock Collection." *Rolling Stone* 760 (May 15): 46–100.

Westbrook, Lynn. 1990. "Evaluating Reference: An Introductory Overview of Qualitative Methods." *Reference Services Review* 18 (Spring): 73–78.

Whitlatch, Jo Bell. 1992. "Reference Services: Research Methodologies for Assessment and Accountability." *The Reference Librarian* no. 38: 9–19.

———. 1998. "Enhancing the Quality of Reference Services for the 21st Century." *Reference & User Services Quarterly* 38 (Fall): 15–16.

Wolfe, Paula. 1996. "Evaluating Internet Resources: Criteria for Evaluation as a Collection Development Extension." pp. 213–17 in *Information Across the Waves: The World as a Multimedia Experience. Proceedings of the 21st Annual Conference of the International Association of Aquatic and Marine Science Libraries and Information Centers*, eds. James W. Markham and Andrea L. Duda. Fort Pierce, FL: International Association of Aquatic and Marine Science Libraries and Information Centers (IAMSLIC).

World Wide Web Consortium. 1999. "W3C HTML Validation Service." http://validator.w3.org/. (Last accessed April 11, 1999.)

———. 1999. "Web Content Guidelines 1.0." http://www.w3.org/TR/WAI–WEBCONTENT/. (Last accessed July 16, 1999.)

Zakon, Robert Hobbes. 1998. "Hobbes' Internet Timeline Version 4.0." http://info.isoc.org/guest.zakon/Internet/History/HIT.html. (Last accessed March 5, 1999.)

Zammuto, Raymond F. 1982. *Assessing Organizational Effectiveness.* Albany, NY: State University of New York Press.

Zweizig, Douglas, and Eleanor Jo Rodger. 1982. *Output Measures for Public Libraries: A Manual of Standardized Procedures.* Chicago: American Library Association.

INDEX